Understanding Undergraduates

Most university teachers have ideas about the typical good or not-so student in their classes, but rarely do they share these thou~~ht~~ keeping quiet about the preconceptions – or s~~t~~ ers put themselves at risk of missing key ev beliefs; more importantly, they may fail to no~~t~~ support and encouragement.

In this unique work, the authors explore ~~t~~ beliefs about their students' performance and ~~...s~~ are well-founded, which are mistaken, which mask othe~~r~~ ~~underl~~ying factors, and what they can do about them. So is it true, for instance, that British Asian students find medicine more difficult than their white counterparts, or that American students with sports scholarships take their studies less seriously? Is it the case that students who sit at the front of the lecture hall get better grades than those who sit at the back?

By comparing students' demographic data and their actual performance with their teachers' expectations, the authors expose a complex picture of multiple factors affecting performance. They also contrast students' comments about their own study habits with their views on what makes a good learner. For each preconception, they offer clear advice on how university teachers can redesign their courses, introduce new activities and assignments and communicate effective learning strategies that students will be able to put into practice. Finally, the authors explore the ramifications of teachers' beliefs and suggest actions that can be taken at the level of the institution, department or programme and in educational development events, designed to level the playing field so that students have a more equitable chance of success.

Ideal for both educational developers and university teachers, this book:

- reveals general tendencies and findings that will inform developers' own work with university teachers;
- provides practical guidance and solutions for university teachers to be able to identify and address students' actual – rather than assumed – needs;
- explores means of addressing and challenging people's natural tendency to rely on preconceived ideas and stereotypes; and
- explains an action research method that educational developers can use on their own campuses to unravel some of the local preconceptions that may be hampering student success.

Celia Popovic was Head of Educational Development at Birmingham City University, and is now an educational developer at York University, Toronto, Canada. She is book review editor of *Innovations in Education and Teaching International*.

David A. Green is Director of the Center for Excellence in Teaching and Learning at Seattle University, USA, having previously been Head of Educational and Staff Development at Birmingham City University in his native UK. He is co-editor of the *International Journal for Academic Development*.

The Staff and Educational Development Series
Series Editor: James Wisdom

SEDA is the professional association for staff and educational developers in the UK, promoting innovation and good practice in higher education. SEDA offers services to its institutional and individual members through its Fellowship scheme, its Professional Development Framework and its conferences, events, publications and projects. SEDA is a member of the International Consortium for Educational Development

SEDA
Woburn House
20–24 Tavistock Square
London
WC1H 9HF
Tel: 020 7380 6767
www.seda.ac.uk

Academic and Educational Development: Research, Evaluation and Changing Practice in Higher Education, edited by Ranald Macdonald and James Wisdom, 2002

Assessment for Learning in Higher Education, edited by Peter Knight, 1995

Benchmarking and Threshold Standards in Higher Education, edited by Helen Smith, Michael Armstrong and Sally Brown, 1999

Changing Higher Education: The Development of Learning and Teaching, edited by Paul Ashwin, 2006

Computer-Assisted Assessment in Higher Education, edited by Sally Brown, Phil Race and Joanna Bull, 1999

Education Development and Leadership in Higher Education: Implementing an Institutional Strategy, edited by Kym Fraser, 2004

Educational Development Through Information and Communications Technology, edited by Stephen Fallows and Rakesh Bhanot, 2007

Enabling Student Learning: Systems and Strategies, edited by Gina Wisker and Sally Brown, 1996

Enhancing Staff and Educational Development, edited by David Baume and Peter Kahn, 2004

Facing Up to Radical Change in Universities and Colleges, by Steve Armstrong and Gail Thompson, 1997

Flexible Learning in Action: Case Studies in Higher Education edited by Rachel Hudson, Sian Maslin-Prothero and Lyn Gates, 1997

A Guide to Staff and Educational Development, edited by Peter Kahn and David Baume, 2003

Inspiring Students: Case studies in motivating the learner, edited by Stephen Fallows and Kemal Ahmet, 1999

The Management of Independent Learning, edited by Jo Tait and Peter Knight, 1996

Managing Educational Development Projects: Effective Management for Maximum Impact, edited by Carole Baume, Paul Martin and Mantz Yorke, 2002

Quality Issues in ICT-based Higher Education, edited by Stephen Fallows and Rakesh Bhanot, 2005

Researching Learning in Higher Education: An Introduction to Contemporary Methods and Approaches, by Glynis Cousin, 2009

Reshaping Teaching in Higher Education: Linking Teaching with Research, edited by Alan Jenkins, Rosanna Breen and Roger Lindsay, 2003

Resource-Based Learning, edited by Sally Brown and Brenda Smith, 1996

Teaching International Students: Improving Learning for All, edited by Jude Carroll and Janette Ryan, 2006

The Realities of Change in Higher Education: Interventions to Promote Learning and Teaching, edited by Lynne Hunt, Adrian Bromage and Bland Tomkinson, 2006

UNDERSTANDING UNDERGRADUATES

Challenging our preconceptions of student success

Celia Popovic and David A. Green

Routledge
Taylor & Francis Group

NEW YORK AND LONDON

First published 2012
by Routledge
2 Park Square, Milton Park, Abingdon, Oxon OX14 4RN

Simultaneously published in the USA and Canada
by Routledge
711 Third Avenue, New York, NY 10017

Routledge is an imprint of the Taylor & Francis Group, an informa business

British Library Cataloguing in Publication Data
A catalogue record for this book is available from the British Library

Library of Congress Cataloging in Publication Data
Popovic, Celia.
Understanding undergraduates : challenging our preconceptions of student
performance / Celia Popovic and David A. Green.
    p. cm.
College teaching. 2. College students. 3. Academic achievement.
4. Education, Higher–Great Britain. 5. Education, Higher–United States.
I. Green, David A., Ph. D. II. Title.
LB2331.P58 2012
378.1'25–dc23   2011040093

ISBN: 978-0-415-66754-8 (hbk)
ISBN: 978-0-415-66755-5 (pbk)
ISBN: 978-0-203-81690-5 (ebk)

Typeset in Adobe Caslon and Trade Gothic
by Cenveo Publisher Services

Printed and bound in Great Britain by
CPI Antony Rowe, Chippenham, Wiltshire

For Rad and Bryan

Contents

List of figures

List of tables

Acknowledgements

We thank all the university teachers and students involved in this study, and the administrators who made it all possible, as well as the many participants in workshops at ICED and POD who contributed to our understanding of the power of stereotypes.

We are particularly grateful to the colleagues who reviewed chapters, giving us invaluable advice and generously sharing resources: Fiona Campbell, Phil Carey, Julie Hall, Alison Holmes, Eric Kristensen, Deandra Little, Katarina Mårtensson, Sue Morón Garcia and Kathryn Plank.

Rebecca Jaynes has worked patiently and with good humour to locate references and remedy wayward citations. We are thankful to have her as a colleague. Meanwhile, Matt Byers has solved our electronic quandaries, enabling us to work seamlessly across an eight-hour time difference.

We are grateful to James Wisdom for his encouragement to write the book and his guidance from the outset. We are both, of course, indebted to SEDA as a community that has supported us in our careers as educational developers.

Many people contributed to this book in one form or another, some of whom we refer to directly. We would like to single out the following for particular mention: Joyce Allen, Ann Austin, Sven Arvidson, Jim Austin, John Bean, Brenda Broussard, Derek Bruff, Vanessa Castañeda, Lisa Coutu, Lynn Deeken, Bob Duniway, Theresa Earenfight, Diana Eastcott, Jenny Eland, Bob Farmer, Peter Felten, Barbara Grant, Marion Green, Peter Green, Sue Green, Mick Healey, Therese Huston, Angie Jenkins, Ruth Lawton, Bridget Middlemas, Jacquelyn Miller, Anne Mohundro, Larry Nichols, Monica Nixon, Bianca Popovic, George Popovic, Millie Popovic, Rad Popovic, Christina Roberts, Bryan Ruppert, Lynn Taylor, Pam Taylor and Trileigh Tucker.

Series Editor's Introduction

Travelling on the London to Brighton railway is always more special than other journeys – for lovers it is a romantic line, promising escape; for children, the squealing excitement of a day at the seaside; for the great actor, Lord Olivier, it was being served kippers for breakfast.

As we settled into our seats for the journey to London after a SEDA conference, David and Celia started the conversation with 'We think we have a book for SEDA', and by the time we reached Victoria, they certainly had.

The book, too, is a very special journey. It takes us, whether we are teachers or students, to some of the most important places in higher education – the assumptions, the preconceptions and the stereotypes we use to get through our working days. These are the beliefs which shape our actions, the clutter and lumber of the half-understood ideas in our heads which we use to make choices, the prejudices and instincts we use to try to teach well and study successfully.

And here they are – itemised and analysed, tested with evidence, valued and challenged. Written in the most accessible language, it is clear to read – but it is also hard to read. This is a book of revelations and occasional discomforts. But do not despair – the authors have exercised all the skills of good educational developers in their text, and guide us humanely through the practices with which we can re-shape our work. Driven by explicit values and by research, practice and experience, the authors offer us insights which we must not lose from higher education. It is ever more important to listen to our students, and also to listen to ourselves.

James Wisdom
Visiting Professor in Educational Development,
Middlesex University, UK

1
INTRODUCTION

Before you read on, jot down some brief responses to the following questions:

1. What makes a good student?
2. What makes a poor student?
3. What do you think your *students* believe makes a good student?

We aim to provide our own answers to these questions in the next seven chapters, along with responses to a fourth question:

4. How do we overcome our preconceptions about good and poor students so that they don't get in the way of learning?

Many of us have beliefs about the really able and the most challenging students. Yet most of the time, we keep those thoughts to ourselves or only share them with a small group of trusted friends, in what Goffman (1959) would call 'back stage conversations' – ones that shouldn't be heard in public. Some university teachers don't feel they can air these views with anyone at all. Such experiences can leave us feeling isolated, concerned that we might act unfairly or that no one else shares these worries. A doubt nags us that we may be missing a part of the puzzle, that maybe we could have reached that group of disenchanted students last year if we'd somehow acted differently.

At other times, we're not even conscious of the automated thought patterns we draw on, but they may well affect our expectations of our students. We notice the student whose phone keeps vibrating and the one at the front who looks terrified, but we may not realize how our brain tags and stores this information, creating neat packages tied to preconceived notions of who will or will not succeed in our courses.

This book is the fruit of an international research project that sought to unearth some broadly held preconceptions and test them out.

Through interviews with 38 university teachers in 14 subject areas at four institutions in the UK and USA – followed by questionnaire responses and end-of-course grades from 1,241 students taking those teachers' first-year courses – we're able to present you with findings on the validity of the 37 frequently cited preconceptions. For each pre-conception, we also offer strategies you can employ to help students achieve their potential regardless of acknowledged or unacknowledged stereotypes.

Given the potentially discomfiting nature of the topic, we're mostly writing as if to individual university teachers or to educational developers, like us, who work directly with those teachers. We hope, though, that you will want to share our findings, and your thoughts on them, within your 'significant network' (Roxå and Mårtensson 2009) of close, trusted colleagues, and also with your wider network of departmental and cross-university collaborators, since we believe learning and teaching practice is enhanced by working in groups (Bruner 1966; Lave and Wenger 1991; Vygotsky 1987).

To give you a flavour of what is to come, we'll provide some responses to those initial questions from the teachers in our study:

> [Good students are] very independently minded but very thoughtful, and seem to have really been exposed to interesting debate […] and it often seems to be that their parents have pushed them in interesting ways.
>
> (US-Constantia-8)

> A career goal is very important, that sets out a long-term aim so they can work towards their dream.
>
> (UK-Baskerville-5)

> Students who expect it to be just like the high school course, who come with the idea of 'this is how they would need to prepare', that's definitely a negative […]. Students are often trained in high school to study in a particular way: you memorize terms. Students who are prepared to say 'I have to go beyond memorization' are in general set for success.
>
> (US-Delphin-6)

While it may be no surprise that university teachers describe good learners as 'Punctual, hard-working, devoted, organized and independent', would it surprise you to know that these are the views of students, too?

And why do they choose the courses they take? Perhaps these views resonate with comments you have heard from your own students:

> Because I want to do well in life and feel that this course will help. Also I enjoy what I am studying.
>
> (UK-Arial)

> I came to the campus a couple of times and really liked the atmosphere.
>
> (UK-Baskerville)

> To piss my dad off.
>
> (US-Delphin)

> I love this city. Strong [degree] program coupled with a liberal arts education that emphasized philosophy and spirituality.
>
> (US-Constantia)

> It's close to home
>
> (US-Delphin)

> Because I left education a long time ago and wanted to have a complete change of career.
>
> (UK-Arial)

As you discover students' motivations in this way, perhaps you find that your expectations of their performance shift.

Background to the research

This research had its genesis in a doctoral thesis by one of the authors (Popovic 2007). She investigated differences in performance by medical students at a UK university. This revealed that teachers had beliefs about the types of student they expected to perform well or poorly. In discussing the issue with teachers, Celia realized that many teachers shared common beliefs about some students – beliefs that turned out to be unfounded. Her analysis of exam results revealed that student performance was not linked to the factors identified by the teachers. Teachers, in contrast, had constructed rationales to account for links that Celia's study revealed as untrue. Because these unspoken beliefs had not been tested, the teachers believed underperformance was beyond, and therefore not, their responsibility. Once it was shown that there was no link between certain characteristics and performance, it was possible to open the dialogue to investigate the implications of these beliefs. We explore teacher beliefs from all four institutions in this study – both well-founded and not – in Chapters 4, 5 and 6, and some of it has been published elsewhere (Popovic 2010).

The most significant challenge presented by this project was the one attributed to George Bernard Shaw – 'America and Britain are two countries divided by a common language'. Not only were we confronted with two different educational cultures but also our shared language is not universal. Seemingly obvious words (term, evaluation, assessment, course, module, staff, faculty, lecturer) can have quite different meanings in the two countries. This linguistic conundrum has permeated the writing of this book as we have tried to ensure accessibility to all speakers of English, not just the countries in the study. You have already seen us use the phrase 'university teacher' to describe what in the UK would be called a 'lecturer' and in the USA 'faculty' – neither of those terms translates meaningfully. Occasionally, you will see us include an American–British translation in parentheses where it aids clarity. Throughout, we have tried to minimize the potential for confusion and ask you to bear with us if our wording seems unwieldy.

Why do we care?

In discussing the question of teacher expectations, we found we were both personally invested in researching further and disseminating our findings to help inform university teachers and educational developers ('faculty developers'). To explain that interest a little better, we interviewed each other and report our comments here. We hope it's helpful for you to see where we're coming from in writing this book.

Celia Popovic is an Educational Developer at York University in Toronto, Canada. Before this appointment, and for most of the time the research was conducted, she was Head of Educational Staff Development at Birmingham City University in the UK.

1. Which of your experiences relate to the topic of preconceptions?

Not only do teachers make assumptions about students but the reverse can also be true. I clearly remember a tutorial where I hesitatingly suggested that some people might question the existence of God. My previous, sheltered experience at boarding school – with compulsory church attendance on Sunday and an underlying adherence to Church of England beliefs and values – suggested that all figures of authority were in agreement. I was completely shocked when the tutor revealed she was an atheist, and was amazed that the walls of the tutorial room did not collapse. That recollection reminds me that students can make false assumptions about teachers, too: that stereotyping is not always one-way traffic.

In my personal life, when my middle daughter, at the age of four, expressed relief that the family was not moving house, I discovered she thought people relocated because *someone else* put a 'For Sale' sign on the front lawn. To a four-year-old child, this was a rational explanation. To her mother, it suggested a deeply insecure little girl for whom existence was a totally random experience. Having reassured my daughter, I thought about how much we take for granted about shared knowledge, and the understanding of rules and consequences. On another occasion my son, then aged five, casually mentioned his disclosure at school circle time that Daddy had to wear an ankle bracelet 'so that the police know where he is'. Appalled, I said, as calmly as I could: 'but George that simply isn't true is it?' To which George replied, 'No, but everyone was *very* interested.' As far as George was concerned, he had been asked to tell the class something about his family that was interesting; the minor detail that this should also be true, had escaped his attention, or perhaps was never articulated. These personal anecdotes might seem irrelevant in a book concerned with higher education, but for me they encapsulate the essence of this study – What is it that we take for granted, both as teachers and students, what do we assume, what do we articulate, and how accurate are we in our assumptions? Could the student who frustrates their teacher by apparently missing the point in an assignment, or the one who plagiarizes others, be examples of the same responses as my children: guilty of not applying the rules, but innocent of deliberately breaking 'the law'?

2. How do these issues relate to your own work with students and university teachers?

I have worked with students at every level, and now work mainly with academic colleagues. I also work with MA and PhD students investigating pedagogic issues, some of whom are also university teachers. I try to ensure that assumptions are fully examined, that expectations are clearly expressed, and that motivations and prior knowledge are explored, in an attempt to avoid the house-moving or the ankle-tag experience with my students.

With my colleagues, I like to explore preconceptions and generalizations. I am surprised by how frequently teachers say that students no longer want to learn for the love of the subject. Often this view is based on two assumptions: the first is that students are different from the teachers' peers; the second is that current students' motivation has no bearing on the choice of subject. In some cases both of these assumptions may be correct. However, it is not always so. Certainly in my own case, I studied English and American Literature because I loved reading. I completed the essays every time they were due, not because of this love of the subject: I did it in order to meet the requirements of the course. If I didn't ask repeatedly about the criteria for a First, or what was needed to pass, it wasn't because I didn't want to know, but because the climate at that university at that time did not encourage such questions. Was I so very different from the average literature student today?

I am interested in the subtext – What is really going on? Are our assumptions correct? This is what led me to embark on the research that has culminated in this book.

David A. Green is Director of the Center for Excellence in Teaching and Learning at Seattle University, Washington, USA.

1. Which of your experiences relate to the topic of preconceptions?

From my undergraduate days, I recall some outrageous comments from my teachers, particularly statements that were sexist (in a subject where 80 per cent of students were women) or latently homophobic – an uncomfortable experience for me as a recently out gay man (though my teachers at the time didn't know this). The sense of being an invisible minority has stuck with me.

In the last 15 years, I've worked with students from a far broader range of backgrounds than I could have imagined during my horrendous first teaching position as a postgraduate. And I've discovered, often through a painful process of trial and error, that it's best to presume nothing but good intentions from students. One student would be on the verge of falling asleep during group work; it's only once I asked what was going on that I learned that he and his girlfriend (also a student at the same university) had a new baby, no family support and were juggling full-time studying with full-time parenting in shifts. Another would ask questions five minutes out of sync with the rest of the group, to the point where I put her in touch with the counselling service; it turned out she was experiencing the start of her first psychotic incident and had to interrupt her studies for a year. Then in my first use of online discussions in the late 1990s, two first-generation university students anonymously posted strongly worded messages because they felt unable to tell their best friend face-to-face that her homophobia was unacceptable and damaging their friendship. Each year, my students continue to surprise me.

2. How do these issues relate to your own work with students and university teachers?

Issues of identity led me to develop an activity for the first class in my course on Cultural Taboo and Transgression at Seattle University, and people might like to borrow and adapt it. Ten minutes into the first session, after students have briefly introduced themselves (name, major, year of study, reason for taking the course), I ask them to write down everything they think they know about me. (I tell them that I can't be offended because I realize they don't know me. It turns out that I *can* be offended, but it's important for me not to show it and to remain open-minded!) After two or three minutes, they get into threes to pool their ideas for five minutes before volunteering the items they have noted. Typical examples include: male, British, wears a suit, married (they always check for rings), punctual – and I type them up, projecting them on screen. I then ask them to tell me which categories they chose *not* to mention, and type up that list, too – for example, ethnicity, sexual orientation and religious beliefs. Not only does the exercise enable the whole group to discuss the kinds of presumptions they automatically make in a very short space of time but also it opens up a debate on aspects of people's identities that are somehow off-limits or too risky. To round off the activity, I go through the first list of items and score them – 1 for correct, 0 for incorrect, and occasionally 0.5: for instance, I'm a registered Civil Partner under UK law, but that relationship is not recognized in the USA, so I can't give them a full point for 'married'. My students discover all these things on day one, and our subsequent discussions are all the more open as a result of this level of candour. (See Chapter 8 for further development of this exercise.)

In the USA, I do a lot more one-on-one work with university teachers than I did in the UK. Rather than hearing sweeping negative statements about student groups as a whole, I instead hear about more specific situations or difficulties with individual students. This provides me the opportunity to help teachers unearth some of their own preconceptions and to separate those notions from factual observations. This might be a matter of shifting colleagues' attitudes from 'I hate students who are late to class' to 'I hate it *when* students are late to class', but this shift from the individual to the individual's behaviour is a significant step in the process. In this role, I'm constantly learning more and developing greater appreciation for the factors affecting my students, their behaviours, and their chances of success. My long-standing interests in culture, identity and communication have propelled me to study and relay the tricky issue of preconceptions of learners.

Overview of the book

We have written this book for university teachers and educational developers who are interested in improving student learning. The starting point for our work has been an investigation of our own and our colleagues' expectations of students. This rapidly led to a focus on beliefs.

In **Chapter 2** we set the scene for the research by exploring the current literature on the key issues facing first-year or freshman students and their teachers. This chapter includes details of the data collection method for the study so that you can replicate it if you wish.

Chapter 3 provides a comparison of the UK and US higher education systems. Although they have many similarities, there are key differences that had a bearing on the teachers' responses and on the subsequent findings. Here we also describe our four universities, focusing on the main issues that influenced the project.

We then present our findings based on where they arose. **Chapter 4** explores beliefs common to university teachers in both the UK and USA. We share what the teachers told us and how this compared with the students' performance. It is paradoxically heartening and discouraging to find that there are some universal problems and challenges. Heartening that we are not alone; discouraging as it suggests an element of inevitability. However, since we suggest practical approaches to deal with the common themes, we aim to leave you encouraged and not downhearted.

In **Chapters 5 and 6**, we focus on country-specific aspects: teacher perceptions and student performance in the UK and USA, respectively. In both, we contextualize the issues so that the findings will be relevant to teachers in higher education regardless of country.

Chapter 7 presents the students' points of view. What do they think makes a successful student? Do their espoused study behaviours match their actions? We suggest ways to help students re-conceive strategies for their success: What do your students need to know to help themselves, whether this is addressing behaviours they can control, or ways to minimize the negative aspects of characteristics that they cannot?

Finally in **Chapter 8**, we offer some practical strategies for working with colleagues: What can we do to reduce and respond to stereotyping and prejudices at the institutional and departmental level and through educational development?

How well do we understand our undergraduates? This book will help you answer that question.

2
UNDERSTANDING THE RESEARCH CONTEXT

In this chapter, we describe the methodology used in the study, but first we give a brief overview of what we see as current thinking regarding students' attitudes to education and their learning. Rather than providing a thorough reprise of studies that are well documented elsewhere, we focus on key issues that pertain to our later findings and provide some pointers for exploring issues in greater depth beyond this study. In later chapters we expand on many of these topics in the context of our own findings.

The intention of this book is to help university teachers think through the spoken and unspoken presumptions that can interfere with a positive learning experience; at the same time, we hope to boost teachers' job satisfaction by encouraging a more nuanced approach to understanding undergraduates. As educational (or faculty) developers who collaborate with university teachers on a daily basis, we frame our approach to our work around the six values of the UK's Staff and Educational Development Association (SEDA, n.d.):

An understanding of how people learn
Working in and developing learning communities
Working effectively with diversity and promoting inclusivity
Scholarship, professionalism and ethical practice
Continuing reflection on professional practice
Developing people and processes

The last two values are intrinsic to the work of educational development; we will use the first four values to structure our discussion about the current research in higher education that contextualizes our study.

An understanding of how people learn

The first SEDA value leads to a consideration of key learning theories and what constitutes effective learning. A review of the literature in this field reveals substantial, long-standing support for a model of education that is student-centred, activity-led and social constructivist, particularly where the aim is to encourage deep approaches to learning and higher-order thinking. We briefly discuss each of these below.

Research into education in general has shown that students learn more effectively when the learning is student-centred (Knowles 1980, 1990; Weimer 2002), when they are able to have some control over the pace and content of the learning, and when there is sufficient opportunity for student interaction, activity and reflection (Gibbs 1992; Kolb 1984; Laurillard 2002; Race 2007). Indeed, being learner-centred may also assist student retention (Zepke et al. 2006). But what do we mean by learner-centred? Ramsden (2003: 106–16) discusses theories of university teaching as progressing from 'teaching as telling' to 'teaching as organizing', and finally to 'teaching as making learning possible'. Whereas the first theory is teacher-centred, presuming that learning arises from good lecturing, the second theory acknowledges that students need to engage in learning through activities, and emphasizes the development of active-learning techniques. Many university teachers find themselves working with this second model. The third theory, though, shifts teachers' thinking to a more scholarly process, where they adapt the class – and the variety of learning activities in their repertoire – in response to how each group of students engages or struggles with the course material.

Students' approaches to learning also considerably influence their ability to apply and extrapolate from the new ideas and theories they study (Gibbs 1992; Marton and Säljö 1976a, 1976b; Marton et al. 1997). Those students taking a surface approach aim to replicate the content of a class without creating meaning from it for themselves; although this rote learning may prove successful in certain classes, it reduces the likelihood that a student will be able to remember and use that information in future courses or outside experiences. In contrast, students who demonstrate a deep approach see learning as a process by which they transform what is taught so that their understanding of the subject, and possibly their view of the world, is changed. Deep approaches lend themselves to identifying relations across and between topics and between personal experience and more abstract representations of theory and practice. Importantly for university teachers and educational developers, approaches to learning are not fixed for any learner: The same individual may take a surface approach in one subject and a deep one in another. The *design* of the learning experience, such as the choice of assignment, can significantly affect whether students choose to take a deep or a surface approach to their studies. For example, Scouller (1998) demonstrated that essays encourage a deeper approach than multiple-choice answer papers. Teachers can influence their students' approaches to learning through course design and those who see teaching as 'making learning possible' are more likely to promote deep approaches (Ramsden 2003).

Course design can also influence students' motivation. Given the importance of results, it is neither unreasonable nor surprising that at least some students are motivated primarily by the grade they are awarded, rather than a love of the subject. Elton (1996), building on the work of Herzberg (1968) and Maslow (1954), gives a comprehensive rationale for the need to consider and manage student motivation. Put simply, he argues that humans are motivated by a hierarchy of needs, where basic needs must be met before higher ones can be considered. For student learning, a basic need would be to feel confident that the course covers the subject matter to be assessed. If students doubt this, they may be unable to engage in higher-order thinking. A lack of clarity over assessment methods can lead to considerable demotivation, withdrawal or rebellion. Elton argues that, in order for students to be genuinely motivated to learn the subject, they first need a clear overview of the ways in which their work will be graded, a sense that they will be rewarded for the important aspects of the course (rather than for unimportant 'busy-work') and to see that the course prepares them well for these assessments.

These conflicts can be minimized, by ensuring constructive alignment (Biggs and Tang 2007), where the material and skills tested through assignments align with the intended outcomes for the learning experience, and where the teaching and learning methods build students' skills and knowledge in ways that will help them complete the assignments successfully. Biggs argues that the content, the teaching and learning methods and the assessment strategy must accord with each other if the student is to experience the optimum learning opportunity.

However well the assessment activity aligns with learning outcomes and learning opportunities, this may still not be sufficient to ensure that students progress seamlessly to the next stage of learning. Meyer and Land (2006a) have identified threshold concepts as the possible key to learning, or to the barriers that some students face. They contend that each discipline has its own threshold concepts – key topics that are transformative, irreversible, integrative, troublesome and bounded (Meyer and Land 2006b: 7–8). These concepts stump students most often, so they find themselves intellectually circling on the verge of comprehension, but not quite making it through to enlightenment. Effective learning involves students moving across these thresholds, so-called because once passed, a learner's view of the world, or at least of the subject, is irreversibly changed. If we apply this to higher education pedagogy, for example, one such threshold concept might be student-centred learning (Green and Pilkington 2006) – that gulf between Ramsden's second and third theories of university teaching (2003). Celia remembers the first time she encountered this as a novice university teacher. Her experience of university until then had been of a mainly didactic, teacher-centred approach. Once she grasped the implications of student-centred learning, she could not return to her previous way of thinking about teaching, as her core beliefs about what constituted education had been changed. Since threshold concepts are transformative, it is difficult to put oneself back into the pre-threshold mindset, such that teachers who have passed through the threshold often cannot understand why their students struggle with a topic. Identifying the threshold concepts in your discipline not only helps highlight potential sticking points for students but also reveals concepts that could ignite a passion for the subject in your students, since by definition they reach to the heart of the discipline.

These troublesome concepts require students to engage in higher-order, complex thinking about an academic discipline, typically well beyond the level expected in secondary schooling. Perry's scheme of intellectual and ethical development (1970), based on in-depth interviews with Harvard students (in other words, not your average undergraduate), has led to many subsequent studies that aid course design to promote such higher-order thinking (for a good overview, see Pascarella and Terenzini 2005). Perry's scheme begins with 'dualism' – black-and-white, simplistic thinking using absolute categories – where many first-year students find themselves. Their tendency here is to rely on an authority figure (like a teacher) to give them 'the right answer'. Next is 'multiplicity', where students recognize alternative perspectives, but either still defer to the teacher's opinion on a topic or believe that *all* views are equally valid, regardless of the varying quality of evidence or analysis. The somewhat depressing finding is that most graduating students are still at this stage of development (Pascarella and Terenzini 2005: 163). 'Relativism' is the third stage, in which students see knowledge as contextual and relative – a transformation in their thinking that might also cause 'analysis–paralysis', where judging the validity and applicability of competing evidence may delay a student's progress. In the final stage, 'commitments to relativism', individuals test claims and propositions in an integrated, systematic way. The research tells us undergraduates are very unlikely to reach this stage, yet offering it as a goal is an incentive to stretch intellectually. Some teachers who are themselves at the final stage of understanding may find it difficult to empathize with their less sophisticated students. This difficulty resonates with Meyer and Land's work on threshold concepts.

Working in and developing learning communities

SEDA has an appropriately broad definition of 'learning communities': students, university teachers, educational developers, colleagues who support students – all fit under this large umbrella. We discussed the audience for this book in Chapter 1 as the teachers, educational developers and colleagues who support students. Here we focus on students.

The learning community of students in our study largely comprises first-year students (freshmen): we recognized this group as in particular need of support as they enter the novel learning experience of higher education. All student groups represent diverse needs and approaches, but this comes into particular focus when addressing first-year student groups. First-year students often find themselves faced with new ways to study, in unfamiliar surroundings, and frequently encountering new ideas and approaches (Tinto 1993; Upcraft et al. 2005); the majority have recently left school and are developing as young adults at the same time as entering a new phase in their education. Some might be dealing with adult life for the first time, learning to live away from their families, to manage their finances and personal lives as well as their educational experiences. Others may be stepping back into education after a break, bringing different sets of life experiences and motivations to study. For all these reasons, first-year students are likely to be vulnerable and to have a diverse range of needs.

Many institutions have focused on supporting first-year students in particular, as student drop-out rates tend to be higher at this stage than later (Cook and Rushton 2008; Upcraft et al. 2005). The loss of a student in the first year of their study represents a significant event for the individual, but it also means loss of income for the institution, income that may be hard to recover. With the expansion in student numbers and an increase in 'non-traditional' students entering higher education, many institutions are concerned with the need to support students as they transition into higher education (UCAS 2010).

Tinto (1993) suggested that institutions with low student attrition were more willing to become engaged in students' social and intellectual development. In his examination of student retention, he identified four main causes of premature departure from a degree programme: difficulty, adjustment, isolation and incongruence.

Those who leave because of the intellectual difficulty of the work are relatively unusual. Adjustment involves separating from the past life that preceded the course and adjusting to the new; students who leave for this reason usually do so in the first few weeks of the course and may well successfully join another course. Isolation arises when students fail to form friendships or connections with others, be they students or teachers. Incongruence, in contrast, occurs when – despite interacting with fellow students and teachers – students feel they do not fit in with the institution as a whole. Although these situations are sometimes unavoidable, much can be done to reduce the chances of attrition if universities, programmes and teachers address these four causal factors.

Social support in the first year, combined with adequate guidance in choosing the right degree programme and institution, are vital to reducing attrition, according to both Wilcox et al. (2005) and Cook and Rushton (2008), who found that the wrong choice was the main reasons for students to leave in the first year. Attrition may also be countered by institutions taking action to create an institution–community–student partnership (Moxley et al. 2001), rather than leaving it to chance. Moxley et al. (2001) urge teachers to encourage students to discuss and reflect on their roles as students; this is particularly necessary as students are transitioning between different types of educational provision. Many students' experience of didactic teaching at high school does not prepare them for the style of learning expected at university (Cook and Rushton 2008; Wilson and Sweet 2003), despite a shift in schools, focusing on course work and continual assessment. Students may need to be supported, perhaps by a personal tutor ('academic advisor') and through tailored programmes to develop their independent learning skills.

According to research in the UK, students often experience a dip in confidence around six weeks into the first term (Cook and Rushton 2008), with a second dip in confidence – and the time some students consider dropping out of the course – towards the end of one term and the start of the next, around Christmas in UK universities. In many institutions, programmes hold end-of-module exams in January. Students may feel daunted by the prospect of returning to university: worried about their ability to perform well in these exams. Cook and Rushton's research at the University of Ulster found the main reasons students gave for leaving by January of the first year was 'personal', 'course unsuitable' or 'to go elsewhere', and they conclude that since these students 'leave before they have the opportunity to fail [...], this indicates dissatisfaction with their early experience' (Cook and Rushton 2008: 23). It may also be triggered by concern about possible failure. These dips in confidence coincide with peaks in disruptive student behaviour (often politely referred to as 'classroom incivility' or 'classroom impropriety'), according to Boice's large-scale, three-year study in the USA (1996), where mid-term and end-of-term exams were found to heighten anxieties. Viewing these studies side by side suggests university teachers need to accentuate their support and encouragement in the build-up to assessment periods. We will discuss ways to support students in some detail in Chapters 4–7.

Working effectively with diversity and promoting inclusivity

First in this section, a note on terminology: when talking about diversity, we are using the term in its broadest sense – literally the very varied and different backgrounds and experiences of the students themselves – not in the narrower sense sometimes used in the USA, where diversity can act as a shorthand for ethnic or racial diversity. In this section, we'll discuss only those aspects of diversity that pertain to the findings in our study.

Levels of participation in higher education (HE) have been increasing in both the UK and USA: between 1999 and 2009, participation rates in the UK increased from 56 per cent to 70 per cent of 18 year olds (Department for Education 2011a); in the USA over the same period, they grew from 45 to 50 per cent of 18 to 19 year olds, with smaller increases for students in other age ranges (Aud et al. 2011; National Center for Education Statistics 2011). Multiple factors account for this growth: the increasing number of colleges and universities offering degree programmes; a higher level of attainment at secondary school, with a greater proportion of schoolchildren opting to stay in school to age 18; national and regional schemes aimed at widening participation in HE; and more sophisticated recruitment and retention practices, including additional opportunities for students to receive academic, financial and personal support (HEFCE 2006; Provitera McGlynn 2007).

This increase, in turn, means that our classes are more diverse than ever, that our students' experiences vary more noticeably, and of course, that it takes more effort on the part of their university teachers to find commonalities to draw a disparate group together. The wealth of publications on student diversity in recent years attests to the fact that this gradual change in the make-up of our classes is causing teachers and university leaders to step back and re-evaluate both their pedagogic approaches and their institutional support mechanisms (see, for instance, Brown-Glaude 2009; Carroll and Ryan 2005; Harper and Quaye 2009; Massey et al. 2003; Ouellett 2005).

Race, ethnicity and performance

Concern over a perceived link between performance and ethnicity has led to several studies in the last 20 years (Coker 2003; Ferguson et al.

2002; Hurtado and Carter 1997; McManus et al. 1995). In the UK, for example, attention has focused on the perceived underperformance of Black and Minority Ethnic (BME) groups compared with the majority white group. A HEFCE (2010) study found a large difference in final achievement on degree courses, with only 37 per cent of BME students in their study achieving the highest two degree classifications (a First or a 2:1) compared with 62 per cent of white students. In the USA the focus tends to be on African-American students (especially men) and Native American students, again in comparison with their white peers (Demmert 2001; Harper and Quaye 2007). Much of the debate is complicated by multiple factors, with affluence and access to social capital proving to be the most important factor in both countries (Popovic 2010), affecting enrolment to higher education and performance once there.

What Tinto calls 'incongruence' might explain the underperformance of some students from minority ethnic groups. Incongruence arises from a mismatch between students' expectations about the nature of the university experience, perhaps based on an idealized notion of college life, but can also arise from perceptions of cultural fit. Such cultural or ethnicity-based issues are often complex and nuanced. Steele (2010: 140–2) discusses the kinds of cues that individuals in any minority may identify in a given situation (How many people here are like me? Do people segregate in social settings? Is prejudiced language challenged?) and explores the impact of these 'contingencies' on individuals' success and comfort in that setting. Similarly, Chavous (2002) studied the role of student background, perceptions of ethnic fit and racial identification for African-American students at a predominantly white university. While cautioning against viewing all African-American students as a homogenous group, he found overall that African-American students tended to be from less advantaged backgrounds than white students, and to perform worse academically than white students from the same background. He questions whether non-cognitive factors related to experience and race-related belief systems have an impact in adjusting to university life; he concludes that ethnic minority students who experience being in a minority at high school have fewer problems adjusting to university than those who had attended schools where they were in the majority. This gives a more sophisticated explanation of why poor African-American students tend to perform worse at university than more affluent

African-American students – the latter were more likely to have mixed socially and academically with white people before coming to university, while their poorer African-American peers may have had very little previous experience of white culture and faced difficulty in settling into the new white-dominated environment.

Gender and performance

There is compelling evidence in both the UK and USA that girls outperform boys at every level of education (Francis 2000; Sax 2008), with increasing numbers of women entering university (in the UK for instance, 42 per cent women in 1970, 55 percent in 2006) and more women than men achieving a First or 2:1 at the end of their undergraduate degree programmes (Purcell and Elias 2010). However, this apparently positive picture for women is complicated by several culturally determined factors. Purcell and Elias's long-term study exposed significant differences in gender perceptions of ability and self-confidence in choice of subject studied, and in willingness to live away from home, all of which contribute to a persisting gap between graduate earnings for men and women. Sax (2008) likewise reported that female students in the USA are less confident, despite typically higher grades, and curiously that women with major financial worries performed better than expected. She also found engineering to be the only subject where women can be predicted to score lower than men.

Men are still more likely to study subjects that lead to traditionally higher paid jobs in the built environment, engineering and science, while women are more likely than men to study health-related subjects and public services and care-related vocational qualifications. Women are also less likely than men to apply to the most prestigious universities (Purcell and Elias 2010). This may be connected to a similar reluctance to study far from home and to a reported lower self-confidence. Once graduated, some women's pay is lower than men's because of lower weekly hours worked, perhaps caused by demands on their time for domestic and caring duties, and a tendency to work in female-dominated (and lower-paid) workplaces. In brief, it is generally still the case that women and girls perform better in education but are rewarded financially less than men once they graduate.

Dyslexia and performance

Positive recruitment policies and a general raising of awareness has led to more students with disabilities being able to attend university. In most countries, however, people with disabilities still face huge challenges to gain admittance to higher education and to complete courses once there. The only disability raised by teachers in this study was dyslexia, a learning difficulty that is thought to affect between 5 and 10 per cent of the UK population (LSIS 2004; Parliamentary Office of Science and Technology 2004; Pennington 1991) and between 10 and 17 per cent of the US population (Jones-London 2006). It primarily affects 'the skills involved in accurate and fluent word reading and spelling' (Dyslexia Action, n.d.). Fry, Ketteridge and Marshall (2003) claim that typically, dyslexia accounts for half of all students reporting a disability at UK universities. It can affect people with a wide range of intellectual ability. People with dyslexia tend to have difficulty in processing the link between the spoken word and writing; their verbal memory, ability to organize, and decoding skills may be less fluent than those without dyslexia. With appropriate support, these difficulties may be overcome and need not prevent people with dyslexia succeeding with academic work. In both the UK and USA, appropriate support may include amendments to the assessment requirements, for example by allowing more time in exams and the provision of specialist equipment, including software (Fry et al. 2003; Goldius and Gotesman 2010; Gravestock 2006; Jacob et al. 1998; Waterfield et al. 2006). We discuss ways to support students with dyslexia in Chapter 5, where we also argue that such adjustments are usually beneficial to all students, regardless of learning disability.

Generational differences

Research into generational characteristics and attitudes might help us understand some of our reasons for thinking that 'students today aren't what they used to be' – a commonly heard indication of bafflement among university teachers, though we wish to stress a few caveats along the way. Categories provided by Howe and Strauss (2000), in particular, have shaped people's views of the so-called 'millennial generation': namely, people born roughly between 1982 and

2000, though exact dates vary depending on author, as does the generation title (Generation Y, Net-Generation and Digital Natives being among other contenders). While Howe and Strauss aren't saying that absolutely all individuals born in this period will bear the same traits, they do argue that seven core characteristics are more prevalent among millennials: they are special, protected, confident, team-oriented, achievement-oriented, pressured and conventional (Howe and Strauss 2000: 174–88).

These broad-brush characteristics can easily become a convenient, but dangerously simplistic, tool by which to rationalize classroom situations and surprises. To overcome such simplification, Nilson (2010) recommends that teachers think about how they might tap into these characteristics in their courses, while fully conscious that not all students bear such attributes in the first place. For example, setting clear policies on late assignments or speed of returning homework might dovetail a teacher's need for workable ground rules with the students' need for certainty and protection. Educational developers Kathryn Plank and Todd Zakrajsek (2011) have used the millennial research in workshops as a foil to explore whether one generation's attributes are truly unique (they are not), which can lead to productive discussions about the prevalence of particular attitudes and behaviours on a specific campus and strategies to help students expand their repertoire of attributes during their studies. At the same time, participants examine how the educational context has changed since many university teachers were students (particularly in relation to technology), and how these changes affect teaching and learning, too. In this way, an oversimplified framework becomes a heuristic for thinking more broadly about students, the learning context and the skills teachers can help them develop.

Some commentators on this generation suggest that there has been a change in relationship between parents and children. Twenge (2006), for instance, argues that these children have become accustomed to having their views taken into account much more than was the case in previous generations, citing examples where teenage children have affected parents' job choices or significant purchases. The suggestion is that this has led to a changed attitude in students, who, accustomed to having their views taken seriously, expect to be treated as equals in the classroom. Furthermore, there has been a change in the behaviour of parents, too, who feel entitled to engage with every aspect of their children's lives, even when those children are adults. Parents who descend on the dean or other senior managers to complain about perceived unfairness in assessment or to plead for special treatment have been dubbed 'helicopter parents' (Redmond 2008).

Whether or not these stereotypes of students and their parents are valid, some teachers have commented on the perceived link between this form of parenting and an increase in classroom incivility. The perception is that an indulged generation of young people feel entitled to challenge and question at every turn, at times in a way which their teachers perceive as lacking in respect for authority or expertise. For the purposes of our study, we'll leave aside the fascinating debates and complexities of power relations in the classroom (see, for instance, Bourdieu and Passeron 1965/1994), other than to acknowledge that power is inevitably unevenly distributed in an undergraduate class, and that respect is better earned than demanded.

Stereotyping and microaggressions

Steele and Aronson coined the term 'stereotype threat', which they describe as 'being at risk of confirming, as self-characteristic, a negative stereotype about one's group' (1995: 797). In other words, concerns about fitting a cultural stereotype can trigger anxieties that lead individuals from stereotyped groups to underperform (in a similar fashion to the Chavous study we mentioned earlier). Initial studies focused on stereotypes that African-Americans were less intelligent than whites (Steele and Aronson 1995) and that women were less intelligent than men (Steele 1997). In both cases, individuals belonging to the stigmatized group performed less well when the stereotype was stated directly or even alluded to (for instance, with the phrases 'personal factors' and 'verbal reasoning'). Later studies have detected the negative influence of stereotype threat for a range of groups (for instance, Clark et al. 2011; Gonzales et al. 2002; Shapiro 2011; Steele 2011), through complex psychological and physiological processes (Schmader et al. 2008), and have found that the stereotype need not be a negative one: if the stereotype is that one group excels in a particular subject or type of test, that can generate performance anxiety, too (Aronson et al. 1999; Stone 2002). Of concern for university teachers is the finding that stereotype threat can be triggered by individuals who do *not* themselves harbour prejudices against particular groups, but whose comments or actions lead students from stigmatized groups to doubt whether they will be treated fairly.

A separate body of research helps us think more precisely about the nuances of everyday interactions and how these might be received by members of groups different from our own: microaggressions, which Derald Wing Sue (2010b: 3) describes as 'everyday verbal, non-verbal, and environmental slights, snubs, or insults, whether intentional or unintentional, that communicate hostile, derogatory, or negative messages to target persons based solely upon their marginalized group membership'. So an inappropriate comment that goes unchallenged or uncorrected – 'That's so gay', 'There's no need to be a bitch about it', 'Man up and grow a pair' – might heighten anxieties among negatively stereotyped students and lessen their chances of success.

These two areas of research tell us that if we, as university teachers, are truly to support all students in our classes to achieve their potential, we need to become much more adept navigators of hot moments in the classroom with the confidence to respond appropriately. For many teachers, this will be a new and challenging skill to develop.

Scholarship, professionalism and ethical practice

This SEDA value encourages us to refute the false binary between research and teaching that prevails in some universities. Historically, many academics, particularly those whose primary function was research, defined themselves first according to their subject (Jenkins 1996): they were geographers or astrophysicists, psychologists or art historians, and scholarship resided in those fields. Yet at the time of writing, teachers in many countries find themselves faced with increasing demands in their roles. In some US research-intensive institutions, for example, professors who were accustomed to teaching one graduate-level class per year are now faced with 100 or more undergraduates, since budget cuts and ensuing job losses have left holes in the teaching schedule.

Professionalizing the teaching side of academics' roles lies at the core of educational development organizations like SEDA in the UK, POD in the USA and their international parent organization, ICED.

Founded by pedagogical activists and experts, these groups encourage academics to become not only better university teachers but also more scholarly teachers – improving their practice firstly by drawing on the higher education knowledge base, and then by making our own contributions to the field. This requires a transfer of learning to occur (Bransford and Schwartz 1999), where researchers come to apply scholarly methods not only to their subject but also to the teaching of their subject.

The literature on higher education teaching and learning runs the gamut from highly controlled empirical studies to anecdotal reports of individual successes. As educational development has evolved (Grant et al. 2009), we have seen a move away from an anecdotal approach towards an evidence-based approach to HE pedagogy. In this book, we aim to add our own empirical data to that evidence base, as well as providing interpretations and successful practices based on varied sources in a range of disciplines.

While there is substantial literature on the first-year experience and student diversity, we find a lack of information on university teachers' perceptions and beliefs about their students. Research has long existed on schoolteachers' perceptions of their pupils and the possible effect of those perceptions (for instance, Crano and Mellon 1978; Rosenthal and Jacobson 1968). Our interest here – and our contribution to the field – was to locate the perceptions of university teachers and to analyse whether or not these perceptions are valid.

Investigating teachers' preconceptions about students and their learning pulls us into potentially difficult territory. In Chapters 4–6, you will see that, more often than not, teachers' beliefs were refuted by our student data. As with any social scientific research, ethical considerations played a vital role in the design of the study to enable us to gain insights into teachers' beliefs and students' learning, while protecting the individuals involved.

Research methodology

Four universities were involved in the study: two in the UK (specifically in England), and two in the USA. In Chapter 3, we describe these universities, along with a brief outline of higher education in both countries. We focused on courses with a historically wide range of performance, not courses where most students either did well or most poorly. These are all first-year courses, but (as we'll discuss in Chapter 3) US courses are often open to students from all four years. At each location, we invited teachers to participate in the research. As a result, our interviewees were self-selected rather than random subjects.

In phase one of the study, one of the authors interviewed all 38 teachers, using a protocol that had received ethical approval in each institution. To help focus our interviewees' responses, they were asked specifically to discuss students taking the first-year courses we had identified for inclusion in the study. Interviews were recorded and transcribed verbatim and the resulting data were then analysed using an inductive approach (Cousin 2009), based loosely on grounded theory (Glaser and Strauss 1967) to identify specific themes.

Themes that were mentioned by at least three teachers were highlighted as potential factors believed to affect student performance. Factors mentioned by only one or two people were discounted in order to anonymize individual responses and minimize more idiosyncratic ideas, but also because preconceptions – or stereotypes – only become meaningful when they are more widely shared (McGarty et al. 2002). In the event, there were very few of these, since most aspects were raised by several teachers. Naturally, a degree of interpretation was involved, as not all teachers used precisely the same terms. However in the interviews, teachers were asked to give examples of the behaviours they identified, rather than simply a label.

While some themes were common at both the US and UK institutions, others were particular to one country. Consequently, the design of the student survey was tailored for each setting (see Appendix 1). As we explained in Chapter 1, differences in American and British terminology could lead to confusion, so we also adjusted our wording where necessary for the student surveys in each setting.

In phase two of the study, we surveyed students taking the first-year courses taught by our 38 university teachers. In total, 1,241 students from 14 subject areas completed the surveys. With the students' consent, we collated their final grades for that subject at the end of the course. We used these grades as our benchmark of student performance, with students ranked from highest- to lowest-scoring in each course, and then divided into quartiles. The results were analysed to establish which of the teachers' beliefs were supported. In other words, did the students who performed best in each course have the expected characteristics, and did the worst-performing students conform to their teachers' negative preconceptions?

In all four institutions, we underwent ethics approval (UK) and institutional review board approval (USA). In the UK, ethics committees directly reviewed the interview protocol from phase one, but – surprisingly – deemed it unnecessary to review the student surveys. In the USA, however, we went through a two-phase approval process, where firstly the interview protocol was approved, followed by the student survey.

Before we present the results of this research in some detail in Chapters 4–7, in the next chapter we explain the context for the study, describing the four institutions involved, and comparing the different higher education systems in both countries.

3
HIGHER EDUCATION IN THE UK AND USA

Key differences between the education systems in the UK and USA influenced the teachers' responses in our study. In this chapter, we provide a brief overview of each system as it affected the project – mostly so that you can read up on any system that is unfamiliar to you – and we provide salient information about the four institutions in the study. It is important to recall that the UK's four countries – England, Northern Ireland, Scotland and Wales – exercise varying degrees of autonomy when it comes to education policy and practice. Since our study involved two English universities, you will note a slant towards that context.

We chose these universities to reflect a range of institutions in each country so that we could explore a wider variety of issues. While preserving the anonymity of participants in the study, we give you as much relevant detail as we can about the institutions and have renamed them after typefaces. Both English universities are large and publicly funded; one is mainly vocationally oriented and teaching-focused (Arial), the other more traditionally academic and research-focused (Baskerville). In the USA, one university is medium-sized, private, and more teaching-focused (Constantia), while the other is large, public and research-intensive (Delphin).

The UK educational context

Getting to university in the UK

Most British students enter university directly from secondary school or after a 'gap year' when they gain work experience or travel. These traditional students have typically completed seven years in secondary education. After five years – at age 15 or 16 – they sit GCSE (General Certificate of Secondary Education) exams unless they are in Scotland, where they sit Scottish Qualifications Certificate (see below). The government has set a target of five GCSEs at grade C or above for the general population in England, Wales and Northern Ireland; in 2010, 75.4 per cent of schoolchildren met this benchmark (Department for Education 2011b). Most pupils are required to take English, mathematics and science, but can usually choose other subjects. Some leave school after GCSEs, while others continue in education for a further two years – referred to as the sixth form – to complete A (Advanced) levels. Government figures show that 74 per cent of 17 year olds are still in secondary education (compared with 98 per cent at 16), but some of these will be retaking GCSEs or studying vocational courses (OECD 2009: 303). A typical sixth-form student studies four or five subjects in the first year (the 'lower sixth') before taking AS exams. Many then drop one or two subjects and continue with the remaining three or four in the second year (the 'upper sixth'), ending with A2 exams. Grades from AS and A2 exams are combined to provide a final A-level grade in each subject.

Scotland's school system differs from the rest of the UK in that pupils complete Standard Grade or Intermediate exams at ages 15 or 16; then most continue for a year to take Highers. Technically, Higher qualifications provide entry to university, but most students who want to earn a degree continue at school for a final year and sit Advanced Higher exams. Unlike the A-level system elsewhere in the UK, the Scottish system favours breadth of study over early specialization. In some respects, as you'll see, this makes it a little closer to the US secondary school system.

The gradual narrowing of the curriculum in the rest of the UK means that schoolchildren have to make critical subject choices when they are only 14. For instance, if you hope to study medicine (an undergraduate subject in the UK), you need to be sure to choose chemistry as a GCSE subject. Without it, you are unlikely to make it to medical school.

Pupils who hope to progress to higher education apply to up to five universities through a centralized clearing system (UCAS: University and College Admissions Service) during their penultimate school year. By this time, they have already chosen the exact programme (in US terms, 'major') they wish to study and their choices have been considerably limited under the narrow A-level system. UK degrees are specialized from the outset (unlike the liberal arts approach in US higher education), so students will not have the prerequisite knowledge for many programmes. Once at university, students rarely transfer to another degree programme, and if they do, they often have to begin their studies from scratch, losing any credits they have accrued in their original programme.

University entry requirements vary based on institution and subject. As you might expect, more popular subjects at the most prestigious universities require the highest grades; typically, the minimum requirement for entry into any degree programme in the country is two A-level passes. With pressure on university places increasing due to cuts in funding, entry requirements are inevitably rising; at the same time, pupils are achieving year-on-year improvements in A-level grades, leading to accusations that A levels have become easier or that schoolteachers teach only how to pass exams, rather than building up the wider range of intellectual skills required for further study. While this claim is contested, you'll see that it arises among the UK university teachers in our study.

Pupils who don't attain the grades they need to attend their preferred universities can apply to other institutions and degree programmes through the UCAS Clearing system once they receive their A-level results in August each year. This month-long scramble for places throws a lifeline to both underperforming students and less popular programmes. Again, Clearing was raised as an issue in our interviews with teachers.

British universities

British universities fall broadly into two main categories: research-intensive universities (like Baskerville) and teaching-led universities (such as Arial); in addition, smaller specialist institutions and colleges of further education offer some higher education programmes.

Research-intensive universities in the UK offer mainly degrees in 'pure' subjects (using Biglan's 1973 framework), such as philosophy, history and the natural sciences, while their vocational programmes are mostly in the higher-paid professions – medicine, dentistry, law and their ilk. These universities are divided into formal and informal groups, such that the higher education literature features a confusing range of monikers. The Russell Group represents the self-styled 'top 20' universities in the UK: large, prestigious institutions that receive some income from teaching, but give greatest emphasis to world-class research and externally funded projects. This group modelled itself after the US Ivy League and includes Oxbridge (Oxford and Cambridge) and the 'redbricks' – a term technically referring to six Victorian-era civic universities, but often used to describe any research-intensive older institution. The 1994 Group was established in response to the Russell Group and comprises smaller research-focused institutions, keen to ensure that they still influence the national research agenda despite their smaller size. The 1994 group includes many 'plateglass' universities – those founded during the expansion of higher education in the 1960s.

In contrast, teaching-led universities are mostly those that were designated polytechnic colleges during the expansion of higher education in the 1960s, but which gained the 'university' title under the Further and Higher Education Act of 1992. For this reason, they are often referred to as 'post-1992 universities' or 'new universities'. Many of these institutions, including Arial, were amalgamations of several older colleges with an emphasis on applied education. So while both research-intensive and teaching-led universities may offer degrees in art, the redbrick is likely to emphasize art history, while the former polytechnic will specialize in creative art and design for practitioners. There are many areas where post-1992 institutions continue to excel, particularly in their approach to teaching skills: these institutions took the lead in ensuring that university teachers were well prepared for classroom interactions and pioneered certificate programmes on teaching in higher education.

Several smaller institutions have evolved from specialist colleges in fields such as education and agriculture. As they expand and develop their programmes, some of these colleges are granted the title 'university college', and eventually 'university', following a lengthy accreditation process. There is currently only one private institution in the UK with university status, attracting two-thirds of its students from other countries (HESA n. d.). Some higher education courses are also offered at colleges of further education (FE; similar to US community colleges).

These colleges often attract students from historically under-represented groups as well as those who are returning to study after years in employment, or are studying part-time while working. The UK government has provided some additional funding to encourage non-traditional and minority students to return to education under the title 'widening participation'. FE colleges work in collaboration with a university to deliver initial higher education courses; to obtain a full degree, students have to transfer to a university for a final year or two of study (HEFCE 2009).

Undergraduate degrees in the UK

Most UK undergraduate degrees take three years to complete, while foreign language courses are four years long (with a year abroad) and some business degrees are four-year 'sandwich' programmes, where the third year is spent working in industry. Specialist professional degrees like medicine, architecture and veterinary science take longer. In Scotland, degrees usually take four years to complete and lead to a master's qualification, rather than a bachelor's, more akin to the traditional system in many mainland European countries.

British degree programmes are made up of modules that can vary in credit size, duration, contact hours, and so forth. In total, a bachelor's degree entails 360 credits, with each credit equivalent to 10 hours of study – whether in class-contact time or private study – for the average student. That equates to 40 hours' study per week during term time. The syllabus for an individual course may well tell students how much private study time is expected, based on this credit system. Science and engineering programmes, for example, tend to require more class-contact time in labs and are therefore meant to assign less homework, while humanities subjects require students to read extensively outside class and have fewer contact hours as a result. The average student is expected to undertake roughly the same amount of work in any discipline to earn a degree.

On many British degree programmes, the first year's grades do not count towards the final qualification, but instead represent a hurdle that students must pass in order to continue. Universities hold 'resit' exams at the end of each summer to allow students a second chance to pass the year. Since programmes typically follow a cohort model where each group of students progresses in lock-step, passing on schedule allows students to proceed with their friends and maintains the sense of community that can keep them buoyed. Within this cohort model, many programmes offer a range of option courses (electives) alongside compulsory classes taken by the entire group.

With rises in tuition fees, students are increasingly questioning 'value for money' in terms of time with their teachers, access to resources and the likelihood of future earnings. What most students don't see, however, is the extensive British quality assurance system, which surprises university teachers in many other countries. Degrees are carefully monitored to ensure consistency both within the institution and across the sector. University teachers have some freedom in designing class content and assignments, but within a set protocol that states how many coursework assignments and exams will be set, which topics will be addressed, and what learning outcomes successful students will be able to demonstrate through their work. Student work is often marked blind to reduce the risk of bias, then 'second marked', where a colleague either re-marks papers or moderates a sample of papers to check the grading is fair and appropriate. For modules where the grades count towards the final degree qualification, all programmes must appoint external examiners – subject experts from other universities who approve exam questions in advance, check for consistency in grading and alert the university to any discrepancy compared to the rest of the higher education sector. This highly regulated and complex system provides *some* reassurance of consistency across institutions, yet the administrative burden on university teachers is very high and sceptics argue the system acts as a fig leaf to hide the fact that practice varies widely between institutions.

The social and financial context

University for many students marks their first experience of living away from home. Most first-year students live in university-owned accommodation and in subsequent years share rented houses with friends. Most universities encourage this socializing, with many bars on campuses and in university halls of residence (the drinking age in the UK is 18), and they support their students' unions, which organize social events and student societies and help students develop their interests beyond their immediate academic studies.

The experience differs somewhat for students from less affluent backgrounds, who in previous generations would most likely not have been able to attend university. While financial support for widening participation has been available, it's widely acknowledged that the scheme has not been as successful as intended; young people from the least affluent sectors of society remain the least likely to reach university. Those who do continue their studies more often live at home while studying, creating a dynamic where they're less able to mix with other students later in the evening and build up a wider social network. Beatty-Guenter (1994), Tinto (1993) and Cook and Rushton (2008) emphasize the importance of ensuring that all students feel part of the institution; these potentially isolated students may need even more support than their peers.

Tuition fees now present an additional sticking point. In the past, UK students at university were not required to pay tuition fees, while cost-of-living expenses were distributed by the government based on family income. In 2006, the Labour government introduced fees, in part as a way of funding an expansion in the sector with the specific goal of increasing access to under-represented groups. Fees were capped at around £3,000, with the least affluent eligible to apply for a government loan. Students could also apply for a means-tested grant and for university bursaries. The average student starting a degree in 2010 can expect to leave with a debt of more than £20,000 (NUS, n.d.). The Conservative–Liberal Democrat coalition government has allowed universities in England, Wales and Northern Ireland to increase their fees from 2012 to compensate for less financial support from central government (not to generate additional income); it has been surprised to find that most universities plan to set their annual rates at the maximum of £9,000 – three times the previous level. The picture across the UK is complex, as devolved government in Wales and Scotland has led to different policies for students in those countries; for example, Scottish students attending Scottish universities do not pay any fees and Welsh students attending Welsh universities pay less than other UK students. Concerns about the fate of less affluent English students continue to loom.

The US educational context

Getting to university in the USA

Most American schoolchildren receive 12 years of education (to age 18) before they can enter university, with their grades for the final four years (junior high school and high school) typically included in their transcripts of academic achievement, expressed as a Grade Point Average (GPA). In certain states, pupils may be allowed to leave education earlier (as young as age 14), though latest census data show that 80.5 per cent of 18 to 24 year olds graduated from high school (US Census Bureau 2011). The curriculum remains broad throughout this schooling: while requirements vary from state to state, most pupils study English, mathematics, science and social sciences (which often means history), plus other elective subjects.

Pupils may also take Advanced Placement (AP) courses if they excel in their studies: these courses demand more from learners and are intended to equate to freshman (first-year) courses in higher education. Some universities and colleges accept AP credit in lieu of their own courses, so students can graduate more quickly, while others exempt students from specific freshman subjects, but won't count the credit towards a final degree.

For entry into university, pupils also take a national, standardized, privately-run test (usually either the SAT Reasoning Test or the ACT) so that university admissions officers have more uniform data than a simple GPA for courses taken at school, or information on extra-curricular activities and a personal statement. These standardized tests are intended to measure reading, writing and mathematical skills – in other words, preparedness for higher education – while the ACT also has a science reasoning component.

Standardized testing as a whole has increased in US high school education since the 2001 No Child Left Behind Act, where states are required to assess pupils' academic performance in order to receive federal funding. As you might expect, such testing is not without its detractors. Of particular concern is the idea that schoolteachers are 'teaching to the test', where they focus their energies on the kinds of questions they expect to appear in the tests, rather than encouraging their pupils to develop a deeper understanding of the material.

This issue arises in our interviews with university teachers in the USA, and is mirrored in the concerns of our UK interviewees.

As in the UK, most American students enrol in universities and colleges (these terms are basically synonymous) direct from high school, usually applying during their final year of schooling. Over 400 universities use the Common Application system, similar to the UK's UCAS, though with the additional ability for each institution to require specific further information as part of its application process. The majority of institutions, though, use their own separate application forms and require students to apply to each institution individually. Students incur a fee for each individual application.

Commonly, the application deadline is January each year, though two schemes – the binding Early Decision and non-binding Early Action – have earlier deadlines, while larger institutions often use a rolling admissions process all year and can accept new students at the beginning of each teaching term. Students are offered a place, rejected, or put on a wait-list of reserve candidates who might be able to attend the institution if spaces become available. The data for reaching these decisions varies by university; typical applications can contain standardized test scores, a transcript of school grades, a personal statement, sometimes a specific essay related to the particular focus of the institution (to identify whether the student is a good 'fit'), evidence of extra-curricular activity and community service and letters of recommendation. Some institutions will also consider aspects such as family connections, state residence, first-generation status, ethnicity, religious affiliation, work experience and class rank. As in the UK, institutions vary greatly in the grades they expect of prospective students.

American universities

The Carnegie Classification Framework has been used since 1973 to provide both broad and more nuanced categories to describe the diverse higher education institutions of the USA. Using the simplest of its categories, universities and colleges fall into six main groupings: doctorate-granting universities, master's colleges and universities, baccalaureate colleges, associate's colleges, special focus institutions and tribal colleges (Carnegie Foundation for the Advancement of

Teaching 2010). As many of these titles suggest, the classifications are based on the highest degrees awarded, where, for instance, doctorate-granting universities (like Delphin) award at least 20 doctorates per year, while master's universities (like Constantia) award fewer than 20 doctorates, but more than 50 master's degrees per year.

Broadly speaking, the doctorate-awarding institutions emphasize research over teaching, though they may still enrol large numbers of undergraduate and graduate students each year. The research focus of these institutions means that undergraduate classes may be taught by postgraduate students under supervision. Occasionally, this group of universities is still referred to as Research I or Research II – former Carnegie classifications. It includes the Association of American Universities (the country's 62 leading research universities), which itself incorporates seven of the eight elite Ivy League schools in the north-eastern United States, after which the British Russell Group was modelled.

Master's-level universities and baccalaureate colleges (often called liberal arts colleges to reflect the broad curriculum they offer) tend to focus more on teaching, though an element of research is typically expected. Liberal arts colleges, awarding mostly bachelor's degrees, in particular have a reputation for small class sizes and higher contact between students and their university teachers. A potential surprise to outsiders is that a high percentage of PhD students in the natural sciences completed their bachelor's degrees at liberal arts colleges, rather than research-intensive universities: for many students, the level of personal attention and learning support from full-time university teachers – rather than graduate teaching assistants – sway them in favour of these prestigious smaller colleges.

Associate's colleges are most often community colleges – similar to British FE colleges – and especially welcome students with non-traditional academic histories. They award associate's degrees after successful completion of two year's full-time study, after which students must transfer institution to gain a full bachelor's degree. Most teachers at these colleges have a master's degree in their subject and they typically teach far more classes than their university counterparts.

A further difference in US higher education is the number of private and religiously affiliated universities and colleges. Private colleges mostly charge higher tuition fees than the state-run public institutions, though many offer scholarships and bursaries to their students. Universities with a religious affiliation might select students based on their faith; others welcome people of different faiths.

Undergraduate degrees in the USA

Bachelor's degrees in the USA are designed as four-year, full-time programmes. In reality, they are flexible, allowing students to take fewer or more courses in a term depending on circumstance, motivation, or availability of courses. The US Department of Education records the percentage of students who complete their bachelor's within six years of study, so university leaders attend to those progression rates more than the four-year rate. Unlike in the UK, certain professional courses, such as medicine and law, cannot be taken at undergraduate level.

Most US undergraduates begin their higher education by studying a 'liberal arts' curriculum, meaning that they should become well-rounded individuals with a good grasp of the different fields of study: often humanities, social sciences, natural sciences and fine arts. Since study at most universities begins this way, students need not decide their major (area of specialism) until later in the programme – sometimes even into their third year of study. The liberal arts curriculum gives undergraduates a taste of various disciplines and an opportunity to consider whether, say, anthropology would suit them better than their intended physics major. Some vocationally oriented programmes (such as nursing or engineering) tend to be more restrictive and tie students earlier (more like the UK system).

Students in many universities choose their courses with the help of academic advisors – either regular university teachers or trained professionals who help them piece together their degrees, ensure they fulfil requirements, that they have the correct prerequisites, and that their chosen courses will fit the academic timetable. The level of flexibility in this highly modularized system makes coordination between teachers challenging. As most students don't generally progress in lock-step, their teachers have little chance of knowing exactly which courses they have already taken, or which discipline-specific skills they are sure to have practised. A striking difference between the US and UK systems, therefore, is the degree of individual autonomy for university teachers – US teachers have almost complete control over all aspects of their courses: from creating the syllabus, to choosing assignments, to policies on grading or late work. There is no external oversight at the level of the individual course; there is no system of second-marking assignments; and there are no exam boards. From a British perspective, this freedom can feel both exhilarating and precarious. Exhilarating in that you are suddenly able to make changes partway through a course when you realize it's not supporting your students' learning as you had intended and a better approach has presented itself; precarious in that it depends on the fundamental integrity of the individual teachers – a level of trust in the goodness of human nature long since absent from UK universities. Quality assurance procedures in US higher education are a comparatively light touch: individual courses are typically approved in skeleton form by each university's governing academic body, while each university's degree-awarding privilege is regulated by a regional accrediting organization, and each programme must demonstrate through one form of assessment (usually a final-year essay) that its graduating students meet the learning objectives of both the programme and the university's core undergraduate programme.

Students build up credits in each subject and the title of their degree reflects those credits: each institution stipulates the number of credits required in a discipline for it to be considered a major or a minor, and students can graduate with complex degrees, such as a double major with additional minors. Equally, students may prefer to maintain a broad educational base during their four years, leading to a single major and no minors.

Unlike the UK system, all grades usually count towards degrees and appear on transcripts. Rather than having 'resit' opportunities later in the year, students who are failing may be allowed to redo specific assignments while the course is still in progress (at the teacher's discretion), and if they ultimately fail, they have to retake the course from scratch – or pick an alternative course if possible.

The social and financial context

Students' living arrangements reflect the institution they attend: those studying at remote, rural universities tend to live on campus (some places make this a requirement, at least for freshmen students); those attending their local institution more often stay at home, or move into shared housing with other students – often their friends from high school. This latter situation, combined with the modular degree system, can make it harder for students to build strong friendships with their college peers: there is less chance of studying with the same students, or of happening upon them socially in the evenings. Yet, the difficulty of creating the 'social glue' that enhances the learning experience is often counteracted by well-resourced student affairs or student development divisions in universities: highly qualified professionals who engage students in extra-curricular (often called co-curricular) activities. This can range from centres that support minority students to events encouraging students to grapple with societal problems through dialogue, from intercollegiate and amateur athletics to volunteer and community work. The good-deeds culture runs deep in the USA. Community work provides a good 'service' line on students' CVs, too, presenting them as more rounded individuals.

In comparison with the UK, tuition fees at US universities are high, and higher still at many private institutions. But, in addition to government loans, many universities offer scholarships and bursaries to students based on need. Even so, the average debt for a US student graduating in 2009 was $24,000 (Cheng and Reed 2010), a 6 per cent increase on the previous year, raising concerns for less affluent students, some of whom opt to attend community college for their first two years of study to reduce the cost, but may find the transition to a four-year university more problematic as a result. For many US students, the only way to keep loans down is to work part-time while studying. In 2010, the average first-year student was working in the range of 6–13 hours per week in paid employment (NSSE 2010), while final-year students were working longer hours. Sometimes, this work is done at the university itself – staffing helpdesks, catering, working as department assistants, and so on – but the NSSE survey found that between 25 and 54 per cent of seniors were working in the regular economy. These are not necessarily jobs that will provide beneficial work experience for when students graduate. You'll see that some students in our study were working more than 40 hours per week to make ends meet.

Universities involved in this study

We have renamed the four institutions in this study after typefaces beginning with A, B, C and D, simply to make the text more readable. Arial and Baskerville universities are both in the UK, while Constantia and Delphin universities are in the USA. Here we provide some useful background information to contextualize the results we present in subsequent chapters.

Arial University

Arial University is situated in a large English city. Though its origins date back to the mid-nineteenth century, it is categorized as a post–1992, teaching-focused university, having become a polytechnic on the amalgamation of its constituent colleges, en route to university status.

On numerous campuses across the city, Arial delivers undergraduate and postgraduate courses in a broad range of disciplines, most of them still vocationally oriented, though a few traditional, 'pure' subjects remain. Arial supports 25,000 students, of whom 21,000 are undergraduates. Atypically for the UK university sector, half the full-time students at Arial come from the immediate area and live at home, and a large percentage are from ethnic minorities, reflecting the ethnic diversity of the city as a whole.

Arial also offers a large portfolio of part-time programmes. The vocational focus of many degrees has led to strong local and national ties with employers, with some programmes requiring work-based learning. Courses are well subscribed, with six applicants for every place and a typical entry requirement of between three Cs and three Bs at A level.

Of the university's 2,400 employees, around 2,000 are full-time university teachers. The *Guardian* league tables in 2010 ranked Arial roughly halfway down the table and reported a student–teacher ratio of 19:1. While the university prides itself on its teaching expertise, there are also several pockets of research excellence.

The subjects surveyed at Arial in this study are built environment, sound engineering and architecture.

Baskerville University

Baskerville is a large research-intensive university and one of the oldest, established around the turn of the twentieth century with roots that date back to the early 1800s. Around 25,000 students are enrolled at Baskerville, two-thirds of them undergraduates. As a whole, Russell Group universities like Baskerville attract nine or ten applicants for every undergraduate place. Its courses typically require between three A grades and three A* grades (the highest) at A level. Students are recruited from all over the country, as well as locally, and from overseas, particularly at postgraduate level. Baskerville lies in the top 25 (out of 117) institutions in the *Guardian* league table, while the Academic Ranking of World Universities (the Shanghai Ranking) ranks it in the top 100 universities. The university itself claims that it is one of the top 10 UK universities targeted by employers for bachelor-level graduates.

Baskerville offers most of the traditional subjects available in HE, including medicine, natural and life sciences, law, engineering, modern languages, humanities, social sciences and education. It employs 6,000 people, and while its own publications don't tell us how many are directly involved in teaching, the *Guardian* newspaper indicates a student–teacher ratio of 16:1. Most students are housed in purpose-built halls of residences and flats or in private rented houses near the campus. Students at Baskerville are likely to feel part of a community that may have little to do with the host city, but traditionally many remain in the area following graduation.

Students and teachers involved in this study were in the school of medicine.

Constantia University

Constantia University is a medium-sized, private, not-for-profit, religiously affiliated university in the west of the USA. Despite its religious affiliation, Constantia does not require students or employees to be of any particular religion, simply to be willing to engage in questions of faith and belief systems – including agnosticism and atheism – and to demonstrate a willingness to contribute to the university's social justice mission.

Of Constantia's almost 8,000 students, 55 per cent are under-graduates and 45 postgraduates, with the graduate programmes mostly in vocational areas (such as education, law and ministry). They are taught by 700 academics, two-thirds of whom are full-time, including almost half who are either tenured or tenure-track. The average under-graduate class size is 20 students – a student–teacher ratio of 13:1. Unlike at larger, research-intensive universities, classes are only ever taught by university teachers, never by graduate students. *US News and World Report* ranks Constantia in the top 10 universities in the West in its category; its six-year graduation rate stands at over 70 per cent.

Undergraduate programmes cover a broad range of traditional sub-jects from the humanities, arts, social sciences, natural sciences and professions, the latter comprising nursing and health professions, as well as various business-related fields. Though high school GPA is not the only measure used for admitting undergraduates, average GPAs hover around the 3.5 mark (out of 4.0). The four-year bachelor's pro-grammes at Constantia are centred on an integrated core curriculum: a required liberal arts sequence of courses, as in most US universities, but with a particular emphasis on philosophy and theology, reflecting the university's faith-based origins. All four subject areas surveyed at Constantia for this study contribute to Constantia's core curriculum and as such, the participating students could be majoring in any of the 60 or so bachelor's degrees on offer, while a number have yet to declare their major.

Constantia's undergraduate population is mostly female (six women to every four men) and it prides itself on being the most diverse private institution in the region, with 35 per cent of its US under-graduates coming from minority ethnic groups. Constantia's under-graduates predominantly study full-time and have an average age of 21. Although annual undergraduate tuition fees are in the region of $31,000, around 80 per cent of undergraduates receive financial aid averaging roughly $25,000. In addition, as you will see, many students are working long hours in paid employment to cover the cost of their studies – not the stereotypical 'rich kids' we might imagine at a private institution.

Traditionally teaching-focused, Constantia has been shifting to a point where teaching and scholarship share almost equal weight in decisions about tenure – the system by which university teachers become permanent employees after a six-year probation, during which time they demonstrate their suitability in terms of teaching, scholarship and service to the university. At the same time that research requirements are increasing, university teachers are still expected to maintain close contact with their students, who were promised small class sizes, to be known by their instructors by name, and to receive personal attention and support if they need it.

An additional change that is reflected in the findings here is that Constantia has joined Division I athletics, which entails participating in at least 14 inter-varsity sports. Student-athletes are on scholarships that require them to maintain a certain GPA in order to continue to play for the team; if their grades slip, they will not be allowed to play until they attain the set academic standard. At the same time, teachers have to make accommodations for students to be able to attend away games. Some Constantia teachers see Division I athletics as an expensive diversion from both education and the overall university mission, a tension that you will see reflected in some of the concerns raised in this study.

Subject areas surveyed at Constantia were biology, literature, environmental science and philosophy.

Delphin University

Located in the western United States, Delphin University is a large, research-intensive, doctorate-awarding public institution. Established in the second half of the nineteenth century, Delphin's original focus was on agriculture and agricultural research for the people of the state; one of its key goals now is to provide a liberal education 'as citizens'. Delphin is known for outstanding research in areas such as education, human sciences, agriculture, sustainability, water and land resources and engineering; its research focus has led it to promote undergraduate research since the 1970s, with almost two-thirds of university teachers saying they have worked with undergraduates on a research project in the last two years.

Delphin's enrolment stands at almost 22,000 students, with almost 3,000 on master's or doctoral programmes. Sixteen per cent of undergraduates study at Delphin part-time. Almost 900 academics work here, creating a student–teacher ratio of 17:1, while the average class size is between 20 and 29 students. Only half the academics teach undergraduate students. Like Constantia, Delphin has more female than male students (53 and 47 per cent, respectively); 75 per cent of its students are in-state (paying $4,500 per year to study here), 15 per cent are from other states (paying almost $13,000 in fees), and a further 10 per cent are from other countries.

Delphin offers over 170 undergraduate degree programmes covering the humanities, arts, social sciences, natural sciences, veterinary sciences, agriculture, environmental sciences, business, education and engineering. To be admitted, undergraduates must have at least a high school GPA of 2.5 (out of 4.0), as well as taking standardized tests. All undergraduates complete a general education programme before progressing to their chosen major. It comprises not only the typical courses across the broad disciplinary spectrum but also courses that will build students' academic and interpersonal skills, including courses that emphasize communications and quantitative reasoning.

Delphin University is located in one of the numerous western US states with a large Mormon population – members of the Church of Jesus Christ of Latter-day Saints, the common acronym for which is LDS. Approximately 80 per cent of Delphin's students are LDS Church members and the traditions of the church have an impact on study patterns: most men aged 19–25, and some women (aged 21–29), go on a mission for 18–24 months, so the average age of undergraduate students at Delphin is a little higher than is typical, at just over 22. In addition, as you will see, some university teachers expressed concern that female students were marrying and starting a family before graduating; this in part accounts for the high number of students studying part-time at Delphin – some of them are already raising children while completing their degrees. The university works hard to create an environment that enables female students to graduate. Delphin's six-year graduation rate currently stands at almost 60 per cent.

At Delphin, we surveyed teachers and students in anthropology, art and design, biology and engineering.

From these four institutions in two different countries, we interviewed 38 university teachers across 14 disciplines and surveyed

1,241 students taking those teachers' first-year classes. In the next three chapters, you see which presumptions were common to teachers in both countries or in only one country and will find out which presumptions were upheld by the student data.

4

Understanding beliefs shared by teachers in the UK and USA

Chapter 4 describes the common themes identified by university teachers in both countries. You will remember from Chapter 2 that we asked teachers to tell us the key characteristics of students who perform well, and those who do less well. We then surveyed students to identify those with the characteristics. Finally we compared exam or assessment performance in our interviewees' classes with survey responses to see if students achieved the expected levels of performance.

Altogether, teachers in both the UK and the USA raised 10 preconceptions in common, four of which proved to be upheld when we analysed the students' academic performance, while another six were not upheld by the data. By 'upheld', we mean that there is a statistically significant correlation between the preconception and final grade. These are summarized in Table 4.1.

We will now examine each belief in some detail to elaborate on the teachers' thoughts about their students and then consider practical responses to each item in light of the research findings. As you'll see, responses to these preconceptions vary in length: some demand far more detail to be able to respond appropriately, while others can be dealt with relatively swiftly.

Shared preconceptions that were upheld

1. Successful students expect to develop different study habits from those that worked at high school

University teachers in the UK and USA were concerned about students who didn't realize that study at university is different from that

Table 4.1 Summary of preconceptions and their validity: beliefs common to teachers in both the USA and the UK

UPHELD	NOT UPHELD
Successful students:	Teachers believed that successful students:
1. Expect to develop different study habits from those that worked at high school 2. Are punctual for lectures and classes 3. Keep up with assigned reading 4. Prefer to sit towards the front in class	5. Perform some paid, voluntary or service work, but not excessive hours 6. Choose to come to university of their own volition, rather than to please others 7. Belong to particular ethnic groups (white in most cases) 8. Have a particular gender (differs depending on the subject studied) 9. Talk with their teacher and ask questions 10. Actively form their own study groups

in high school. They recognized that students who have been success-ful so far are likely to continue with behaviour that has worked well in the past. Of course, such behaviour may well work at university too, depending on the course design, teacher behaviour and assess-ment strategies; but it may not. This interviewee recognized that uni-versity teachers had to intervene to help students change some of their practices:

> So students won't do well until we readjust their attitudes.
>
> (US-Delphin-11)

Apparently the problem lies in the typical high school approach to learning:

> Students are often trained in high school to study in a [...] note-card way [...]. You memorize terms and that's biology [...], so students who are prepared to say 'I have to go beyond memorization' are in general set for success. Students who are focusing on 'I need to memorize these terms and not work at the bigger picture' often do poorly.
>
> (US-Delphin-11)

Like many of his colleagues, this teacher does not dismiss memoriza-tion, but says learning by rote is insufficient. Successful students must also learn to make links and create knowledge and understanding for themselves, to take what we discussed in Chapter 2 as a 'deep approach' (Marton et al. 1997).

Some teachers elaborated on this to include a general approach to learning. They felt high school students are helped by teachers in their approach to learning as well as in the specifics of a subject. One teacher complained that despite, as he felt, explaining to students in great detail about what they would cover in class, and giving them guidance about what they needed to learn, each year students complain:

> that exams are unfair because they don't match what goes on in the lecture. They don't know how to compare [course work] to the exams. [...] There is always a disconnect between student expectation and what I see as the reality of the course. I think I've been clear what my expectations are, I think I'm telling students this is what you need to know, this is important [...] and they say 'no it's not fair, we didn't know that'.
>
> (US-Delphin-11)

Clearly, one person's idea of clarity will differ from another's, but this comment reflects a frequently stated concern that even when they have revised and rephrased their materials based on feedback from students and colleagues, teachers are told that they have not been clear. Some students, especially those who have been particularly successful in their pre-university work, expect to continue to find the work easy.

> I mean, not that they're not prepared in terms that they have the skills to write or to read, although that's an issue as well. But I've had a lot of students who things have come really easy to in high school and find out that it's not going to be like that anymore and so are just assuming that they're already successful before they've actually done the work.
>
> (US-Constantia-1)

Several teachers said some students have not been properly prepared for university by their high school teachers:

> [for] some it's a lack of preparedness, that they're actually coming into the classroom without having the same skill set.
>
> (US-Constantia-3)

Some schoolteachers may question whether it is their responsibility to prepare schoolchildren for university, or simply to see them safely through the school curriculum, regardless of whether the pupil aims to attend university or not. A UK university teacher complained about the approach taken by high schools, which involves breaking down the curriculum into 'bite-size' chunks of information. He claimed that, in an attempt to raise grades, teachers oversimplified the subject, leaving students ill-prepared for undergraduate study, which requires an ability to synthesize and analyse as well as merely memorize.

In our study, we asked students whether they expected to need to adopt different study habits at university from those that worked at school. We found those students who were more likely to agree about the need for new study habits performed best.

What we can do

Once students arrive on campus they need support in the transition to university life. The move from school to university can feel both overwhelming and liberating. Students are suddenly away from the constraints of home, perhaps for the first time; teachers and parents aren't keeping tabs on progress; and they may feel they shouldn't need to ask for help if it seems that everyone else is coping. All these factors may combine to leave the first-year or freshman student feeling unsure about whether or where to get help, or in a state of self-delusion, erroneously thinking that all is well.

In the first few days and weeks (potentially during orientation – see Chapter 5), we suggest that you make it very clear to your students that they'll need to **expand their range of learning methods** to excel at university. Try to get them into that mindset quickly, so that they don't have too many nasty shocks. As a starting point, consider your course design. Katarina Mårtensson at Lund University in Sweden encourages teachers to incorporate a session early on in which students reflect on their own preferred – and so far successful – learning strategies and to share their approaches in small groups. You collate the ideas, then discuss which strategies would probably work at university and what new strategies students might need to adopt to succeed at this higher level. If the students are all used to being top of the class, point out that the rules have changed, so they need to play differently and 'up their game'.

Throughout your course, support students in developing new skills. **Devote small amounts of time to exercises that model new ways of**

studying (say, 15–20 minutes each) and schedule them so that they occur at the point when students can put them into practice immediately – how to structure an assignment, how to use study time outside of class, and so on. While you might think this is only suitable for new students, we have been surprised in our own classes to find final-year students who are still unclear about how to read critically or how to take good notes in class. For some, it may be a refresher, but for many, it's an eye-opener to see how you would tackle an article, engage with a text, or map out a topic for an assignment. And students who already have well-rehearsed, effective learning strategies can share those with classmates as part of these short discussions. We provide a concrete example of an activity on developing reading and note-taking skills in Chapter 7.

Many students have not yet reflected on their productive times of the day. If you **include a short exercise where they work out when they are most alert or most drowsy**, you can encourage them to capitalize on the times when their brains are best for higher-order cognitive tasks and to reserve less demanding tasks (formatting, planning, searching for sources) for their low points.

Draw on the skills of your discipline to show how you would tackle a problem (see also the discussion concerning tenacity in Chapter 6). For example, when a history teacher heard on the grapevine that her first-year class was fomenting rebellion due to panic over assignments and course material, she used the historian's question–asking approach firstly to find out how individual students were feeling about the course and what was creating stress, and then used these responses to open a conversation on the subject in the next class. After a series of questions to probe the issue from different angles, she gave students a mid-term evaluation on 'the most difficult thing about studying history' and discovered the actual source of anxiety was the lack of a textbook; her students couldn't make sense of historical monographs, having only ever read pre-digested chunks of information while at high school. In response, the teacher ran a session in the following class on 'how to gut a book', explaining how history graduate students are taught to read and decipher a text and establish the argument being presented, including use of the index to see how important a point or topic may be to the author. The combination of questioning like an historian and then problem-solving with the tools of an historian defused the situation while also giving freshman students learning skills typically known only to postgraduates.

Make use of other students to model behaviour: buddy up students from more senior years with first years/freshmen. In some universities, students write alternative study books for their junior peers, covering 'things I wish I had done differently' and 'lessons I have learnt'. You do need to be careful, though, to avoid permitting students who failed first time around and who are retaking the course or re-sitting exams to infect the new cohort with ideas about the minimum work requirement. This was particularly the case with a group of students at Baskerville, where re-sitting students spread rumours about the irrelevance of aspects of the course. The teacher had to challenge these claims by reminding the class they were made by people who had been unsuccessful first time around. In this case the teacher harnessed the views of students who had passed the course, countering the unhelpful comments of those re-sitting.

A simple adjustment to the alternative study books is to **ask for focused feedback from students in your class**, in addition to any formalized end-of-course feedback they provide. Request specific advice for next year's students, including what they wish they had done differently. You then **compile the students' informal feedback and advice**, cluster the comments under headings and hand it out in the first class next time you run it. You might even want to include it in your syllabus. Since you have control over the use of the feedback, you can point out to your new students the advice that you consider particularly helpful and that which you don't. It is worth providing *all* of it, rather than editing, so that the students can read dissenting comments; this shows them that you are both open to feedback and confident enough in your teaching to take a few knocks without making it personal.

Cultivate a sense of professionalism and progression that engages students from the outset at a level that is achievable but which presents a certain amount of challenge. First-year courses are sometimes designed to be as easy as possible in a genuine attempt to smooth the route of students out of school and into HE. This can be misguided, as most students embarking on a course expect it to be challenging and, particularly where it is vocational, as in law, education or medicine (all undergraduate degrees in the UK), students expect to feel like prototypes of their future selves (lawyers, teachers, doctors). If their first experience is that the work is easy, or worse still, boring, because it involves going over old ground, they can easily be demotivated. This was the case for medical students at Baskerville: having faced huge challenges to achieve the highest grades in their A levels, they arrived at medical school excited at the prospect of becoming doctors. Because not all students had taken biology A level, the course started with a gentle overview of basic concepts. The majority who had studied biology found this far too easy to engage them. Even if the course becomes more challenging a few weeks later, as was the case with the medical course, the damage may already be done. Some students will have switched off and will rapidly fall behind with the increased pace and complexity of the course. It's important to get the right balance, though, as failure is equally demotivating. The key is in knowing your students and understanding their entry knowledge and expectations. **Build in opportunities for formative assessment** – which can be fairly informal – to find out what your students find meaningful, difficult or challenging. Some teachers find classroom response technology (clickers) extremely useful for gathering feedback swiftly; you can use them during a lecture to gather instant information about students' levels of understanding (see Bruff 2009 for greater detail on this). At Baskerville, the course was changed to make it more challenging from the outset, with a separate additional course for the students who had not taken biology A level. The problem was identified during a consultation committee meeting between students and their teachers. Towards the end of year, students were asked about any changes that they would recommend for future iterations of the course. Students from more senior years can be invaluable, too, in retrospectively identifying 'wrinkles' in the curriculum – and in recommending solutions.

Regular feedback from students will also help you monitor progress and the degree of challenge: **use an informal mid-term course evaluation** to gauge what course corrections might aid your current students' learning. Many example evaluation forms are posted online – often in a format where you can change the wording to match your circumstances. One that we particularly like lists only constructive statements (see Huston 2009 for an example): one column is headed

'I like the way the teacher...', below which are comments like 'uses real-life examples' and 'explains concepts'; the second column is titled 'I would like the teacher to...', and the comments below include 'use real-life examples' and 'explain concepts more clearly.' With this phrasing, you can find out what's going well and what changes the students would like, and it's all expressed positively, making it easier to digest. Much simpler systems include 'stop–start–continue', where students write on a scrap of paper the things they dislike about class ('stop'), things they would like you to introduce ('start') and what's going well already ('continue'). In all cases, the important factor is to use mid-term course evaluations early enough that you have time to collate the feedback, select a few changes for the rest of the term, and report back the results of the feedback to your students. Reporting back – if possible by handing out or emailing a typed-up list of all the comments you received and a tally of numbers against checked items – helps close the loop and allows students to see whether they are an outlier or the mainstream in their views about the course. Research into these informal evaluations in the USA suggests that using them – and making some (but not all) changes – can lead to higher scores in final course evaluations (Lewis 2001).

If you identify a pattern of under-preparedness among your students, we suggest you take it up with your university leaders and that you give them this concrete suggestion: many universities in the UK **offer summer school programmes** or work closely with schools in the vicinity to explain to pupils what will be expected in HE and how to adapt their study skills. For example, the University of Nottingham runs an extensive liaison service (University of Nottingham 2011) targeting local schools and colleges, but also provides some services to school-leavers from across the country. They offer campus visits and summer courses, and visit schools and colleges to encourage pupils to consider higher education. Much of this work is targeted at children from socio-economic groups that are under-represented in UK higher education. Research into widening participation, as it is termed in the UK, has shown that students from disadvantaged backgrounds may need greater encouragement to attend university than more affluent students (Gorard et al. 2006; Stuart 2003). These students also need advice and guidance about how to study at this level.

2. Successful students are punctual for lectures and classes

Many teachers believed successful students are more likely to attend their classes on time than those who perform less well or fail. One teacher from Arial explained he expected students to succeed:

> [for] reasons […] like turning up on time, actually paying attention and listening.
>
> (UK-Arial-5)

His view is supported by this US teacher:

> you identify the ones you think will do badly: Oh, there's the redhead – she's *always* late to class.
>
> (US-Delphin-9)

Many teachers also mentioned attendance as a key factor, though not all of them kept an attendance register. Asking students about their attendance partway through a course was likely to generate unhelpful data, so instead we asked them to rate their own punctuality. While there was some scepticism that all students would report honestly, the survey results showed the full range of responses. (We discuss attendance further in Chapters 5 and 7.)

Teachers in both the UK and the USA remarked on a perceived change of attitude among students in recent years: whereas in the past students expected to have to put in some effort in order to do well, some students now expect to excel merely by being on the course, echoing some of the generational research we mentioned in Chapter 2. In the UK this has been linked to the introduction of course fees, which has led to a perceived commodification of higher education (Cheney et al. 1997). The 'bargain' used to be that the teacher or university would provide the environment and resources necessary for learning and the student would provide diligent study. Now the bargain – as allegedly perceived by some students – is that the student provides the fees and the teacher or university provides the degree: in this line of argument, money has replaced student effort. Note, though, that in the USA, where university fees have long been the norm, teachers report a similar shift in attitude, suggesting that money is *not* the cause:

> And so that seems to be changing. At least their expectation about what attendance means. […] There are now students who feel like they should

still make A's without coming to class. And I think in the past it was always just assumed if you don't come to class you probably don't deserve an A, you're not going to get an A – nobody's going to complain about not getting an A. But that seems to have changed a little bit in the last couple of years.

(US-Constantia-2)

The link between punctuality and performance is more complex than a straight correlation. We divided each class into quartiles according to performance. The students with the highest grades were less punctual (by their own admission) than students in the second-highest-performing group, but more punctual than the worst-performing group. Students in the bottom group were the least punctual. This suggests students who do well can afford to be a little tardier than weaker students or that better students are harder on themselves in evaluating their punctuality. So teachers are right in thinking the least punctual perform worst, but those who regularly arrive on time may not be the strongest students.

What we can do

Punctuality is catching: if you as a teacher are always on time, arrive ahead of the start of class, are well-prepared and behave in a professional manner, you will find it easier to insist on similar behaviour from students. If, on the other hand, you're regularly late, or create the impression that you are ill-prepared and chaotic, then students may feel justified in mimicking you. At the start of a new course **consider agreeing guidelines for mutual expectations**, spelling out precisely the behaviour that you expect from the students and that *you* agree to exhibit as well. Devising these guidelines takes around 20 minutes of your first class session and if your students are struggling to produce ideas, encourage them to think about behaviour that irritates them in classes, then re-formulate a positive expression that avoids that behaviour. So if latecomers are an irritation, you may agree to 'be punctual'. We suggest you have a few agreements prepared. For example, our own priorities would be: punctuality, participation and courtesy towards one another (while not necessarily respecting one another's views) and not using mobile phones without prior consent.

Please don't laugh at the next suggestion! If you know that you have a problem with over-running the end of class, we suggest that you **invest in a clock** if one is not provided in the classroom. Provided you check it, this strategy does work. Some teachers enlist the help of students to remind them when there are five minutes left, but this can be counterproductive if it encourages students to watch the clock all session, rather than engage in their learning.

You can encourage students to be less tardy if you habitually reward punctuality by **giving out important information at the start of the session** and letting students know that you will do so. **Avoid rewarding lateness** by recapping all that has been covered each time a late arrival joins the class: if students are late, they need to catch up on material by consulting with their classmates, not with you. Similarly, **avoid punishing punctuality** by making the rest of the class wait for latecomers or complaining to the punctual students about their tardy peers.

Students may arrive late because of their own poor time management. Those who have few outside commitments may view their week as a mass of leisure time interspersed with occasional classes. This isn't necessarily something that you are best placed to address, so **find out when your learning centre offers student workshops on time management and encourage your students to attend**. If you have developed good organizational skills, **share your own strategies for keeping on top of your workload** and ensuring punctuality. For more advice about developing time management, see Chapter 7.

3. Successful students keep up with assigned reading

Having designed a course to include particular readings, it is hardly surprising that many teachers believed it important for students to do the required work. Our interviewees identified problems with class discussions where students failed to complete the pre-session readings, thereby frustrating the intended lesson plan, and they contrasted this with strong students as those who clearly engage with the wider reading:

> But people who ask me questions out of the book – so that it's obvious to me that they've actually been reading it – they tend to be the ones that do the best in the class.
>
> (US-Constantia-2)

Of course this teacher may perceive these students as the better ones because they match the teacher's expectations, while the students may be strategically trying to please the teacher without having completed all the reading. Nevertheless, our research showed a correlation between high performance and staying on top of the reading, with students in the top quartile far more likely to say they keep up than those in the other three quartiles.

What we can do

Most of us are programmed to respond to immediate gratification. Faced with the choice of reading seemingly irrelevant tomes, or spending time developing new friendships, many of us will choose the latter. Simply telling students that reading will help them is most likely not enough incentive. It may be necessary to **spell out precisely the advantages of doing the work, and the disadvantages of leaving it**. When designing a course, consider whether the reading is relevant at that stage, in that particular week, why it is relevant and what you expect the students to gain from it. **Make sure that you are not overloading students in one week, and leaving them little to do in another**, especially if you have no way of knowing which other subjects your students are taking and how the work is spread out. If you're teaching a cohort of students who take the same subjects at the same time (as is the case in many UK universities and a few subjects, like nursing, in the USA), see if you can **work across course teams to minimize the heavy weeks**. You might also find ways to **align assignments and readings** so that skills developed in one subject can help students with a later assignment or task in another.

How can you gauge what workload is manageable? In the UK, each course you teach states the number of hours of study, including both in-class and out-of-class hours. These are described as 'notional hours of learning' (QAA 2009: 6), meaning that they represent the workload for your *average* student – some will complete tasks more quickly, others will require longer. Under this credit scheme, a full-time undergraduate student would be expected to study for a total of 40 hours per week, including class-contact time. The US Department of Education is in the process of formalizing the use of the Carnegie unit, which dates back to the early 1900s and measures credit hours, stating that one hour in class should equate to at least two hours of study out of class, while at the same time allowing for variation based on different modes of course delivery (US Department of Education 2008: 5). For a full-time student, this credit-hour system would lead to a total workload of roughly 45 hours per week, including class time.

Let students know how long it should take them to complete the reading and take notes. Working this out is tricky: students will take much longer than you to read the same text and, increasingly, they make it to university with little experience of reading entire books. Anecdotal discussions suggest it takes students around three times as long as the teacher to complete tasks, but it depends what level of reading you expect. Carver (1992: 87) reports that that the typical university student performs casual reading (called 'rauding') of non-technical text at 300 words per minute; academic reading with the intention of remembering ideas (and including some unfamiliar vocabulary) runs at around 200 words per minute, while reading for accurate recall is at 138 words per minute. If you can at least provide a guideline of how long a reading should take, as well as some basic reading strategy guidelines (see Chapter 7), it will help students develop their time management; for those who find it takes much longer than you expected, you can **remind them of learning support on campus to improve their reading and note-taking skills**. Once you feel comfortable with the approximate workloads you have calculated, you can either **let students know how long the work should take on a session-by-session basis, or add this information in your class schedule**. All this may sound like an awful lot of work with little return. In fact, course overload has been found to be a key cause of disruptive student behaviour ('classroom incivility'; see for instance Boice's influential study of 1996), as well as leading to a surface approach to learning (Gibbs 1992). Undertaking an audit of the time required to complete the course reassures you that your expectations are reasonable; publicizing this to your students reassures them that you are supporting their development – all while creating a setting that promotes a deep approach to learning in a positive classroom environment.

While it is not helpful to 'spoon-feed' students, since they do need to learn how to learn in this new context, it is equally unhelpful to assume that all students will know instinctively that they must complete all the reading. Some students, particularly in the early weeks, will not know how to cope with an enormous list of further or wider reading: Are they supposed to read every book on the list? If not, which ones are most important? If parts of books are relevant, which parts? (See also Chapter 6 on reading around the subject.) And what does 'reading' mean to you? Should they read every word, skim read, or take notes? Help the students to help themselves, and **ask yourself what is the point of each reading**. Be sure that you can clarify this question when asked by your students, and consider annotating your reading list in your syllabus or schedule so students have a formal record.

Having set reading in one class, **build in references, exercises and discussions that make use of the reading in the next session**. Students will quickly learn whether it is worth their while to read, and those who diligently read around the topic the first time may not be so keen later if their underprepared peers seem no less advantaged as a result. **If the class turns up with few or none having done the reading, send them away (or keep them in class) to do it, rather than précis the work for those who made no effort**. Some teachers may consider this too risky, particularly in the age of high tuition fees. Maybe we are fuddy-duddies on this issue, but here is our thinking: university teachers' responsibility is to the integrity of the institution's degree programmes, not to compensate for students' lack of preparation. We have never heard of a situation where a teacher has had to dismiss the class more than once for not having prepared for class: students realize you are serious about the work and that they need to make the effort in order to succeed.

Beware of the overlap between reading content and class content: somewhere between a half and a third is ideal in most subjects. If there is too little overlap, students question the need to do the reading if they never discuss it in class. Too much overlap and they may not see a need to read since the teacher covers the material anyway, or they may decide there is little point in turning up to lectures if they can read the same material in the comfort of their own room at the time of their choosing. **Make it difficult for students to keep up in class if they haven't done the reading**. In this case, a little frustration need not be a bad thing. To structure this process, you could **introduce Just-in-Time Teaching (JiTT) methods** in your class (Simkins and Maier 2010). In this approach, you set students reading along with questions on that reading to complete. They must answer the questions and send responses to you (by email or on a message board) ahead of class – we suggest 24 hours to allow you time to prepare – so that the class directly builds on your students' answers. That might mean you spend more time on, say, the third section of a chapter because that's the one area where the students were clearly confused, or perhaps you devote time to discussing one student's response because it draws out the issues you consider to be key to understanding the topic. If the Just-in-Time approach is unappealing, then a much simpler version is to list the key topics from the chapter and **ask students to vote at the start of class on the section they understood** *least*: that then becomes the main topic for class. The likelihood is that you already have an excess of material, so this should not create additional work for you. But it does keep your classes unpredictable and interesting – and you're far more likely to see those metaphorical light bulbs appearing over your students' heads if you can help them think through topics they found especially challenging.

The **'Pass Notes' system can be used to link punctuality, out-of-class reading and an end-of-course exam**; it was used successfully by marketing teachers at Birmingham City University for a course with poor final exam results and chronic lateness. At the start of class, each student hands in a single page of handwritten notes on that week's reading. Each weekly page is stored in an envelope with the student's name on it, and, during the end-of-course exam, the envelope of notes is returned to the student. The exam is based on the readings and students can only refer to the notes that that they personally handed in. No late notes are accepted without a doctor's note or documented exemption. If you tell students that they can only hand in the notes at the very beginning of each class, then you will also improve punctuality. This system incentivizes students to stay on track with the reading and to show up on time.

4. Successful students prefer to sit towards the front in class

Many teachers commented on a perceived link between where students choose to sit in class – particularly in a large lecture theatre – and subsequent performance. They tended to connect location with troublesome students and punctuality. Teachers told stories about small groups arriving shortly after the start of a lecture, sitting at the back of the room and giving the appearance of being detached from the class. Behaviour typically included sending text messages, listening to music, in some cases eating and drinking, and even – in one extreme case at Baskerville – two students smooching! In contrast, teachers identified the 'keen' students who sat at the front of the class appearing to concentrate and engage in the session as those who would perform best.

It's worth problematizing the location issue beyond questions of students' attitudes. Might it be the case that teachers are better able to interact with students in the front of the class, since it's easier to respond to their non-verbal cues and to hear their asides to one another, leading to some unexpected learning opportunities? Do the students at the front experience a 'higher quality' of class because their reactions help shape the teacher's delivery and organization of the class?

Whatever the cause, the virtually universally held belief that students sitting near the front perform better proved to be correct in our study. Students who self-reported a preference to sit at or near the front of the class did perform better than those with no preference or those who preferred to sit at or near the back.

What we can do

Unless you have either a very small group or a cleverly designed teaching space, it is often not possible for the whole class to sit near the front. There is nothing magical about those first one or two rows. Students who are focused, determined and keen to learn may be more likely to sit near the front because they want to be involved and they don't want to miss anything. As a teacher, you can influence this. Rather than waiting passively for your students to present themselves and select where they will sit, you can change the dynamic. **Move away from the front**. By walking among the group, seeking eye contact with individuals, asking questions and engaging students, you break down the impression of anonymity in class. If the group is small enough and the furniture will allow, **seat everyone in a circle for discussions**. If you use slideware, invest in an inexpensive remote control for forwarding the slides, so that you aren't stuck behind a podium. Use a wireless microphone for larger rooms or if you have voice problems.

Move students around very frequently, too, so that they work with different people during break-out activities. You can get the students to do this themselves by asking them to form groups of, say, five or six, but they have to conform to certain criteria; for example, you may decide each group should contain men and women, people from different cities or regions, a range of educational backgrounds – you determine the criteria to suit the group. It may take a few minutes to settle the class, but the students will appreciate the opportunity to hear completely new perspectives as they work with and get to know students they may not otherwise have met. Another technique, to create different groups quickly for classes of up to 36 students (six groups of six), is to **construct a grid** so that groups can be organized vertically, horizontally, diagonally, and so on. Figures 4.1 and 4.2 provide two examples using a class of 25 students, while Appendix 2 gives you blank 6 × 6 grids to populate with your own students' names. Groups with more than six members become unwieldy; so if your class is larger than 36, you would need to create a longer grid; it doesn't matter if your class size doesn't lead to evenly-sized groups, just use the grid as a starting point, and ensure that group sizes don't differ by more than one person. If you mix groups from day one of class, students will typically not object, though you may need to cajole them a little so that they move around swiftly: **set a time limit for getting organized** and

1. Allie	2. Ben	3. Charlotte	4. Daoud	5. Ella
5. Ferdi	1. Gina	2. Hazrat	3. Isabel	4. Johannes
4. Kate	5. Lyle	1. Mumtaz	2. Niall	3. Olivia
3. Paul	4. Queenie	5. Ryan	1. Shushanna	2. Tom
2. Ursula	3. Vince	4. Wendy	5. Xavier	1. Yolanda

Figure 4.1 Example of using grids to mix student groups – diagonal groups

1. Allie	2. Ben	3. Charlotte	4. Daoud	5. Ella
4. Ferdi	5. Gina	1. Hazrat	2. Isabel	3. Johannes
2. Kate	3. Lyle	4. Mumtaz	5. Niall	1. Olivia
5. Paul	1. Queenie	2. Ryan	3. Shushanna	4. Tom
3. Ursula	4. Vince	5. Wendy	1. Xavier	2. Yolanda

Figure 4.2 Example of using grids to mix student groups – knight groups (across two, down one, as a knight in chess)

give students an immediate one-minute task to get the groups focused. Two suggestions to make this simpler: **post the group numbers or names around the room at the start of class** so that you're ready for the first group activity; put the group names on regular sheets of paper in plastic wallets (so you can reuse them) and be sure to use a large point size so everyone can see. (If you have groups that will be in the middle, put those signs on a centre table, or wait until the groups are ready to form.) This is even faster if you **give the groups colour names** instead of numbers, and type the names onto sheets of the appropriate colour ('red' on a red sheet, 'yellow' on yellow, etc.). This might sound over-the-top organizationally, but David's experience has been that students identify their colour designation more easily than a group number or name, and the visual impact of the colours makes the group locations around the classroom easier to find. And all it takes is five or six sheets of coloured paper and a black-and-white printer.

Among other things, regularly changing groups is a good way not only to move students to the front or rear of the class to mix them up but also to **promote discussion between groups of students who do not normally sit with one another**, be that due to gender, race, appearance or participation level. Promoting intergroup dialogue, particularly between students of different races and ethnicities, is found to be effective in enhancing critical thinking and analytical skills (Pascarella and Terenzini 2005); requiring students to work together in class may mean they're more likely to have those informal intergroup dialogues outside class, too. We see this as social engineering for the common good and there is no harm in explicitly letting your students know you are doing this intentionally to enrich their learning and broaden their experiences.

Sharing the findings of this research may also help – some students may not realize that their success or failure can be self-determined through something as simple as seating.

General preconceptions that were not upheld

Of the 10 beliefs that were voiced by teachers in both countries, our research tells us six are unfounded: we did not find a correlation between those beliefs and student performance. You may be wondering why we choose to discuss these items if they're untrue.

Regardless of their veracity, these preconceptions can influence how university teachers conduct their classes, interact with students and perceive the environment around them. The consequences could be negative for many learners, as well as their teachers. By clarifying and considering each issue in this section, we intend to provide broader context and a choice of strategies to help support all learners in your courses.

5. Teachers believed that successful students perform some paid, voluntary or service work, but not excessive hours

Several teachers said outside work affects students' performance. This belief was partly upheld, but not entirely. Some felt students who combined work with their studies, and in particular worked excessive hours, were less likely to excel than those who did not need to work at all. Others thought students who did a small amount of paid or voluntary work were more likely to perform well, because this demonstrates self-discipline and good organizational skills – skills they apply to academic work as well as to extra-curricular activity:

> I've definitely had a handful of students who had so many responsibilities in terms of their work that it's made it difficult for them to get all their work done. I guess it depends on why they're working; if they're working because they have to, I think that can really get in the way; if they're working just to have some extra money, that's different. Students who've brought up in class that they are regularly doing volunteer work, those students, on the whole I would say, seem more successful just insofar as they usually have some sort of sense of responsibility that keeps them coming across every meeting and doing the assigned readings.
>
> (US-Constantia-1)

Teachers in both the UK and USA commented on the burden of debt that many students incur to complete their studies. This is particularly acute in a recession, with fewer graduate-level jobs available than in previous years. Purcell et al.'s (2009) comments on the increased debts faced by students from the least affluent backgrounds are mirrored by this teacher:

> I can't imagine to be graduating right now with the kind of debt these guys have and what they're facing for jobs. Because I have friends who

have children in that situation and it's, like, $1,000 a month just to pay their debt loan. I mean, that doesn't leave you any money if you're waiting tables.

(US-Constantia-2)

This teacher compared the demands faced by his students with his own experience:

I see a lot of students who are working 20 hours a week. That's the maximum they can do here on campus, but some of them have jobs off-campus and work more than that and for some of them, that works, you know? It depends on what they do, how they use their time and if they're really good at time-budgeting. One of my best students works at a sporting goods store. I know […] she's working well over 20 hours a week and she's an honours student and she's bright, she's really good. So far be it for me to say, 'You can't do it'. It's just, *I* couldn't.

(US-Delphin-8)

Some students, though, don't manage to combine excessive paid work with academic study successfully:

Middle-class parents [here] don't think they have a responsibility, their kids don't think they have a responsibility, so one of the consequences of that is that there will be kids that get into trouble financially because they are not quite good enough to get scholarships and they start working part-time jobs to make ends meet and they just can't get it all together.

(US-Delphin-10)

A distinct difference in working culture between the UK and the USA affects student performance. In the USA, it is not uncommon, while still not yet the norm, for students to work full-time hours (40 or more hours per week) while simultaneously studying full-time at university. Our research found that working *extensive* hours does have a negative impact on student performance. In the UK, students are increasingly likely to seek work, particularly in vacations, to offset the cost of their education. Some UK students work in term-time as well.

For those students who worked under 10 hours per week in either country, there was no correlation between paid work and performance. Some students who combine work and study may have greater self-discipline than those who do not, as teachers expected. Work, be it paid or voluntary, can be a wonderful opportunity to widen students' learning by linking theory with practice. However, for every student who is well-organized and applies the lessons learnt in paid work to their study, there are others who struggle to meet commitments and whose studies suffer. Similarly, some students who do not choose or do not need a job may be just as well organized as those who work.

We found that teachers were right in their belief that excessive hours of work adversely affected student performance, but they were wrong in their belief that students who did a moderate amount of work performed better academically than those who did none.

By 'excessive', we mean anything over 12 hours a week: that was the threshold where we began to see a negative impact on students' performance. This is broadly in agreement with Wenz and Yu (2010), who found that hours worked in term-time had a modestly negative effect on grades. Their more detailed study suggests that students who are motivated to take up employment for financial reasons perform less well than those who are motivated by a desire to develop career-motivated skills, but they perform better than those who are simply seeking general work experience.

What we can do

Paid work is something of a double-edged sword for students: many need the money to help pay for fees and living expenses, and a strict schedule for paid work might help them organize their study time better – good practice for self-management when they graduate. Yet too much work negatively affects their grades, their ability to concentrate in class, and their ability to engage in out-of-class activities that make university a more balanced experience. Understanding this tension presents a dilemma for some teachers: Should we reduce the work load in acknowledgement of students' commitments or should we turn a deaf ear to students' pleas about conflicting demands? Our personal view is that a teachers' primary responsibility is to uphold the quality of the university's degrees. If we don't do that, then students will graduate with a faux qualification and employers will quickly come to realize that graduates from, say, Delphin University, are not of the right calibre.

In your classes, you can **encourage students to be strategic about their paid work**. Can they find work on campus to save them travel time and develop skills that may help both their CV and their academic performance (for instance, by tutoring in mathematics or working as an assistant to a teacher)? If they work off-campus, can they find a part-time position that connects with their intended career or with their studies? We also suggest that you let them know about the impact of paid work on grades, based on this study. More than 12 hours is problematic: if they're expecting straight A grades, they'll need to reconsider their priorities.

Although there is a danger that paid or voluntary work can overload students, there is also an opportunity for out-of-class activities to augment the classroom experience. Some teachers have used such activities to help students make connections between their studies and future employment or community contributions. As with any course design, it is important to think about balance and workload for you and your students. **Remember to ensure that any out-of-class activity is friendly towards students with work or care-giving responsibilities** (see Chapter 6).

When you design your course, consider whether you can **move beyond the immediate classroom to engage students' eagerness to do good in the world**, both in terms of physical delivery as well as subject matter. There are many ways to do this, some of which are more easily incorporated into certain disciplines than others. Service learning is becoming increasingly popular in the USA, whereas in the UK, institutions are encouraged to address sustainable development regardless of discipline. We'll discuss both approaches briefly here to give you a flavour of how outside work might expand the scope of courses.

Service learning integrates classroom learning with community service. Examples include biology students investigating the toxicity of local rivers and its impact on biodiversity or a statistics course where students investigate the cost of buying organic produce from a supermarket or farmers' market, then setting up a stall at the farmers' market to share results with the shoppers. When Stacey Jones ran this latter project at Seattle University, her students found that farmers' market prices were similar to (and in some cases lower than) prices in supermarkets, a finding which has since been used by the local farmers' market association to support the introduction of farmers' markets in poorer areas and the use of food stamps at farmers' markets. For this particular course, service learning – in comparison with case studies on the same topic – increased the likelihood that students saw statistics as a relevant part of their professional education, even though their final grades were unaffected (Hiedemann and Jones 2010). A class at Delphin created a path with a bridge over a small stream in a local park area. The students were able to put their mathematics skills into practice as well as developing problem-solving and teamwork skills. The local community benefited from the improvement to the pathway, too. In another example, accountancy students at Constantia, under the guidance of their teacher, helped people in a poorer area of town to complete their tax returns. (In the USA everyone has to do this, whereas in the UK, most employees have tax deducted at source by their employer.) Tax advice is expensive, with the result that wealthy people are able to ensure that they don't overpay tax, while poorer citizens can't access this advice. The students were able to inform their clients of their entitlements, safe in the knowledge that their advice was validated by their teacher.

While service learning is gaining momentum in the USA, Education for Sustainable Development (ESD) is growing in significance in the UK, where many universities have included reference to sustainability, global citizenship or internationalization in their learning and teaching strategies. Increasingly, university teachers are encouraged to regard their responsibility as HE educators as something wider than 'merely' initiating students in the canon of a particular discipline. ESD is concerned with helping students understand their role in the world and the impact of their actions and choices on their immediate environment and on the world as a whole. While some consider this to be irrelevant and outside the scope of higher education, many people find it an appropriate, comfortable fit. The issues raised by ESD link with those of employability, as an ability to see beyond one's immediate impact and to think strategically in an ever-changing world, plus a willingness to work as part of a team, are all qualities that are valued by most employers. Thus, ESD can combine with employability to improve students' chances of gaining employment while taking responsibility for the wider environment. When students at Exeter University took part in a project to identify their peers' views on sustainability, they found that while students were interested in finding ways to live sustainable and socially aware lives, they were put off by the perception that they were being lectured to by 'left-wing liberals'. Students were, however, interested in pursuing a Green Award that would reward engagement in sustainability-related activity.

6. Teachers believed that successful students choose to come to university of their own volition, rather than to please others

Several teachers said stronger students tended to have greater control over their lives than their weaker peers. They claimed students who made a decision to come to university on their own initiative (regardless of subject studied) performed better than those who passively accepted university as the next check-list item after high school. This teacher expects students who are passive not to ask searching questions and to perform less well than their more active peers:

> You know there's a sense of passivity among the students who are sort of 'Well I'm at college because that's what you do,' you know? [They] wait for things to come to them. [...] And I don't want to say this, but there hasn't been the same sort of challenging questioning, it's just more, kind of, 'follow this programme'.
>
> (US-Constantia-4)

In our study we did not find a link between students who came to university of their own volition and subsequent performance, nor between those who attended merely to please others and their performance.

But why should it be the case that the student who actively chooses a particular course is expected to perform better than one who follows the advice of teachers, parents, peers or others? Might guidance from those who know the student well prove more useful than the potentially ill-informed choice of the student? Most students in this study chose their degree programme or institution at a young age – usually 17 or 18 – from a position of relative ignorance. The student who at 17 thought sound engineering was the course for him might feel differently six months later when the workload is not as expected, and the links seem weak between the work required now and any future benefits. In contrast, the student who has the support of parents, friends and former teachers may have greater stamina to persevere.

Internal motivation is important, but it would be a mistake to under-value the power of external motivation.

Cultural context figures prominently here, too. Both the USA and UK are characterized as individualist – rather than collectivist – cultures where people tend to prioritize themselves and their immediate families, as opposed to larger 'in-groups' of extended family members (Hofstede and Hofstede 2005; Trompenaars and Hampden-Turner 1998). So this particular belief may stem from a perspective that privileges individualism above collectivism. As participation in university-level study increases, giving access to more students from minority cultures and from other countries, we cannot presume that individualist values resonate with all our students. Given that most teachers *and* students in this study hail from individualist cultures, it's perhaps surprising that individual choice transpired not to be important to success.

What we can do

Students' performance can be enhanced by tapping into their motivation, whether it's driven by an individualist or collectivist desire for success. **Consider including a session on 'how to take control of one's life'.** A longer session of this sort was offered at Arial, initially to teachers, for them to use for themselves but also as a stimulus for student-focused sessions. The day-long workshop, influenced by the work of Peter Hawkins (1999), encouraged participants to take stock of their lives, their career aims and their personal ambitions. Participants followed a series of exercises that culminated in the production of a comprehensive career plan. The group considered various employability-related skills, including networking, communication, setting realistic objectives, work/life balance and the value of reflection. In the UK in particular, there is an increasing emphasis on employability: it has been recommended that British universities should be required to publish employability rates in each subject (Department for Business, Innovation and Skills 2010) so that potential students can base their HE choice on comparisons of the same course at different universities. Students who fail to show initiative in their studies may take an equally passive approach to developing their employability skills. It is in the interests of students, but also the institutions, to address this passivity and to help them to realize how much influence they can have over their careers.

In the USA, students have significant choice over which courses to study, and often in which order. In the UK, once students embark on a degree programme there may be little choice. Several programme teams have been successful in devising alternative paths that lead to the same qualification, with some offering significant choice, such as the arts, media and design master's degree at Staffordshire University in the UK, or an entire module consisting of negotiated study at London Metropolitan University. Is it possible and appropriate to **build greater flexibility into your own programme**? Help students identify ways in which they can exert control over their studies. Some of them may be unnerved by flexibility, and they'll need support in making appropriate choices. Start by asking them why they are at university, what they aim to get out of the programme, and what they can do towards achieving those ends. In programmes where your students do have choice, you can compile examples of pathways through the programme that focus on particular areas of interest (sometimes called 'concentrations' in the USA) so that students have a sense of the range of options available. For example, you may be able to show how one selection of modules might be better suited to someone with, say, an interest in global issues, while another might be particularly suited to someone passionate about feminism. To give students more concrete examples of how these paths through the degree might lead them in different career directions after graduation, **collate alumni portraits** and post them on the programme webpage.

7. Teachers believed that successful students belong to particular ethnic groups

Some teachers were reluctant to talk about student ethnicity, but most made candid observations, usually qualifying them and giving thoughtful reasons for their beliefs. Those teachers who expressed an opinion expected students from an ethnic minority to perform less well than the white majority. As we discussed in Chapter 2, some studies do describe a link between poor performance and certain ethnic groups (Chavous 2002; Ferguson et al. 2002). While it is possible that some differences may be found in subgroups of students involved in this study, overall we did not find a statistically significant link between performance and ethnicity.

In the UK, teachers expected students from African-Caribbean backgrounds to perform less well than white students. Their views were more complex regarding another large ethnic grouping – British Asians (which in the UK generally refers to people whose heritage is from the Indian subcontinent). In particular, teachers presumed that British-Pakistani and British-Bangladeshi students would perform less well than British-Indian and white students.

Baskerville teachers who expected British-Pakistani students to underperform rationalized that these students were more likely to have to work for a family business or that females were expected to perform domestic duties, which they did not expect of white students. Although there were individual cases where female British-Pakistani students were expected to help at home and all British-Pakistani students were more likely than white students to live at home while studying, we found that British-Pakistani students were no more likely than white students to have to work for a family business. There was no statistical link between any of these factors and performance.

So the teachers had noticed what they perceived to be a pattern, and then made sense of it based on their limited data and supposition. Reasons for underperformance, though, were linked to factors other than ethnicity: it was only when we conducted this study that we were able to identify precisely each students' ethnic group (we asked them to self-identify), and the degree of social affluence.

What we found in the case of Baskerville was a link between ethnicity and socio-economic grouping and performance. (For a summary of similar findings, see Eggens et al. 2008: 554.) Students from more affluent socio-economic backgrounds tended to perform better than those from more deprived backgrounds. At Baskerville, medical students from a British-Pakistani background were more likely also to come from more socially deprived households than white students. Because British-Pakistani students stand out in person among a majority of white students and on paper because of their Asian names, teachers noticed more of these students failing the exam. However, they didn't notice the prevalence of failures among white students from socially deprived environments. It was only when we examined the socio-economic background of the students that we were able to make this link (Popovic 2010).

In the USA, one teacher spoke at length about the effect of ethnicity on student performance, echoing our findings from the UK. She explained that most students in her class:

> come from a type of background where they've received a solid education before coming here, have access to resources and wealth.
>
> (US-Constantia-3)

The minority from a less privileged background tended also to be from a different ethnic and cultural background:

> there are ways that the culture of the classroom is such that it can lead to some students having a marginalized experience. Students of colour, students that are coming from other [social] class backgrounds. [...] When you are part of two different cultural systems – when you spend the majority of your time in a certain space, and then a little bit of your time in another space – there's a way that it makes it even harder for you. [...] I feel that there is then this pressure for students to assimilate and acculturate in order to succeed, we expect them to behave in a certain way.
>
> (US-Constantia-3)

So in a similar fashion to our Baskerville findings, this teacher alluded to the conflation of ethnicity and social class, with a knock-on effect in higher education. She went on to discuss the issues faced by Native American students:

> Navajo students in particular are encouraged to listen, they're not encouraged to draw attention to themselves, and this is from their cultural community – from their home environment. And so as a result, what was happening in classes was they were not performing as well as other students, because the classroom was established and set up in such a way that it encourages a certain type of participation that the students were not comfortable with. You need to understand where students are coming from – at least acknowledge that students are coming from different backgrounds that might have different expectations for behaviour.
>
> (US-Constantia-3)

With very few exceptions, teachers in the USA believed that Native American students did not perform well, and that they were highly unlikely even to gain university admission, let alone excel once they arrived, despite a certain amount of government intervention. However, as the previously quoted teacher observed, this perspective ignores the complexities of different expectations, where cultural norms may be misinterpreted by teachers from the dominant culture. Tinto (1993) and others have exposed this culture clash before, and it may well be a common experience. In our research we had only a tiny proportion of Native American students. They did not perform exceptionally well or exceptionally badly compared with their cohort. The difficulty for this group seems to occur earlier in the students' careers – the challenge lies more in increasing the number of Native Americans who enter higher education and only subsequently in finding ways to help them integrate authentically once they are there. Perhaps the real challenge is to find ways of supporting high schools to encourage Native Americans to aspire to university, and to make the learning environment in university more conducive to them.

Another teacher talked about the difficulties faced by African-American students who had performed well at school and were tired of being singled out by their schoolteachers as having bucked the expected trend for African-Americans to perform badly. This teacher believed that African-American students performed better than average (contrary to the more common expectation) because they had worked exceptionally hard to get into university. To explain the following comment, the AP programme is an advanced class for students with above-average ability.

> some of my African-American students have been in the AP programme [and] have reported that they got sick of being targeted by the AP teachers. It's like, 'Well, tell us about the black experience'. And they were also sort of alienated by other African-American students saying, well, 'You're not really a part of us'. And I had one student who opted out of AP and went into the other classes. But she was wonderful to have in class because she spoke about it in this very interesting way. So I really, really appreciate the African-American students that I've had here. […] I feel like they have a little bit more intention.
>
> (US-Constantia-4)

So the caution to take away from this slice of the research is that in most, if not all, cases, issues that were thought to relate to ethnicity were instead linked to class or social affluence: we disregard the hidden diversity of social class at our peril.

What we can do

Most university teachers would be appalled at the suggestion that they might be racist. Yet in the UK and USA at least – and despite claims to the contrary in the wake of Barack Obama's election to the US presidency – we do not live in post-racial societies and some ethnic groups feel the effect of this more than others. In both countries, a white European heritage tends to bring individuals privileges that are denied to people of colour (see Feagin 2010 or Rothenberg 2008 for a discussion of white privilege). Within the broad 'white European' category there are subsets of people who suffer from stereotypical views and from verbal slurs and worse. As liberal educators we may believe that we are not prejudiced and that we are 'colour blind', but that is a disingenuous claim since we are all affected by invidious stereotypes.

Recalling the negative impact of stereotype threat (Steele and Aronson 1995; see Chapter 2), **be conscious of the stereotypes that exist in your discipline and work hard to avoid them**. This is more difficult than it sounds. Singling out any group of people – whether by mentioning them directly ('Muslim students tend to struggle with this') or acting indirectly (for instance, by *never* calling on African-American students to speak in class in an attempt to avoid picking on them) – signals that your expectations of students differ. Instead, it's helpful to **offer the same support for everyone and the same reassurances**. We know that people *intend* to do this, but in an effort to be supportive, we may inadvertently trigger anxieties. Similarly, where there are positive stereotypes in your field (such as 'East Asians find my statistics class easy'), mentioning these could not only worry the positively stereotyped group that they have an unfair reputation to live up to, but also could lead the other students in your class to presume you hold negative stereotypes, too. (We discuss this further in Chapter 8.)

Consider the implicit messages you communicate to students from minority groups and listen out for potential microaggressions between students (Sue 2010a; see Chapter 2). As the name suggests, microaggressions may appear insignificant and fleeting, yet the cumulative effect of these verbal and non-verbal cues can be immensely detrimental. Two examples: (1) An African-American student answers a question and a white student interrupts and says, 'What she means is…' – thinking this is helpful and that the African-American student's response needs somehow 'translating' for the rest of the class. (2) A male student approaches the teacher during a break in a computing class, while other students are in the room, to discuss his difficulties with an assignment and the teacher says, 'Man up! You can do this.' The student feels his masculinity has been assaulted, while the female students in the room detect an underlying message that 'this subject isn't for women'. In either situation, it's essential to **address the microaggression as quickly as possible** – preferably immediately. In the first situation, you could say something like, 'Just a moment – that's an interruption. I'd like [name] to finish her point, then we'll hear your view', while in the second, a swift apology is required: 'I'm sorry, that was a bad choice of words. What I meant to say is…'. In many situations where a student 'microaggresses', you can respond by saying, 'I'm sure you didn't mean to cause offence, so can you rephrase that in a way that doesn't put down others?' Peter Frederick (1995) recommends saying the exact phrase back to the student (and we would include expletives, if there were any), but slowly and with rising, questioning intonation to encourage the student to apologize and rephrase. These hot moments in the classroom are disconcerting for teachers, so having a few lines ready means you're in a better position to respond on the spot and return to a positive classroom environment.

Avoid treating individual ethnic-minority students as 'representatives' of the experiences of all people of that ethnicity. With the constructive intention of inviting alternative perspectives, we may inadvertently put students on the spot, inappropriately expecting them to speak for a group rather than just for themselves. When the tables are turned with questions like 'What do white people think of President Obama?' or 'Do the British like America?' individuals from the white majority in both countries quickly realize they are being asked for terrible generalizations and to speak on behalf of a category of people that is not a group, but is highly diverse. Those of us from majority cultures need to be mindful of the impact of counter-productive global questions.

Keep track of who is participating and find ways to include quieter minority students (while still not expecting them to 'represent' their race/ethnicity). We heard earlier from a teacher who was acutely aware of the difficulty faced by Native American students, who have grown up in a culture where young people are expected to be quiet and listen to their elders, finding themselves in a classroom where successful students regularly interrupt each other. This is not an isolated problem. Teachers in both the UK and USA commented on the differences in approach by students from foreign countries or minority cultures who have similar difficulties. To address these cultural differences, **develop classroom norms that enable all to participate**. One way to do this is to control discussions by inviting people to contribute, rather than allowing the group to determine who will and who will not speak. If you have a particular problem where one or two students dominate the class, **consider using a token**, for instance a ball, which 'allows' a person to speak. Participants may only speak when they are holding the ball. Despite unsettling reminders of William Golding's *Lord of the Flies* (1954), this can help give space for quieter students to engage. At times it may be useful to point explicitly to behaviour in discussions – both the behaviour you want to encourage and any that is less desirable. So if a few students are dominating a discussion, say that you want to hear many voices and different perspectives and for that reason will give the ball to one of the quieter students first. Another strategy is to use smaller groups for discussion since some students find it much easier to discuss in a small group of four or five than a larger group of 20 or more. We provide further suggestions on discussions in Chapter 6 on the topic of independent thinking and debate.

Finally in this section, **consider what examples you use and what books you set**. Are they all from the same background? Is there any diversity of experience or perspective? In one case at Arial, a department realized its programme used many examples from the brewing industry; a sizeable minority of the student cohort was teetotal for religious reasons and so had difficulty identifying with the examples due to a lack of familiarity.

8. Teachers believed that successful students have a particular gender

Teachers shared a general perception that women would perform better than men, particularly in classes with roughly equal gender distribution, or a majority of women. Where there are more men than women – for example, a technology course at Arial with only two women in a class of 50 – teachers expect men to outperform women.

Some teachers noted the contrast between the dominance of men in a profession and the performance of the women students:

> in philosophy as a profession, I think men outnumber women to a surprising degree; let's say of my successful students, more of them have been women.
>
> (US-Constantia-1)

Women were mentioned not only for their academic performance but also for their willingness to engage with the wider university experience, as this literature teacher explains:

> And as far as performance [goes], I still feel that the young women perform overall better – yes – than the young men do. And of course that's not in every case, but at the same time it does seem that there's more of an engagement, more of a commitment to education and taking advantage of other things – other resources that are available, so applying for scholarships, applying for leadership positions. When students approach me for letters of recommendation, by far most of the students who have approached me for letters have been women.
>
> (US-Constantia-3)

This was not a universal view, however, as another literature teacher notes:

> I'm seeing more men, I'm seeing this personality shift of more men seeming to be more outgoing in the classroom, I watch it, they tend to be the more charismatic ones a little bit, not all of them. But the ones who do really emerge and they're really bright and funny and quirky. They're not the cool guys, they're the really quirky ones who are emerging as the leaders.
>
> (US-Constantia-4)

As with all beliefs, it is important to identify underlying reasons. Why do some teachers believe that one gender will perform better than the other, and what, if any, effect does this have on their teaching? Where it is the case, what causes one gender to outperform the other consistently? As we discussed in Chapter 2, some studies have shown a link between performance and gender (Jansen 2004; Purcell and Elias, 2010; Sax 2008), with girls in schools, for example, consistently outperforming boys (Francis, 2000). Stereotypes (not necessarily factually correct) may suggest that women perform better than men if courses require them to negotiate, communicate or empathize; and that men perform better than women if asked to analyse, compute or measure. If teachers hold these stereotypical views (either consciously or not), does this affect their responses to students?

Our research showed no overall correlation between gender and performance for either sex.

What we can do

Gender stereotypes can have unintended outcomes even when teachers' actions are based on the best of motives. For example, some courses attract a disproportionate number of one gender, such as the engineering programmes at Arial where over 90 per cent of students are male. **If the few female or male students struggle, look for ways to engage them**. Forbes and Schmader (2010) report that simply using repeated examples of female mathematicians boosted women's confidence in their mathematical abilities. We have another example for you, though with reservations because it taps into conservative views on gender roles: an engineering teacher at Delphin runs an introductory course aimed at increasing the number of women on engineering programmes. Bear in mind that this is a traditionally conservative part of the country. Her approach is to help women **see how the discipline can appeal to culturally more acceptable female values** such as nurturing, as well as values like problem-solving, which she feels may be less appealing to women in her university and therefore the reason why fewer women than men sign up for the class. Although this may appear to pander to gender stereotypes, it allows students with conservative views on gender roles to explore alternatives without feeling their identities are being assaulted. We admire the teacher for meeting the students 'where they are' culturally and, if you teach conservative students, we wanted you to read this potential model in case it feels comfortable for you. You might find that you can allay students' concerns about your discipline's gender stereotypes and can then gradually challenge students to expand their comfort zones so that they come to see how both women and men can succeed in your field.

Where a subject has a traditional gender imbalance such as the ones discussed here, consider some of the factors we addressed earlier in this chapter under ethnicity, including stereotype threat, global generalizations and microaggressions. As in our discussion of ethnicity, **consider what examples you use, what books you set, what images you choose**. Are they all from the same gender? Is there sufficient gender diversity? For example, one of us was surprised to find *no* female authors on the syllabi of a four-year literature degree. When challenged at a teacher–student committee meeting, one teacher stated that 'There aren't any good female writers from my period', a claim that was easily refuted.

This deliberate approach to address gender imbalance can be applied to other disciplines. In the UK there is particular concern over the small number of men who enrol to become primary schoolteachers. The problem extends well beyond imbalance in degree programmes: many commentators lament the dearth of male teachers, particularly in areas where children, especially boys, have few male role models. In an attempt to redress this imbalance, one course team at Arial examined its promotional material and realized the course was represented solely by images of female participants. Decades of stereotyping will not be reversed when you **change the course promotional material**, nor will gender imbalances be redressed, but it is a start to attracting both sexes to the sector. Steele (2011: 147) reports on the positive impact of seeing members of your own minority group represented in organizational material. Once students arrive, try to **ensure that students from the minority gender on your programme are taught or supervised by at least one teacher of the same gender early in their studies**. The presence of an early role model can help bolster these students' identification with their chosen field of study.

You can retrieve statistics on courses from HESA (Higher Education Statistics Agency) in the UK and IPEDS (Integrated Postsecondary Education Data System) in the USA, and most institutions collate statistics locally through Institutional Research offices. You may want to compare the gender ratio of students on your programme with the national average. **Track participation of each gender over time** to see if the imbalance changes and in which direction, and, if gender is recorded on student course evaluation forms, look for gender differences there, too. Sometimes there are patterns here that might help us discern gender issues which might not be obvious to us.

Finally, if you suspect your programme has gender issues but don't have any hard evidence, **compare grades given to a set of assignments**, firstly when marked anonymously and then with the names showing. We expand on assignment norming processes with colleagues further in Chapter 8.

9. Teachers believed that successful students talk with their teacher and ask questions

Teachers expected successful students to engage with them and to ask questions that demonstrate the students' interest:

> the ones who really get it want to know more than the basics, they seem hungry to learn. They come to me with ideas that they want to talk about.
>
> (UK-Arial-2)

> some students have an intrinsic interest in the topic and they quickly move beyond just 'here's what I need to know for this exam and I need to memorize'. They really want to know, they have a desire.
>
> (US-Delphin-11)

> Students that do really well definitely come in talking to me, I think that's across the board. And not so much just to get help or to have me look at their work; they just come in and have conversations with me about the class material, getting a sense of – you know – formulating their ideas so they can participate more effectively in class.
>
> (US-Constantia-3)

Despite these firmly held beliefs among the teachers, supported by other research (for instance, Watts and de Jesus 2005), we did *not* find a link between those students who said they were prepared to ask questions and talk in class and overall performance.

Superficially this presents a conundrum. Surely teachers are right to expect those who ask questions and talk in class to perform better than others? Our research suggests otherwise. The quiet student who listens, takes notes, reviews his work after class and shares ideas and understanding with peers may be better equipped than the student who does none of these things but does ask questions. Quality is a further factor here. We asked students whether they were willing to ask questions in class in general, so they may have been thinking of lower-order, process-related questions; in contrast, the teachers meant higher-order, testing questions that demonstrate an engagement in learning, an ability to make connections and a desire to expand knowledge. So we have a potential mismatch in definitions. Other studies suggest this may be the case. Using a similar, generalized question in a student survey, Myers (2010) detected no correlation between students' propensity to ask questions and their position on the Perry scheme of intellectual and ethical development (1970); Graesser and Person (1994) found a correlation between the *quality* of questions asked and student achievement, where higher-order questioning was related to higher performance; Veerman, Andriessen and Kanselaar (2002) noted that higher-order questions arise only infrequently in classrooms, while King (1992) proposed an explicit training model to help students learn to pose questions that will transform their thinking. How can we promote engagement with the material and encourage questions that enhance learning?

What we can do

If you want your students to feel able to ask questions, you need firstly to **ensure that you are regarded as approachable**. If a student needs to ask a question, particularly if it seems that no one else requires further explanation, then she may feel quite vulnerable. So when students ask even trivial or superficial questions, avoid discouraging them with a witty but hurtful rejoinder. Be particularly careful when working with culturally and nationally diverse groups: while humour can show some students that you are approachable, ironic humour can cause great confusion among students who are unaccustomed to it. We're certainly not suggesting you excise all amusement from your classes, but encourage you to **think about the target of your humour and the extent to which you use it**. Self-deprecating jokes, where you are the butt, are likely to be less threatening; even so, if you self-deprecate too much, you will undermine your authority and will make students think the class is all about you, rather than about the subject.

Establishing that fine balance between your approachability and your credibility in class may take some experimentation. Studies have examined the ideal psychological distance between teacher and students to create a positive learning environment, focusing mostly on attire (see, for instance, Gorham, Cohen and Morris 1999; Sebastian and Bristow 2008), and have led to mixed results. The advice on approachability is painfully condescending, yet we've seen it work both for teachers who come across as too formal and for those who appear too close to students. In both situations, **review your wardrobe, your form of address in class and your body language**. If students see you as too distant, wear slightly less formal clothes (even loosening a tie can make a difference!), sit on the edge of – not behind – the desk if that is culturally acceptable (we are told it is offensive behaviour in New Zealand, for example), remember to smile, and consider whether you're happy for students to call you by your first name (we'll come back to this). If students are over-familiar with you, wear more formal clothes so that there is a clearer distinction between you and your students, stand up straight, use less colloquial language, and ask students to use your title, not your first name. This advice might seem a bit depressing in its conformism; and we certainly do not intend to patronize. However, in our experience, this simple advice in most cases actually works. **Ask a colleague to sit in on a class** and act as a critical friend (Handal 1999) to get richer feedback to see whether your instincts on your approach-ability and credibility appear right from an outsider's perspective.

Cultural differences between the UK and USA lead to different advice on the question of titles. UK universities are typically more informal, so first names are the norm at most institutions. This does not appear to cause difficulties for university teachers. In the USA, however, practice is more variable, but with a slight preference for using titles. Disruptive student behaviour happens more often to teachers who are lower in status, so anything that identifies you as not being part of the 'dominant' group can work against you. It's therefore more important to set out your credentials early on to demonstrate that you are an authority. For teachers who are part of the dominant group (such as white males), you can demand a level of distance that you don't technically need as a way of supporting your colleagues. For example, David tells his students:

> I would *prefer* you to call me David, but know from the research that using first names causes problems for teachers who are female, from ethnic minorities, on part-time contracts, are physically small or who look younger. So in an act of solidarity with those teachers, I have to insist you call me Dr. Green. And I'd encourage you to think about

that research and how *you* interact with teachers belonging to those particular groups.'

This is wordy, but effective. Students are horrified to think they may be prejudiced in their treatment of their teachers; we hope they also come to appreciate that members of the dominant culture can take action to counteract systemic biases. If this is all too much for you, then a neat alternative is to borrow a line from Lisa Coutu, a communication teacher, who tells her classes of 300 undergraduates, 'I'd like you to call me Dr. Coutu as it reminds me of my responsibility to you as your teacher.'

Make it easy for students to ask for clarification. When you ask a closed question (leading to a quick 'yes' or 'no' answer), most students want to be able to say 'yes,' so change your wording to make 'yes' the response that generates further clarification. For example, rather than 'Is that clear?' or 'Do you understand?', ask 'Would you like me to give you another example of that?' or 'Is it helpful if I go over that again?' If you see smiling faces but have a concern that there might be some misunderstanding, **ask students to give you an example to illustrate their understanding**. You may prefer to ask the class to consider in groups of four or five and then share their ideas, if you think they'll be too intimidated to answer on their own. Similarly, **ask students to come up with questions in groups,** or invite them to discuss which parts of the topic seem counterintuitive. Continue to **give students permission *not* to know things**. If you say, 'Many students find this aspect difficult at first, so who doesn't understand it?', you normalize the lack of comprehension. 'Who'd like me to explain what I mean by a metaphor?' encourages students to express their confusion. The opposite ('Do you all know what a metaphor is?') could imply that everyone *should* know.

Some students – particularly those who feel reverential toward people in positions of authority – may consider their questions too insignificant to trouble a teacher during office hours. To counteract this reluctance, **arrive early to class and stay late to answer quick queries**. If it becomes apparent that a student's question is more complex, arrange a time to meet (perhaps during office hours) or offer to discuss it in class if you believe your answer will help the whole class gain a greater understanding. Doing so also encourages the student to realize that his 'insignificant' question was in fact important. We discuss question-asking further in Chapter 7 in response to the students' own comments on successful learners.

Many key conversations between university teachers and their students happen during office hours, but as the teachers in our study reported, few students seem to attend and those who do are often the ones who are already doing well. So how might you make attending office hours a regular activity for all students? If your classes are small enough, **arrange for *all* your students to come and see you in your office hours** for about 15 minutes. (For larger classes, you might do this in groups of three or four.) You can link names, faces and background information that might help you connect with those students in the classroom. Knowing who among your students is a hockey referee, who plays in a jazz band and who volunteers at the soup kitchen helps you tailor your metaphors, tap into students' interests and builds up a picture of a whole person. Those 15-minute conversations allow you to build rapport, be human (your students may not see you as human in the classroom!) and demonstrate that you provide the kind of supportive learning environment that students need for them to feel positively motivated to succeed. You are suddenly far more approachable and less intimidating. Another ruse that a business communication colleague uses in the first two weeks is to tell a white lie in class and **say how pleased you are that so many of your students have already been to see you in office hours** (even when very few – if any – have attended) and how that demonstrates their commitment to get to grips with the subject. Students who would feel awkward about coming to your office become emboldened because it now looks like the norm.

10. Teachers believed that successful students form their own study groups

Many teachers observed strong students taking ownership of their learning. The most commonly cited evidence of this was informal, student-formed study groups. The first of these teachers combined her observation with gendered behaviour:

> successful female students tend to form study groups and I don't know how they find their study groups; I'll often have upper-class people

[i.e. students in their third or fourth year of study] come in and talk about their experiences and they inevitably talk of the importance of study groups and it seems like they just stumble on that.

(US-Delphin-17)

I don't organize them myself, I let them choose, but I watch how they group up and I can tell the group that is just going to be incredibly successful because they find each other. Or they don't [with] the first paper and then they realize [with] the second paper and I can see them looking across the room, like, 'I want to be with that person' and they self-select. I had just an amazing experience: I had a student with pretty challenging learning disabilities and she didn't get one of the best grades in the class, but she worked so hard and she was one of those who could identify the students in the class who could help her.

(US-Constantia-4)

Teachers believed that those students who form their own study groups, and thereby take control of their learning, perform better than others. Our research did not support this belief. Other studies have produced mixed results: Eggens et al. (2008) found that students were more likely to complete their degrees if they had a large social network of friends and Springer et al. (1999) suggest that students who form study groups perform better than those who do not, although this latter conclusion has been questioned by Colliver et al. (2003) using the same data set. In a study of an introductory biology course, Rybczynski and Schussler (2011) concluded that participation in out-of-class study groups had no effect on academic performance, as did Arum and Roksa (2011: 135) in a separate study, finding that 'Social activities, including studying with peers, have either no consequences or negative consequences for learning'. Our own data cannot tell us whether students in study groups performed better than they would have done without them, or whether study groups helped the students stay on track with their studies.

What we can do

Anecdotally we know that many teachers encourage the formation of informal study groups because this has proved to be a successful strategy in their own studies. It's also possible that those students who formed study groups performed better than they would have done had they worked alone. We do know that students perform better if they engage in dialogue about their learning (Brookfield and Preskill 2005; Vygotsky 1987), and so we encourage you to **facilitate the formation of these groups,** but give students the choice as to whether or not they participate. As part of the facilitation process, you might consider factors such as where students live (so they can meet close to home if they're not near campus), whether they have care-giving commitments (so that these students can support one another with strategies for juggling responsibilities) and which days they're on campus.

Set group-work activities, rather than always setting individual work. Students are often reluctant to take part in group work, and complain if they are given the same grade as the rest of the group, particularly where they perceive an uneven distribution of effort. There are numerous ways to address this, some more complicated than others. Race (2001) suggests techniques such as the teacher allocating the same grade for all members of the group, using, say, 75 per cent of the total marks available, after which the group then allocates the remaining 25 per cent of the marks between themselves; or set a large-group task that is awarded one grade, plus separate individual tasks which contribute to the whole but which allow the teacher to differentiate between group members. See Gardner (n.d.) for an effective, if complicated way for the team to peer assess.

While group work may be unpopular with students, it is popular with potential employers, since most workplaces require team work, not just individual effort And as most of us have discovered, we rarely get to choose the people we'll be working with, so much of the group-work process is about negotiating personalities and managing irritations. It's not surprising that students push back. But don't let that deter you. Group assignments and group work in general provide students with the chance to hone their interpersonal skills and give them a richer trove of experiences on which to draw when they are being interviewed. With that in mind, we suggest you eschew the easy option of allowing students to choose their own groups and, instead, **create groups with the clear intention of social engineering**. So if you notice that your class tends to divide along ethnic or racial lines, ensure your groups are mixed; **separate in-class neighbours and force everyone out of their comfort zones a little** so that they work with different people. For one, you'll **encourage intergroup dialogue** – enabling students from different backgrounds to exchange ideas and get acquainted. Equally, you'll **save students from socially awkward choices**: students don't generally want to have to tell their friends, 'I don't learn much when I sit with you' or 'I'm looking for people who will stretch me', so if you do that work for them by splitting groups differently, you're helping all of them in their development. For shorter activities, keep mixing the groups, as explained in Section 4 above.

Earlier, we also discussed guidelines or ground rules: **ask your students to formulate guidelines as 'group contracts' to help avoid later problems**. Ask the group to discuss their personal preferences and previous experiences of group work. Based on this, the group produces an agreement about the way they want their group to operate. Airing concerns, likes and dislikes in this way can prevent irritation, and if problems do arise further down the line, they can be addressed more easily than if an agreement has not been made.

In this chapter, we have discussed the 10 preconceptions that arose in our interviews with university teachers in both the UK and USA, of which four were upheld in our analysis of students' responses and final grades. Chapters 5 and 6 examine preconceptions raised by teachers in the UK and USA, respectively; only a minority of these beliefs directly relate to differences in the higher education systems of the countries, so we see value in both chapters for readers in all settings.

5

UNDERSTANDING UK TEACHERS' BELIEFS

In **Chapter 5** we focus on UK teachers' preconceptions and the performance of their students. The findings are relevant to those outside as well as within the UK, as we explore the lessons that may be learnt from the research by all teachers. You will remember that we asked teachers at Arial (a post-1992, teaching-led university) and Baskerville (a Russell Group, research-focused university) to tell us the key characteristics of students who perform well and those who do less well. We then surveyed those teachers' students to identify who had those characteristics. Finally, we compared end-of-course exam or assessment performance with survey responses to see if students achieved the expected levels of performance. Full details of the research method are given in Chapter 2.

Preconceptions specific to our UK teachers, and the extent they are upheld or not through student performance, are summarized in Table 5.1.

We'll now examine each of these preconceptions in some detail to elaborate on the teachers' beliefs about their students and consider practical responses in light of the findings.

UK-specific preconceptions that were upheld

1. Successful students engage with the orientation (induction) programme

Most UK degree programmes offer an orientation programme (often called 'induction') at the start the first year, providing a non-compulsory introduction to the academic and social aspects of university life through the context of the degree. Student orientation often provides more than standard information about the programme: it is designed

Table 5.1   Summary of preconceptions and their validity: beliefs specific to the UK

UPHELD	NOT UPHELD
Successful students:	Teachers believed that successful students:
1. engage with orientation (induction) programme	3. attend full-time
2. access course information from the institution's VLE	4. have met previous academic targets
	5. enter the programme prior to Clearing*
	6. have moderate anxiety
	7. enjoy doing things in their leisure time that relate to the programme
	8. do not have dyslexia
	9. feel that they belong at university

*See Chapter 3 for an explanation of Clearing.

to be a taste of what's to come, a chance for students to meet with their teachers in the department, to get to know their cohort of students and to start engaging with the structure of the programme, for example through activities and small assignments related to the subject area. Several teachers, such as this one, told us that students at risk of not achieving did not arrive in time for orientation:

> I think there is [a] correlation between the difficulty that [students] are going to have in week one between those that did the induction week and those that didn't.

> (UK-Arial-6)

Students who miss orientation do so for several reasons. They may not see the relevance of orientation to their studies, have other pressing external demands, such as child care or dependent adults, may not wish to give priority to attendance for less noble reasons (such as leisure activities), or perhaps they are juggling study with paid work. The suggestion is that students' behaviour in the first week of the term is likely to signal their future attitudes.

In the UK many students start a programme in week one of the first term of the academic year. The start time varies between universities, from early September to as late as the first two weeks of October, but some students join courses up to a few weeks later:

> There are some students [who], for their own reasons, don't join the course at the correct time with everybody else. Now it may well be because they haven't originally decided to go to university; they were late getting into the appropriate things; they were originally on a different

university course elsewhere and decided to change to this one. The university has a policy, when it's short of numbers, of allowing students to enrol on programmes up to six weeks late […]. I think any student who enters in week five – and the module's only going to last 12 weeks – is going to have a real problem with the module.

(UK-Arial-6)

Teachers in our study expect these late arrivals to perform less well than the rest of the cohort. By arriving after the start of term, they miss out on the potential of bonding with other students and are less familiar with the programme's academic expectations and the nature of university life. If they have ended up on a programme that they didn't originally intend to take, they may feel demoralized, not excited by the degree, and even less likely to engage with the work.

There are five further main reasons for students to arrive late to the programme. The first, very basic, reason is illness; the second is politics, in that some international students struggle to get their study visas in time, particularly if they are recruited late; the third involves religious and cultural festivals; the last two reasons are both financial – some international students may choose to arrive later to reduce the length of their stay abroad, or to avoid travelling in the peak holiday season, while some UK and international students may also arrive late as they prefer to continue in paid work for as long as they can before starting the studies. Although these causes were not mentioned by our interviewees, we encourage you to bear them in mind when students arrive late.

Only nine students in our survey arrived after the first week, so our numbers were too small to provide valid data linking late arrival to performance. Clearly, though, all these students missed the orientation programme, which we *did* find was linked to poor performance and which is supported by research elsewhere (Hassanien and Barber 2008; White and Carr 2005).

What we can do

There are many ways to encourage students to engage in the orientation programme, and to support students who, for whatever reason, join the course after orientation. We present these strategies in three stages: pre-orientation, during orientation and post-orientation.

Given the importance of orienting students and helping them settle into university life, you'll find this a longer than usual section of the chapter.

Pre-orientation Developments in social media have made it far easier to **contact students before they start their programme** than used to be the case. Many students, particularly traditional school leavers use social networking sites with their peers. This makes it a viable medium to engage with students as they are familiar with the technology, and it can be done without making them feel invaded by teachers who are not part of their usual social group. Some course teams have found that teachers don't need to take a high-profile role on the site; indeed, some don't involve teachers at all. The course team creates, for example, a Facebook site for the course, and then invites the enrolled students to use it to contact their peers. This often leads to the students owning the space and using it to get to know each other a little before they attend.

Some programme teams, in areas where student accommodation is limited, go well beyond expectations in helping students prepare for university life. At the University of Brighton, for instance, certain programmes make the additional effort to **liaise with student services** so that students can get to know others on their course, helping them find future flat- or house-mates. Enterprising students among them also arrange shared car rides through this 'match-making' mechanism.

Increasingly, programme teams **communicate with prospective students through regular newsletters** (whether on paper or sent electronically) aimed at keeping the students connected to the university and their chosen degree, as well as enthusiastic and well-informed. Content for such communications can vary widely, from details about specific modules on offer to profiles of current students, from study abroad opportunities to information about what last year's graduates are doing. If paper-based messages are sent in tandem with other official information – for instance on extra-curricular activities through the students' union – prospective students will feel less bombarded by information and more that they're supported in their transition to a new stage of their academic lives. The steady flow of consistent, supportive messages from the university should encourage students to see orientation as an integral part of their studies.

Since the research tells us that students who engage with the orientation programme perform better than those who don't, **share this finding with the students before they arrive**. Tell them in advance what to expect, the importance of attending, as well as the number of hours of study they'll need to invest in the programme (you may need to make this particularly clear to part-time students), and send them the full or an abridged copy of the programme, along with reminders about things that they'll need to bring. You could **consider including a separate communication for parents and guardians**: they could well be anxious about their offspring (think back to our comments on helicopter parents in Chapter 2), as well as more likely to remember some of the details that you send to their child. Along with information about the orientation programme, include a few pointers for them about how to respond to any concerns early in the student's studies, and how they might be able to respond helpfully to promote the student's independence. (We offer additional suggestions on this in Chapter 6, as well as thoughts on how to help students manage their parents.) An evaluation of orientation at Edinburgh Napier University revealed students most valued the chance to meet with programme and module leaders. As this was not universal practice, it generated a need to adapt the orientation to meet students' needs.

During orientation Orientation provides a fantastic opportunity to set the tone for the entire degree programme, so no matter whether it's a two-hour welcome or a full-week programme, **focus on a high level of organization and professionalism**. Your students will quickly get the message that your programme demands high standards of everyone and that the teachers mirror the requisite effort in the way they run the orientation. Just as your communications in advance need to be clear and polished, your orientation event should sparkle – a term that rarely surfaces in higher education. **Play to the strengths of your colleagues** so that the wordsmiths produce text for any handouts, your charismatic teachers do the bulk of the presenting, those with a good visual eye create any slides or graphics, while your process-oriented colleagues work out activities, timings and student groups. To save you time, refer to your university's communications or marketing team to find out how to lay out documents to be both appealing and easy to read – but avoid over-branding so that the message gets through, rather than only your university's or department's name. (Garr Reynolds' *Presentation Zen* [2008] is a must-read for anyone putting together slides, especially for this tone-setting orientation.)

It is vital to manage students' expectations from an early stage. In attempting to present a polished and attractive initial week, we could give the false impression that university is something that is done *to* students: that their role is to consume the offering passively. **Build in activities and emphasize that students are expected to engage with the learning experiences**, and that the more they put in, the more they will gain. As we discussed in Chapter 2, people are more likely to learn effectively when they are actively engaged in their learning.

To emphasize that your new cohort is valued, **introduce all students to both the senior figures in the department and key teachers**. Programme directors, year tutors and the head of department (in the USA, 'department chair') all need contact with this new group to build connections, and help orient students to the various people they will see in the next few years. If everyone is comfortable displaying photos of the department members on a noticeboard, that will also help students put names to faces and give them confidence that they know who is who.

Some students may feel overwhelmed if you present all the information about their degree programme, the university, expectations, assessment, student life and so forth, all at once. **Use the Just-in-Time, or staged, approach to information**, providing what students need when they need it, and let them know where to revisit the information at a later stage. In other words, orientation doesn't have to be a one-time, one-week event at the start of the year: you can **spread orientation events over the whole year**. By doing so, you find the initial event stripped of some of its less attractive details – for instance, you could schedule a discussion on how to avoid plagiarism at the point when students receive their first assignment – freeing up time for more engaging activities. Orientation should lead students to feel part of a learning community and to retain or create enthusiasm about their degree choice.

Above all **make sure that the orientation is worthwhile**. This is particularly important for promoting socialization among your students. **Create activities that relate to the discipline** that they can work on in teams, leading them to generate a 'product' (presentation, blog, poster) by the end of the orientation, with some kind of prize for the best group's work (for instance, a guide to the city or a local product). **Socially engineer the teams to mix international, home and local students** and create an activity where the best work will come about when these different perspectives are brought together. For instance, you can relate your activity to the city (the students' home for the next three or four years) to encourage the group to draw on local students' valuable knowledge; simultaneously, your international students' contributions are enhanced if the product is designed for an international audience. So while students taking business present on specific areas of the city to an audience of potential investors from abroad, those in history create a blog on the past events in the area for potential tourists, and architecture undergraduates produce a guide to key buildings for an international convention.

Arrange small-group discussions with one teacher, ideally some-one who will continue as personal tutor or advisor for the next year at least. This can be connected to giving feedback on the group activity if you have one. Some colleagues like to make this an informal event, starting with an in-class discussion, which is then continued over lunch. Some teachers are happy to invite students to an informal social event in a neutral setting like a café – whatever would make your entire group feel comfortable and included. Personal tutors (termed 'academic advisors' in the USA) have become increasingly important in recent years, especially in the UK, as the increase in student num-bers and large classes has led to concern over students missing the opportunity to make relationships with teachers, and possibly 'falling through the net'. Thomas and Hixenbaugh (2006) offer guidance on personal tutoring and, through work with their colleague Barfield (Barfield et al. 2006), they provide online case studies of effective personal tutoring.

Post-orientation As the year progresses, **consider building in social events to coincide with likely dips in students' confidence**. As we discussed in Chapter 2, Cook and Rushton (2008) found students lose heart around six weeks into their studies and again towards the end of the first term or semester and start of the second – in British universities falling either side of the Christmas and New Year break.

These times (around mid-term and end-of-term exams and assignment deadlines) correspond to Boice's (2000) findings on classroom incivility, where anxiety peaks and people's fuses shorten. So as well as social events, these may also be good opportunities to **meet with students either in small groups or one-on-one** to discuss progress, comfort levels and interest in the subject, concerns about completing the programme and areas for development.

More generally, the personal tutor system offers a powerful means to support students (Laycock 2009; Neville 2007; Race 2010; Thomas and Hixenbaugh 2006; Wisker et al. 2007) both in terms of general welfare (Myers 2008; Wilcox et al. 2005), and academically, as tutors can help students to engage with their learning by providing feedback (Cramp 2011) or by facilitating the production of reflective portfolios (Ellis et al. 2006).

Personal tutors can also play a significant role in helping students gain a bird's-eye view of their studies. The erstwhile Department of Languages and International Business at Birmingham City University developed a process to facilitate meetings and help students advance academically: each teacher is assigned half a dozen students to support in their first year as a personal tutor; the key role of the tutor is to **act as the only person from whom students can collect assignments for all modules** taken in that year; the tutor skims all papers from each student before meeting one-on-one and then focuses the conversation on any detectable patterns in the student's work – a big-picture level of feedback that's often hard to achieve in higher education. Thus, personal tutors can show students which aspects of their studies they should work on (organization, analytical skills, grammar and mechanics), as well as instances where students were succeeding in one subject, but not yet transferring the same intellectual skills to other courses. This 'meta-feedback' gives students greater confidence in their abilities and a manageable list of areas to attend to in future work.

Ensure that students who miss the orientation can access key information later. Assign each student a teacher (usually a personal tutor) from the department who will meet one-on-one to go over important material and find out how well the student is settling in. Be sure to use your university's virtual learning environment (VLE) or course management system (CMS) to store all important documentation. Help your latecomers access this information in a short meeting if they haven't already done so. If a sizeable number of students arrive late, organize a 'mini-orientation' two or three weeks into the course and require it of this group.

Some students who join the course late may be highly motivated to catch up with their peers. This is easier on programmes with a cohort model: see if one teacher can **devise an activity in which *all* the students re-introduce themselves**. Not only does this help new students identify peers who seem sympathetic or have similar interests but also it could remind all students of everyone's names and interests, aiding socialization.

Even students who are present may not engage well with the orientation, so keep an eye out for them to help bring them into the fold. Follow up to **find out why they were disengaged** and to see whether the department – or any other service on campus – can help those students adjust to their new environment. Ask what put them off and what would have made a difference. Their opinions could help you **redesign your orientation to attract and engage a larger percentage of each cohort**, making future orientations more effective and meeting students' needs better. Involving these students in that effort may help them feel better connected to the department or programme. You may also be able to introduce activities later in the year that respond to their feedback on the initial orientation. There is a wealth of literature on student engagement which demonstrates the benefits of involving students and listening to the student voice in all stages of their university career. In the UK, this is increasingly focusing on the student as producer and co-creator rather than consumer (Campbell et al. 2009; Halbesleben et al. 2003; Kaye et al. 2006; McCulloch 2009).

Cook and Rushton (2008) suggest using a peer mentoring system since more experienced fellow students (from later years on the same programme, for instance) may be perceived as more approachable than teachers. **Allocate first-year students a more senior peer** to befriend them and help them with the transition process. An added advantage of this is that the mentors gain from the experience as well as the mentee, but they do need to be trained and supported themselves.

Attendance registers can flag up when students miss classes, enabling teachers to intervene early. Some universities resist implementing registers, partly on grounds of cost but also arguing that students are adults, not children. Some, including lecturers at Baskerville, argue that compulsory attendance works against engagement rather than helping to enhance it. Despite this, you are more likely to notice if students start to miss classes if you **record attendance** – even when there is no grade attached – particularly in the early weeks before you have learned everyone's name. Several research studies, summarized by van Schalkwyk et al. (2010), have shown a link between attendance and performance, particularly for first-year students. Van Schalkwyk et al. recommend passing on this information to students to encourage class attendance.

2. Successful students access course information from the institution's VLE

Virtual learning environments (VLEs) or course management systems (CMSs) have been adopted in most institutions and provide a significant means to enhance the student experience. Many of the teachers we surveyed were concerned that some students seem to be reluctant to access the information on the VLE, and our survey identified these students as more likely to perform badly than those who did access the material.

Concern around interaction with the VLE is similar to that mentioned under orientation: if vital information is stored on the VLE, students who do not interact with it will not access the information they need to function on the programme. We need to stress that the preconception under discussion here concerns the most basic level of VLE use: *information transfer*. Phil Carey at Liverpool John Moores University distinguishes this from more creative e-pedagogies by referring to it as the virtual filing cabinet. It could well be the case that disengaged students would access and use the VLE if they thought it more interesting and creative.

In our data, we found the teachers were correct: students who fail to access even the most basic information on the VLE were likely to perform poorly.

What we can do

Looking at higher education across the globe, we find diverse use of VLEs. In many countries, there has been an explosion in the development of e-learning, seeing a move from the VLE as virtual filing cabinet, where teachers store their slideware presentations and hand-outs, to the VLE as the hub of the learning experience. Despite this expansion and increasingly complex use, the UK teachers in our study were concerned at a very basic level with students accessing unsophisticated, but vital, information such as timetables, reading lists and classroom locations. Given this context, it is perhaps unsurprising that students who did not access the VLE performed badly.

So how do we ensure that students do access the information initially and then go on to engage fully with the VLE (presuming it is being used as more than a virtual filing cabinet)? At the simplest level, we need to **ensure that students know they need to access the VLE and that they have the ability to do so**, ideally during the orientation. (For latecomers to the degree programme, you – or peer mentors – can run an extra session.) Most VLEs allow teachers to **track who has accessed which pages on the site** (and when), so it should at least be possible to identify students at risk swiftly, allowing you to intervene.

In addition, as with any learning experience, we need to **ensure that engagement with the VLE is worthwhile**. You can have the most adventurous website with amusing apps and opportunities for interaction, but if the students don't perceive the relevance or value of it, they will not use it. Since our interviewees focused on the virtual filing cabinet, rather than the virtual learning environment, we're not exploring online learning in greater depth here. We do, though, encourage you to **access the wealth of resources available** on the topic. For an introduction to VLEs, we recommend Weller (2007); for guidance on structuring e-learning and ensuring engagement, try Salmon (2011), Mason and Rennie (2006) and Bach et al. (2007); Garrison and Vaughan (2008) on blended learning; Salmon and Edrisingha (2008) for guidance on using podcasts; Conole and Oliver (2006) for a summary of e-learning research; and finally Laurillard (2002), Beetham and Sharpe (2007) and Sharpe et al. (2010) for discussions about the underlying pedagogy and the changes to the learning experience brought about by the emerging use of technology.

UK-specific preconceptions that were not upheld

All of the other beliefs expressed solely by UK teachers proved to be unfounded. As we discussed in Chapter 4, an examination of these factors can help to understand teachers' mindsets, and can also give an insight into students' attitudes. We will explore each in turn, suggesting practical approaches that may help alleviate the concerns that underlie the teachers' beliefs and that have been shown to improve the student experience.

3. Teachers believed that successful students attend full-time

Several UK university teachers made a distinction between full-time and part-time students, expecting the former to perform better than the latter. While this may be true in some individual courses, it was not the case overall in this study. (The medical students were all full-time, since part-time study was not available; courses at Arial were offered as full- or part-time, with the majority of students choosing to study full-time.)

In Arial's architecture programme, part-time students were typically employed in an architectural practice, which, according to this teacher, limited their ability to be wildly creative, an issue that does not restrict full-time students who have yet to find employment in the field:

> I think full-time [mode] is more likely to push the field of architecture forward because they are not constrained by the practice of architecture [...] so they are freer to experiment. The whole point about this course is that you are free to explore issues of architecture identity. Part-timers have always got that more practical head on because they are in the working environment, which is [a] good, solid grounding in the technical side of things, but I think it is more difficult for them to turn off that side of things when they are in university, because they are only here one day a week.
>
> (UK-Arial-1)

This view of students being constrained by the work environment might seem out of kilter with the positive benefits usually claimed for practice-based study. While success for this teacher related to students' development of their identity as architects, he did draw a further parallel with our own measure of success for this study – academic achievement on the course:

> But those who haven't [passed the course] probably have far more problems than full-time students have got, such as separating families or

financial problems or children to deal with. That's something with part-timers, kids are often in tow and family illnesses and god knows what.

(UK-Arial-1)

So teachers believed that part-time students were at greater risk of underperforming because of the extra demands on their time. In most cases, part-time students were also working full-time, though some of their employers gave them 'study time' in various guises, from time only to attend face-to-face sessions to more generous leave.

Teachers thought that working students who received no study leave were at greatest risk. Even those with some study leave were likely to have more responsibilities outside work than the traditional full-time school-leaver, because these students also tended to be older and more likely to have dependants. This expectation was partly contradicted by teachers who felt that more mature students would perform better than younger students, arguing that many mature students were more likely to work hard and engage with their studies because they had invested more heavily – in some cases literally, through lost earnings – and were therefore more likely to persevere when faced with difficulty and would put more effort into course work.

According to our research, part-time or full-time study mode makes no difference to a student's likely success on the course.

What we can do

Both full-time and part-time students will benefit from consideration and accommodation of their particular circumstances. It may be easier to support students on programmes with separate cohorts of part- and full-time students than when students in both modes take the same module together.

Put yourself in the shoes of a part-time student. What would you find useful? For example, is it possible to **prepare and publish time-tables well in advance of term**, as is the norm in both US and German universities, where schedules and rooms are announced months in advance? Those students who study part-time often have to fit in other responsibilities and they report frustration with arranging child care or swapping shifts with colleagues, when timetables change at short notice. Try to **keep changes to a minimum and set up a notification system for any last-minute class cancellations**: some departments record students' mobile phone numbers and, if changes have to be made, notify the students by text as well as by university email.

Students often regard the course as the time that they spend in class with a teacher. Because they have, say, 12 hours of face-to-face contact, they may presume that the rest of their time is for non-academic activities (similar to findings in the USA reported by Arum and Roksa 2011), and for part-time students with additional responsibilities beyond their degrees, this perception may be all the stronger. **Make it clear to students from the outset the number of hours that you expect them to study each week**. As we discussed in Chapter 4, this equates to 10 hours of study for every credit in the UK, so a 20-credit module requires on average 200 hours of study, including class time.

Some students may benefit if you **give clear guidance about the best way to use their time**. For example, if a module is delivered as a one-hour lecture, followed two hours later by a one-hour seminar, encourage your students to plan how to make best use of the intervening time. While networking and peer support matter, it is very easy to spend the whole time chatting.

Organizing the week in detail may not come naturally to many undergraduates, who could do with developing the life skills of self-organization and time management. So if you can, **show students how you block out your own time** for class preparation, grading and scholarship so that they have a model from which to work. (Personal tutors may be best placed to discuss these issues with students in individual tutorials.) Remind them to use their time on campus for activities that can only be done while they are there, such as visiting the library, and to find appropriate spaces where they can complete more mentally demanding tasks without distraction. Do remember, though, to **value socializing as well**, since students who feel part of a group and can work with others are less likely to struggle than those who feel isolated (Tinto 1993).

Part-time students may be particularly vulnerable to feelings of loneliness and isolation on campus. If they already have well-established social and family networks, they may simply not feel the need to make friends with fellow students or get involved. **If you set group assignments, consider the needs of part-time students**. Will they function better if they work exclusively with other part-time students or would they prefer mixed groups? Will they be able to complete group tasks successfully if they have less unscheduled time for out-of-class meetings? Can you incorporate time for group meetings in your regular class time? More broadly, **encourage all part- or full-time students to form their own study groups** (see Chapter 4 for more details), and set up discussion boards or online forums for this purpose. These can function both as face-to-face and as online gatherings, but most importantly, create the opportunities for socialization that make university study more enjoyable, even if they might not improve academic performance.

4. Teachers believed that successful students have met previous academic targets

Our interviewees suggested that previous academic achievement predicts future performance, a factor that has been identified in a range of studies cited by Eggens et al. (2008). The two aspects that were mentioned – not always by the same teacher – were UCAS points (in other words, success at A level) and whether or not students had at least a grade C in GCSE mathematics and English or the equivalent in other qualifications systems (as explained in Chapter 3).

UK universities use the University and College Admissions Service (UCAS) to manage the application process. UCAS converts all relevant qualifications into points, so that students from different educational systems can be compared; since UCAS points measure previous academic ability, a higher UCAS total should predict future success, or so several of our teachers believed.

> We need to look at the mean A-level grade of students and the range. There is a big cluster of students with three to five A grades but this hides a long tail of weakish students. Some have as low as C grade in one subject. These are the really weak ones.
>
> (UK-Baskerville-1)

A minority of interviewees in our study countered that A levels didn't predict student success, providing a variety of reasons, such as the following:

> In the past, 10 per cent [of school-leavers] went to university. Currently it is 30 per cent. The A-level standard is lowering [...]. Some come in

with six A levels – this should raise suspicion. Independent schools – students from there – do worse than others. They are pushed by their parents and schools into doing medicine. They go over past papers all the time […]. By the time they take the A-level exams, they have done the same questions several times already.

(UK-Baskerville-2)

This teacher argued that students with high A-level grades from an independent (private) school were not typically better students than those from a state (public) school with lower grades: they were simply more practised at passing the exams, thereby skewing the results and invalidating them as a predictor of student success.

GCSEs, as explained in Chapter 3, are exams taken when pupils are 15 to 16 years old. While Baskerville's medical programme required a minimum of an A grade at GCSE in both mathematics and English language, other programmes in this study had no minimum requirements for these GCSEs subjects, which teachers flagged as a barrier to student success. This teacher explains why these GCSE grades matter:

Some of the modules have a maths element in them and [students without grade C in GCSE maths] tend to struggle a little bit with this. Mind you, so do some who have grade C [in maths], but that's another story. And the English side again is quite important, and a lot of them aren't able to produce pieces of work that we can attribute marks to, because you can't make any sense of it sometimes.

(UK-Arial-4)

In our research we found a small range of UCAS points in any one course, and very few (less than 1 per cent) who had not achieved grade C in English or mathematics.

We'll raise two potential explanations for this mismatch between previous performance and success to add to the 'teaching-to-the-test' argument presented above. First, UCAS points may not correlate with performance, because in practice the *range* of points held by students on a particular degree programme is low. For example, to study medicine, the standard offer is between 370 and 400 points, which could mean one A* and two A-grade A levels. There is little scope for students to have a range of grades, contrary to the beliefs of teachers like those quoted above. Whereas less selective courses may require lower grades, the reality is that students tend to accept the course and institution that best match their achievement: rarely do students have far higher grades than required for their programme. Similarly, most students do have grade C in GCSE English and mathematics as a minimum, since many A-level courses set that as a prerequisite, though the system varies across the different parts of the UK.

Secondly, programme requirements vary in relation to the subject, as well as the grade. To take, say, French at degree level, a student would be expected to have a grade B in French at A level as a minimum, with most universities expecting an A or A*. The reason for this is fairly obvious in that the programme is designed on the assumption that students share a basic level of knowledge and ability in French. However, some other subjects are rarely taught at A level, so UCAS points may not indicate a student's facility in their chosen discipline at degree level. In our study, entry requirements for the built environment programme were 220 UCAS points (say, two C's and a D grade at A level) in *any* subject. Consequently, when students start this programme, teachers assume less common knowledge and skills:

> We don't specify subjects at all. […] That means that we have people on paper who are going to meet the criteria, right? What we don't have are people who may have the ability to be able to do some of the subjects like […] first-year economics or first-year law. Even though we're starting from a base that you know nothing, you need a certain aptitude to do it.
>
> (UK-Arial-6)

Teachers' underlying concerns about GCSE maths and English derive from students' facility in those subjects, as shown in their assignments, not their GCSE grades per se. Many teachers in HE argue that the standard of literacy and numeracy among students has fallen in recent years and there has been a long-standing debate in the UK press about falling standards (Bradshaw et al. 2009). The UK government has responded to – or possibly fuelled – this debate in England, with wide-ranging changes to the curriculum and the management of secondary schools (Department for Education 2010). The recently introduced Curriculum for Excellence in senior schools across Scotland raises similar issues (Education Scotland, n.d.). Some of these curricular changes include introducing new topics and skills, but such additions may be at the cost of other subjects. So teachers whose familiarity with GCSE English and maths is limited to their own experience may not approve of the changes, perhaps because they notice what has gone, but are not aware of what has been added.

Despite their many concerns about students' prior academic achievement, as well as past research claiming that high school achievement predicts university success (Eggens et al. 2008), we found no significant correlation between grades from secondary school and end-of-course performance in this study.

What we can do

Beliefs associated with both UCAS points and GCSE grades relate to the prior learning that students bring – or fail to bring – to university. Blaming the student or the failings of the education system are easy traps to fall into, but are beyond the control of university teachers. More important, then, is to **check incoming students' abilities in literacy or numeracy** so that first-year courses start from where the students really are, not where we'd like them to be, all the while mindful that a one-size-fits-all approach is unlikely to work with a diverse student body.

Many university teachers don't have first-hand knowledge of current secondary school syllabi, so **find out what academic work a typical pupil does**. If you have a required A-level subject for students on your degree programme, find out what is covered in the syllabus and what types of course work and exams are required: they may well have changed since you were at school. Many A-level courses, particularly in humanities subjects, don't require students to write long essays, as was common 20 years ago. Students are therefore less likely to find this an easy task, and may respond better to shorter essays at first, combined with clear guidance and advice. In contrast to the UK system, US higher education requires all students to develop their skills in rhetoric and argument, so **draw on resources from the USA on 'Writing Across the Curriculum'** (WAC) to help you structure your assignments and support students' writing skills in your subject (a prime example being Bean's 2011 edition of *Engaging Ideas*). As we discussed at length in Chapter 4, many universities have a central learning support centre that you and your students can draw on to help. The Association for Learning Development in Higher Education similarly provides a wealth of information and resources to help support students (ALD in HE 2011).

Many pupils are accustomed to redoing work several times with frequent input from their schoolteacher before they produce their final piece of work. UK university teachers often find this perplexing as they expect work submitted to be the final version, whereas the idea of revised papers is common in the USA. If you **allow students either to submit a draft assignment for feedback or a revised paper based on feedback** for a few extra points, you encourage them to attend to your feedback more closely and they see how they can improve their work and their thinking – without your writing the paper for them. As an incentive for students to produce their best work as early as possible, **cap the maximum additional points a students can earn for a revised essay**. For instance, we'd suggest that a revision shouldn't be able to attain the absolute highest grade (a clear First, or an A). This may run counter to your institution's policies, so check first. The US experience suggests that this is an issue that needs to be handled carefully. In the USA, teachers can be overwhelmed with revisions and an unmanageable marking load, so there is a need to balance the benefits of giving meaningful feedback that is used by students and ensuring a workable practice.

Feedback has been shown to improve student learning (Black and William 1998), but students need help to understand how to use feedback (Weaver 2006). Several studies compared teachers' expectations and students' views on the use of feedback, with most finding tensions between the two (Beven et al. 2008). If the feedback is given after the final mark has been awarded, students may not see the point of it and will fail to read it, not realizing that feedback on one assignment may help with a future piece of work (Duncan 2007). **Communicate the purpose of feedback to students and the different types of feedback they will encounter.** See Chapter 6 for further discussion of how much feedback students can absorb.

5. Teachers believed that successful students enter the programme prior to clearing

A-level results are published in mid-August, triggering a flurry of activity as those students who have met the required grades accept their places at their chosen university. But not all students meet their requirements. Some will be lucky, as their preferred university may still offer them a place, but most will enter Clearing (see Chapter 3). Teachers believed that students who joined a course through the Clearing process are less likely to perform well than those who entered through the standard route.

> Students who come through Clearing might not be as motivated as the ones who chose the course as their first choice. I mean, it depends on if you're wanting to go away to university and you're wanting to go to a nice location, you're wanting to go to a university – maybe Edinburgh or something like that – and be a real student [...], but instead you have to stay at home and come here.
>
> (UK-Arial-2)

The reasons are similar to those discussed above on starting a course late. While some students in this situation will feel rightly pleased at their maturity in taking action to get onto a different degree pro-gramme, others may consider themselves to be 'failed scholars' if they did not achieve the grades needed for their preferred course. However, they are likely to have the same grades as the rest of the cohort on their new programme, so although they might be disappointed with, say, three B grades at A level, they are no weaker on paper than other stu-dents on the course.

These students are less likely to be taking a course that they really want to do and, as the teacher above suggests, they may find them-selves living at home and not being 'a real student'. Getting onto a course through Clearing was regarded by several teachers as likely to affect student motivation, presuming that these students are disap-pointed because they have not achieved their first choice in terms of subject, institution or location.

We found no connection between entering a course through Clearing and weaker academic performance.

What we can do

Despite a lack of statistical evidence in this study, we recognize the psychological angle: these students may feel less confident or optimis-tic about their degree. As with so many of our suggestions in this book, approaches that are designed to help one group of students are likely to benefit the whole cohort.

As we know, enthusiasm is infectious and is appreciated by students. That enthusiasm may come from your current research in the field, consultancy work you're doing, or how you see your subject reflected in current issues in the news and media. Whatever it might be, **offer a glimpse of the insider's perspective**. Not all students will become enthused – and some will still see it as inherently uncool – but you can create a buzz among them nonetheless. To make this more palpable to new students during orientation, **ask alumni to share their success stories,** whether in person or on video, bringing the field to life for students who might struggle to see where their studies might lead them.

To counter a potential lack of confidence among students who joined the course through Clearing, **create opportunities for students to gauge their existing knowledge base** or knowledge that will be helpful as they delve into the field. Doing so in groups should lead them to share their diverse experiences and insights, generating a deeper understanding of their chosen degree, as well as enabling you to identify potentially troublesome misunderstandings that need swift correction before students progress. At the same time, students' realization that they have more background knowledge than they'd thought can build their own enthusiasm with an early sense of success.

6. Teachers believed that successful students have moderate anxiety

This preconception conflated students' need for detailed instructions with high levels of anxiety, on the one hand, and instances of classroom incivility with overconfidence or arrogance, on the other. Our teachers believed that successful students are only moderately anxious.

Several teachers spoke about over-anxious students who seem to be obsessed with access to past exam papers or who need constant reassurance about administrative details such as assignment hand-in dates. They felt that these students, rather than being exceptionally diligent and conscientious, were likely to damage their prospects by allowing concerns to get in the way of their learning:

> They keep knocking on my door asking for the same information I gave them in class and is up on [the VLE]. Some of them are obsessed with

past papers. If they'd just spend the time on the work instead of worrying about the exam, they would be fine.

(UK-Baskerville-B2)

Describing the other end of the perceived anxiety spectrum, this teacher interpreted bad manners in class as overconfidence, which she believed also leads to poor academic performance:

the behaviour is getting worse […] they are much more disrespectful, talk through lectures, that sort of thing.

(UK-Baskerville-3)

As we discussed in Chapter 2, 'classroom incivilities' of this sort are reportedly increasing on both sides of the Atlantic. This teacher went on to describe how this worsening behaviour seems to her to be linked to large class numbers (in excess of 400 in a lecture theatre), arguing that 'they feel braver together than they would on their own. It is something to do with mob mentality'. Her observation was mirrored at Arial:

It does get to a level sometimes where you have to stop and just shout, 'Shut up!' or walk up to a table. Even when you walk up to them, they're paying that little attention that they don't know you're stood in front of them.

(UK-Arial-4)

So, our teachers identify problems with complacency and arrogance and with severe anxiety. We asked students to report how anxious they felt about failing. Our research did not find a link between reported levels of anxiety and subsequent performance, although other studies tell us that too much anxiety does interfere with students' enjoyment of the university experience (Biggs and Tang 2007; Chan and Lee 2005; Owens and Walden 2001). Defining 'too much' anxiety, of course, proves tricky: one person's extreme anxiety will be another person's impetus to deal with a task. While we didn't find a link between anxiety and performance, we did find that women are more likely to *report* anxiety than men.

What we can do

Causes of anxiety vary greatly and most of them are beyond the scope of a university teacher's role, so **remember to tap university services**

at your disposal, especially the counselling centre. For some students, anxiety about failing arises from feeling out of control of their studies. It comes as no surprise that unannounced tests lead to an increase in classroom incivilities (Boice 2000), one of the potential products of a stressful academic environment. You can alleviate anxiety of this sort by ensuring that you **clearly state all information about assessed work and deadlines, attendance and any other class policy and regulations** in your syllabus, as well as online for students to access at any time. Chan and Lee (2005) use chatty radio-style podcasts to convey this type of information: they find that students are more likely to absorb it and to feel less anxious than if the same information is given using more traditional methods. As much as you can, try to **avoid changes to assignment deadlines**, which can create panic and resentment.

To boost confidence around exam periods, **organize revision classes** that allow students to practise using their new knowledge and make it clear what will be expected of them intellectually. Examples of past exam questions (or fabricated ones if the course is new) help students gauge the level of demand required of them.

Further resources and centres on campus help students build capacity to succeed: **refer all your students to the learning centre** for help with time management, study skills and organization, **to the writing centre** to improve their written work, **to careers services** to help them prepare for work after graduation, and so on. Student support services present opportunities to build students' confidence and counteract anxiety – these are great allies who help make your life easier as a teacher and take the pressure off you when you feel you're being asked to be a therapist as well as a teacher.

In a similar vein, **recommend any good study guides,** such as the free online *Moving On* pack (Terry 2007) or books by Cotterell (2008) or Northedge (2005) that help students become more self-sufficient. Leeds Metropolitan University provides another free online resource aimed at improving students' resilience (Poole and Lefever 2009). This is a well-supported field including some discipline-specific guides. Include any internal guides produced by the students' union or by other central offices on campus. Your learner support department may also have diagnostic tests for students to use, either alone or in the context of a one-to-one tutorial, to help them identify any available assistance. **List these references under 'recommended reading'** in your syllabus and draw them to your students' attention early in the course, when the academic demands are beginning to sink in.

UK teachers in our study saw a mild level of anxiety as a positive factor, arguing that students who do not feel *any* concern will not invest the required effort to excel. Some teachers make a point of telling their students that a particular course will be difficult and that they will need to work hard to succeed, claiming this galvanizes students to learn. Others, like philosophy teacher Sven Arvidson in the USA, take a more nuanced approach and **let students know when they're starting a difficult topic in the course**, pointing out a typical student's intellectual trajectory through it – two weeks of utter bafflement followed by an epiphany – and how, with patience and the support of their teacher, students will reach that end point (Arvidson 2011); in a way, this mirrors Meyer and Land's theory of threshold concepts (2006a; see Chapter 2). While he takes this gentle and supportive approach, Arvidson also strongly advocates that we promote uncertainty in our classes:

> Students need to walk out of each liberal arts and sciences class session with a horizon of unease, ambivalence, ambiguity, and vagueness and with the intellectual tools and cognitive lenses of that course's discipline to start to connect that horizon to the ground upon which they walk.
>
> (Arvidson 2008: 96)

We'll address uncertainty further in Chapter 8.

If your notion of 'mild anxiety' is that it presents enough pressure for students to become better organized and stay on top of the work, then refer to Chapter 4 where we discuss helping students keep up with the reading. For larger course-work assignments, like projects and dissertations conducted over more than one term, **incorporate staging-post deadlines by which specific aspects of the work must be completed**. For instance, if one staging post is a graded presentation to fellow students and teachers, outlining a longer written assignment, students have the opportunity to receive early feedback and can refocus their projects, planning and methods to improve their chances of producing a creditable final piece.

As the focus here is on students' anxiety about academic failure, we chose not to discuss the students who suffer from anxiety disorders to the extent that they are medicated. In these cases, it is always best to **refer students to the experts in your counselling service**.

7. Teachers believed that successful students enjoy doing things in their leisure time that relate to the programme

According to some of our teachers, students who spend their leisure time on activities related to the course demonstrate their commitment and engagement and are likely to perform better than those who do not. This most likely mirrors the teachers' own pastimes – English teachers who enjoy reading or writing literature, architecture teachers who like to visit new buildings – though we realize this is not universally true of academics. The teachers in this study believed that students who didn't show an interest in the topic outside class were less committed than their peers and would perform less well. This interviewee was quite distressed as he discussed students on a music engineering course:

> Most of them will be interested in making music [...]. A lot of them actually are in bands and they have to record and mix. They have ideas of setting up their own companies, if you like, recording a record or [they] think they can make money out of it. And then the others – I don't know – they don't know [about the industry], but they don't ask.
>
> (UK-Arial-3)

We did not find a statistically significant connection between subject-related leisure activities and student performance.

What we can do

You may find yourself in the same position as some of our teachers in this study: you love your subject so much that your leisure activities directly relate to it. Those 'star students' who make the same links probably remind you of how *you* behaved as an undergraduate. Remember, though, that we haven't been able to connect this behaviour to student success. Nevertheless, you may see advantages for students who are fully immersed in the culture of the discipline, so you could help the remainder who see the links less easily.

Earlier in this chapter (under Clearing) we discussed the benefits of enthusing students about the subject, and those suggestions apply here, too, including making links with employment opportunities. **Mention upcoming discipline-related events** (exhibitions, performances, book readings and so on) and, if you're willing, offer to meet your students there; **highlight TV and radio programmes** connected to your subject and spend a little time either before or during class to discuss them and how they might align with the course content. Simply to **model your attention to the times when your academic subject arises in the public domain** will encourage students to watch for connections and apply the discipline's ideas and approaches outside class. (We discuss this further under 'current events and politics' in Chapter 6.) When you have the opportunity, **use examples from current cases or stories in the media** to illustrate your points. These connections might seem obvious to you, but are not necessarily apparent to your students. Using common cultural currency, with some well-chosen examples, puts students at ease as they relate your discipline to a familiar context.

8. Teachers believed that successful students do not have dyslexia

As we discussed in Chapter 2, dyslexia is thought to affect between 5 and 10 per cent of the UK population (Learning and Skills Improvement Service 2004; Parliamentary Office of Science and Technology 2004; Pennington 1991). In recent years there have been marked attempts in the UK to support students affected by this learning difficulty. In part this has been accentuated by universities' obligations under legislation such as the 2001 Special Educational Needs and Disability Act (SENDA) to make reasonable adjustments for people with disabilities. Teachers who raised this issue believed that students with dyslexia would perform less well than those without.

> We know that some of our students [are] dyslexic, some don't find out until they come to university and suddenly they understand why they have had certain problems with school. There is support for them, and if I suspect that a student might be dyslexic I tell them to go to student services. I would expect dyslexic students to get worse grades than others. Well, yes, especially in the essays.
>
> (UK-Arial-5)

Our research did not show a significant link between performance and dyslexia. This may be because the adjustments allowed for dyslexia (for instance, a little extra time during exams) and institutional support are having the desired effect, ensuring that the playing field is levelled such that students with dyslexia are not disadvantaged.

What we can do

First, **find out what support is available** for students with special educational needs (including dyslexia) at your university, and how students access it. Encourage students to self-refer, so that they can benefit from this support. While you mustn't diagnose educational needs (and in fact, should avoid pathologizing any student behaviour), you do have a responsibility to ensure that students get the support to which they are entitled. Be sure to **follow your university's procedures to make reasonable adjustments to support students** once the university has assessed them and devised an action plan. Confidentiality issues are important here and require sensitivity, so be sure to know your own institution's policies, whom you can contact and what, if any, support the student wishes to receive. Whatever the situation for your students, the key is **to remember that *reasonable* adjustment is just that**, not a demand for some students to get an unfair advantage over their peers.

Good practice that helps students with dyslexia is helpful for all students. Those with dyslexia may have difficulty organizing their work, absorbing a large amount of text in a short space of time, and expressing themselves in writing. If your course involves a great deal of written material, **ensure that you give students sufficient time to read it**. Provide advance organizers and handouts, for example, available via the VLE (as discussed earlier in this chapter) before class, and let students know that they are there. Making materials available via the VLE presents an additional advantage: it allows students to print out their own copies on paper that meets their needs. For some students with dyslexia, the sharp contrast of black text on white paper makes words appear to dance on the page and they may prefer to use coloured paper, though the best colour varies from student to student. Universities like Liverpool John Moores provide students with dyslexia a supply of coloured paper specifically for this purpose.

As much as possible, **avoid singling out students with dyslexia** (or any other disability) in front of the class, whether by commenting on their disability to the group (we've seen this happen), calling out their names to come and collect any 'special' materials they'll need for the class, or asking them to perform tasks like writing on the board.

When you present data in class, ensure you don't make exclusive use of text. **Consider breaking down information using bullet points, mind maps, diagrams or charts. Give textual and visual descriptions and explanations wherever possible,** too, even in the way you present your syllabus. Research on Universal Design for Learning (UDL) looks into means of supporting brain function in instruction and finds that these multiple means of representation aid students' learning (see, for instance, the 2011 guidelines from the US's National Center on Universal Design for Learning at www.udlcenter.org). Many students with dyslexia – and many without – also prefer to learn by doing rather than by theorizing. Schroeder (1993) found that around 50 per cent of students prefer activities and examples to come before the underpinning theories, a sequence that appealed to few teachers. Does the design of your course facilitate such active learning?

Some courses require more text-based activity than others. If you **provide comprehensive information about the level of text involved in both delivery and assessment,** this may help students with dyslexia to choose the most appropriate course for them. The incidence of dyslexia may be as high as 40 per cent in art and design courses, with evidence suggesting many people with dyslexia are often more artistic and gifted in practical skills (Everatt et al. 1999; Francis 2009; West 1997; Wolff and Lundberg 2002). Consider whether the assessment methods used in your course provide variety and are appropriate tools for the course learning outcomes, regardless of the incidence of dyslexia. Is it appropriate to **replace some text-heavy assignments with other equally challenging and rigorous methods** that do not involve as much text? For example, students could create a DVD, present output from group work, design a poster or e-poster, collate an e-portfolio, record a verbal essay, or attend a viva voce (oral examination). The Student Voice project (Campbell et al. 2009) includes details of two approaches to assessment: Jenny Eland at Birmingham City University encourages her students in Early Years education to negotiate the form of the assessment, including the assessment criteria. This encourages learner engagement as well as making the assessment appropriate for each learner. Bridget Middlemas at Roehampton University has explored equivalences for different forms of assessment, again in consultation with students (Campbell et al. 2009; Middlemas, n.d.).

For more detailed context, approaches and ideas around supporting students with any disability, we refer you to the work by the Geography Discipline Network (Gravestock 2006; Waterfield et al. 2006), Skill UK (www.skill.org.uk), TechDis (http://www.jisctechdis.ac.uk/techdis/home), Achievability Project (www.achieveability.org.uk) and the British Dyslexia Association (www.bdadyslexia.org.uk).

9. Teachers believed that successful students feel that they belong at the university

In line with Tinto's work (1993), teachers believed that students who feel they belong at the university perform better than those who do not. Teachers at Baskerville, for example, argued that students who distance themselves from the rest of the cohort and who regard the medical school as an alien place perform less well than those who identify with the institution and feel at home. This observation was linked to claims about students from Asian backgrounds: some of the teachers at Baskerville thought that British-Asian students were less likely to feel they belonged at the university than their white peers, and that this was a contributory factor in their perceived under-performance (a perception that was unfounded, as we discussed in Chapter 4).

> There is a medical [school] culture of beer and rugby which alienates the Asian students.
>
> (UK-Baskerville-3)

Teachers from the same institution also observed that the university system can contribute to students' feeling isolated:

> But students lose out as they don't know who the tutor is on the time-table – it is left blank because the lead teacher needs to do the timetable ahead of time, and doesn't know at that stage who will be the tutor. Weak students can easily hide in this system.
>
> (UK-Baskerville-1)

At Arial, teachers were concerned about students – largely those who live at home and who may also be part-time – who only attend face-to-face sessions:

> Some of them just drop in for the taught sessions, then dash off to their 'real' lives. They don't seem part of the place.

> (UK-Arial-5)

We did not find a connection between students who said they belonged at university and subsequent performance. However, 27 per cent of students expressed no opinion on this question and only a handful of students (6 per cent) reported that they felt or strongly felt they didn't fit in.

What we can do

The quotes above point to organizational, cultural and situational barriers to feeling a sense of belonging at an institution. While we found no direct statistical link between belonging and academic success (and in fact the only student who strongly disagreed with the statement 'I feel I belong in this university' outperformed most other students), it still behoves us to minimize the chance that students feel ostracized; if they *choose* outsider status, though, that is a valid option that may well work for them.

Organizational barriers should be easiest to remedy. Where teachers realize that a procedure fails to provide important details for students (like the timetable that can't list a personal tutor because one hasn't been assigned yet), then **introduce a system that ensures students have all the information they need**. This sounds so obvious that you may wonder why we even mention it: often these omissions in the system are minutiae that elude many of us, as we don't see the system from the students' perspective. **Ask your students to suggest ways to improve the flow of communication** as a means of combating this natural blind spot.

Barriers created by the culture of the programme may require greater effort. Tinto's (1993) research on retention found that when students saw their teachers as 'human faces' and as part of the institution themselves, then they were more likely to persevere with their programmes. Some of the attitudes expressed by the teachers expose potentially damaging generalizations. We discuss how educational developers and others can support and influence colleagues, including challenging these more destructive views, in Chapter 8.

Building a sense of community on your programme necessitates a positive learning environment, one of three key components of motivation (Ambrose et al. 2010, discussed further in Chapter 6). That positive environment is mostly achieved by ensuring that students feel you are approachable, by building rapport with each group and by knowing your students' names. We've already discussed approachability in Chapter 4, so we'll just say a little about strategies for learning names. The more often you use students' names in class, the more likely you are to remember them, so it's useful at the start of each term to **ask students to say their names before they make a comment** so that you have chance to learn them gradually as they speak up. If after a few weeks you are still struggling with some students, you may want to remind them that they need to make themselves memorable, too, so you can say privately, 'I still don't know your name, so that tells me that you should be making more contributions in class.'

To reinforce the connection between face and name, some teachers **download students' photos** from the university's VLE and put them into tables in a basic document along with the names so that they can learn them. You can take this a stage further by **uploading each student's photo to your 'Contacts' list in your email package**, so that each time you open an email from students, their photo appears at the top of the message. Although potentially time-consuming, teachers who have historically struggled with names swear by it to help put names to faces.

In Chapter 4, we also suggested you **make all your students come to your office hours** (either individually or in groups) for 15 minutes each at the start of the term so that you can find out more about them and help build rapport, showing that your learning environment is supportive and that you care. It's key here to ensure that your students see this requirement as a benefit, not a penalty, so think about framing it as a way to help you work out how to adjust the course to tap into each group's needs and interests. You will most likely have to offer additional times in these first weeks to be sure to see everyone. If you have limited time to see students, make your available times clear, but also provide other means for students to leave you messages. Let students know how soon you are likely to respond (within two business days, for instance) so that you manage their expectations. All these steps should create a welcoming atmosphere on your programme, regardless of whether the majority culture among your students revolves around activities (like beer and rugby) that might rankle their peers.

We also suggest some strategies that help to build communities. As we discussed in Chapter 4, even though some students resist it, we advocate that you **use group work to promote active learning as well as improving students' sense of belonging**. To create a more holistic and complex group-work experience, **choose problem-based learning** (PBL) as a key pedagogical tool on your course. PBL involves complex, 'messy' problems for students to address in groups, and typically, any course content is delivered only at the point when students ask for it, so the experience for them is much more one of discovery than of information transfer from the teacher. Some teachers elect to use PBL for just a couple of classes to help the group bond; while not quite in the spirit of PBL, these smaller-scale group activities may still help nurture a positive, inclusive environment on your course. We recommend Schwartz, Mennin and Webb (2001), Savin-Baden (2007) and Savin-Baden and Major (2004) for further details and case studies on PBL.

Situational barriers are those where the students' other commitments and interests appear to pull them away from the programme – whether because they live at home and still have their school friends nearby, or because they are more motivated to engage in other activities (student politics, music, community work) than those related to the discipline. Provided they are still completing their work and aren't disruptive in class, this should not be a problem.

Ideally, though, students would not have a binary vision of their university lives, where their studies are hermetically sealed from everything else – whether 'everything else' is still on campus or is outside the university altogether. **Engage with your university's student organization** (most often the students' union in the UK) so that you know about upcoming events and make reference to them where appropriate, thereby encouraging students to engage with the wider experience. You may choose to **tailor your course to tap into specific extra-curricular (or co-curricular) activities**. If, say, there is a focus on raising funds for charity (many UK universities run 'Rag Week' for this purpose), can you incorporate course work that could contribute to this? For example, a teacher on a media course linked the end-of-module assessment (to produce a radio programme) with the Rag Week activity. This gave a focus for the students' work, as well as a feeling of authenticity and a meaningful deadline.

In this chapter, we have addressed the preconceptions raised only by university teachers in the UK; our hope is that readers in other countries can transfer these ideas to their own settings, too, since we see much broader applicability across national borders. In the same spirit, Chapter 6 presents preconceptions arising in conversation with teachers in the USA and provides a further set of insights for us to apply in our various educational settings.

6

Understanding US
teachers' beliefs

In this chapter, we present the findings that were idiosyncratic to the university teachers we interviewed in the USA. You will see that very few of the preconceptions raised in this chapter are unique to American higher education; we contextualize them here so that there are points of interest and relevance for all higher education teachers. As with Chapters 4 and 5, we elaborate on the teachers' perceptions of their students, firstly those beliefs that were upheld in our research, followed by those that were not upheld, and in each case explore how we might respond to these preconceptions in support of student learning. As in the previous two chapters, we devote more time to addressing more complex issues raised.

When we refer to an item as being 'upheld', we mean that we found a statistically significant correlation between the teachers' preconception and the students' final grades for that teacher's subject (refer to Chapter 2 for the full research method). In other words, if students with a specific characteristic achieved statistically significant higher grades than their peers without that characteristic, then the perception is regarded as being upheld. Table 6.1 presents a summary of the issues raised solely by university teachers at the US institutions in the study.

US-specific preconceptions that were upheld

1. Successful students actively choose to take the course rather than being required to do so

General education requirements in US universities compel under-graduates to take courses with potentially little direct relevance to their chosen major field of study. For instance, at both Constantia and Delphin universities, students must take a science course that includes

Table 6.1   Summary of preconceptions and their validity: beliefs specific to the USA

UPHELD	NOT UPHELD
Successful students:	Teachers believed that successful students:
1. actively choose to take the course rather than being required to do so	7. use the learning centre or writing centre
	8. regularly attend religious services
2. expect to perform well	9. are independent thinkers whose parents encouraged debate
3. enjoy reading in the discipline	10. show an interest in current events and politics
4. show tenacity when faced with difficulty	11. have at least one parent who attended university
	12. were encouraged to attend university by their families
5. spend a limited amount of time using social technologies	13. are not married
	14. are not student athletes
	15. speak English at home
6. are not in their first year of study	16. come from specific US states
	17. attended a high school where most of their peers expected to go to university
	18. are not in their final year of study

a lab, even if their eventual major will be in the humanities. The teachers who deliver these courses thus face classrooms of motivated students who express an interest in the subject alongside others who might prefer to be elsewhere.

> We get tons of students because biology seems to be the most popular way to go if you have to take a lab science [*laughs*].
>
> (US-Constantia-2)

While teachers commented that students who actively chose the course would perform better than those who were simply fulfilling general education requirements, they also pinned their observations on the underlying question of motivation.

> Let's say that motivation is a primary focus that you might have, which I guess I believe heart and soul. If you've got that, you can get it done no matter what else is going on. You just need to want it worse than anybody else.
>
> (US-Delphin-18)

I don't think there are many students who say, 'I just don't understand at all why I'm here', but [...] the relevancy factor is a big one. Yeah, [if] students think it is irrelevant and difficult – and it is clearly a difficult course – then it is hard to be motivated to succeed because it is a lot of work to succeed.

(US-Delphin-11)

Conversely, teachers expected students who actively choose to take a course outside their major – but demonstrate genuine interest and want to take the more challenging option – to outshine their peers because they are highly motivated.

> they are really good, because they are in there because they don't have to take this – they are interested. They could take an easier biology, but they want to see what a higher-level biology is like.

(US-Delphin-11)

The teachers in our study were correct in their presumption: students who actively chose to take the subject did outperform those who were required to take it.

What we can do

It's probably no surprise to you that students who chose the course performed better overall – their intrinsic motivation to engage with the material is likely to help carry them through to success. Yet many people teach compulsory classes and manage to motivate students to excel, so what are they doing? Positive motivation is succinctly summarized by Ambrose et al. (2010) as a combination of a supportive learning environment, seeing value in the subject and the expectation of success. So this means not only developing a carefully scaffolded syllabus that supports learning and enables students to increase their skills gradually, but also ensuring that students can gain an early sense of success and can see a reason – beyond pure love of the discipline – for studying your subject in the first place.

We've already discussed the first aspect of motivation – a supportive learning environment – in terms of ensuring your students see you as approachable (Chapter 4), and learning students' names (Chapter 5, under 'belonging at university').

The second aspect of motivation is value. If students struggle to see value in your subject, consider how you can **highlight the ancillary benefits of taking your class**. What transferable skills will students develop through the assignments you have created or through classroom activities? Perhaps they'll hone their critical thinking abilities or their use of logic; maybe they'll enhance their data analysis or visual representation skills. Emphasizing transferability may feel like you are betraying the integrity of your discipline, yet if it provides access to the field to students who are initially less enamoured with it, then you may have found a way to expand their worlds academically.

Connect assignments to the real world, rather than setting abstract, traditionally academic papers, as it particularly helps students see value beyond the confines of the discipline. So a philosophy assignment can be translated into a discussion of stem-cell research using the argumentation of John Stuart Mill, or an economics essay can become a briefing paper on the impact of legalizing gay marriage on the local economy or government revenue. In *Engaging Ideas* (2011), John Bean describes 'meaning-making' assignments requiring four key components, leading to the acronym RAFT: a Role (or purpose) for the assignment, a clearly defined Audience, a Format (or genre of writing, such as a business report or a book review), and finally a clear Task for the students to respond to, and ideally that Task should be posed as an Intriguing Problem (easily remembered as TIP). If you are able to **create meaning-making assignments** following these guidelines, you should be able to reach more of your students and enhance their motivation to study: they'll see your discipline as one that can help them address interesting, challenging issues.

Motivation's third component relates to students' expectation to succeed. In the research, this is referred to as 'expectancies', but we find 'expectation to succeed' more immediate. This component consists of both a student's self-confidence and the apparent manageability of the task (Ambrose et al. 2010). Self-confidence appeared in our research as its own item, addressed in the next section; here, we'll focus on the manageability of the task itself.

This one sounds easy: **Set tasks that stretch your students without overwhelming them**. Yet getting the level right is one of the hardest jobs for university teachers. A few approaches can help you at least find the right ballpark. Most eye-opening is to **read your own undergraduate papers** if you still have them. You'll see the grade you received and you already know that you're not typical – you're one of that rare breed that now teaches in higher education. Your own papers can be a shock, especially if you're just coming down from your doctorate and haven't seen the work of mortals in a few years. **Ask colleagues for examples of assignments they set**, plus sample student work if possible. Elicit their thoughts on what worked and what could be improved so that you're already learning from their experience. **Give your own draft assignments to colleagues for feedback** (later we mention giving them to professionals in your writing centre for feedback on the likely perspective of students, too).

Keep in mind your own priorities for your students' learning and **ask whether your assignments align with the intellectual and technical skills** you think most important at this stage in your subject. Biggs's notion of constructive alignment helps you judge this (Biggs and Tang 2007; see Chapter 2): Can students demonstrate they have met the learning outcomes of the course through the assignments you've set? And do your learning and teaching methods help them develop the skills they need in order to complete the assignments successfully? If you align assessment, learning outcomes, and learning and teaching methods, your intentions for student learning are more transparent and the tasks appear more straightforward because you are reinforcing the same issues and skill development.

Students' confidence that the task is realistic can also be maintained if you **set early, small-scale assignments** allowing for swift feedback and, where necessary, self-correction. One approach involves gradually increasing the level of challenge so that students can chart their own progress over the weeks; another argues that the level of demand stay high from the start, while the scope of the task widens in line with students' increasing knowledge of the subject; a third – perhaps more contentious – argument proposes that the demand be high from the start and that students be disappointed with their first grade (worth only a small percentage of the final grade). If you return their papers using edifying language (see the next section), and explain that part of the purpose of a first assignment is for them to discover what each teacher is looking for, they *may* feel motivated. We stress 'may' here because we think this will only work for the few teachers whose communication style successfully balances firmness and support. One mitigating tactic in this third approach is to allow students to drop the assignment with the lowest grade.

2. Successful students expect to perform well

> I think what I've found is [successful students] come through the door
> with a lot of confidence: They're survivors.

(US-Delphin-17)

In keeping with the old adage 'success breeds success', US university
teachers in our study largely felt that students who are confident and
have high expectations of themselves were more likely to outperform
students with low aspirations. Our research did show a correlation
between those students who said they expected an A grade and those
who went on to achieve higher grades. While the teachers considered
confidence a factor, our findings may have simply recorded students'
realistic assessment of their ability. If a student predicted that she
would get a D and proceeded to do just that, does it tell us that her
expectations are self-fulfilling or merely realistic? Had that same
student believed that she would get a higher grade, would belief
alone have led to an improved performance? The findings can't tell us
either way.

What we can do

Self-confidence is the second element of the expectation to succeed
(along with manageability of the task), as discussed above, and constitutes its own factor in our study. We've already discussed providing
your students **opportunities for early success or early correction**
in their learning to boost their motivation; it will also enhance their
expectations of their own performance. For those whose early work
is lacking, you can **offer support or recommend strategies** to help
them catch up with your course. If the number of assignments you
can set is restricted (as is often the case in the UK), you can introduce
early, formative assignments or tests (in other words, ones where
the grades do not count) that mirror the format of a real upcoming
assignment. Practice runs help students work out whether they are on
track with their learning or need to be working differently in your
class.

Similarly, you can **give students a formative quiz or short task in
the first class and return it to them at the halfway point to dispel
their own misconceptions** that they have not learned. So the student

who 'can't do numbers' and the one who 'can never organize an argument' both see evidence of how much they have progressed in the last few weeks of study (Ruppert and Green, 2012). If you hear students groan at their past errors, this tells you how much they've learned. Remind them of how far they've travelled in their learning so that they don't dwell on the errors they made before even starting the course.

You can also **build up students' expectations of themselves by using edifying language** in your responses in class and in your written feedback. So, rather than telling them, 'I'm really disappointed in the work you produced here', rephrase it to help students own their performance to say things like, 'I can understand why you're disappointed in your mark. What can we do to get you back on track for this class?' or 'I'm looking forward to seeing your thinking really develop in the next assignment'.

Perhaps more surprising is the suggestion that you **keep your feedback concise and focused**, based on findings in various US studies (for instance, Ackerman and Gross 2010; Smith 2008; Weaver 2006). Peter Elbow (n.d.) suggests a time-saving and effective method that doesn't require you to produce a fully-fledged rubric (in the UK, called 'grading criteria'): identify three or four criteria which ideally are shared with the students in the assignment brief. Construct a small grid with three categories of 'weak', 'ok' and 'strong', and then grade accordingly. Elbow argues that this helps students to engage with the feedback and move away from focusing solely on the grade.

Keeping feedback concise can feel difficult, especially when you're keen to support struggling students with more comments to help them learn from their poor performance. In fact, Ackerman and Gross (2010) found that those who performed worst in a hypothetical assignment were least able to take on board their teacher's feedback: not only did receiving fuller feedback lead students to see teachers' comments as unfair and to believe the teacher disliked them as individuals but also those who received fuller feedback alongside failing grades also became *angry* and *resentful* when reading it. If you can keep your feedback brief, focused and carefully prioritized on only one or two key areas of concern, your students are more likely to accept it, learn from it, and ultimately build up their own belief in their ability to succeed.

A final area you can work on to enhance self-confidence is to **encourage your students to adjust their mindsets towards their studies**. Psychologist Carol Dweck (2006) distinguishes between individuals with a fixed mindset – those who believe they either can or can't do something – and those with a growth mindset – who believe they can improve with perseverance and practice and who appear to treat each failure as a learning opportunity. In education, when individuals see intelligence as an attribute they can develop, they are more likely to apply themselves in ways that will help them succeed. Dweck (2008: 235) discusses a strategy parents can use with their children, and it can be transferred to university learning, too. It involves three questions:

- 'What did you learn today?'
- 'What mistake did you make that taught you something?'
- 'What did you try hard at today?'.

Some teachers already require their students to hand in reflections on their assignments or use reflection as an overarching theme in their courses (see, for instance, Moon 2004). You can adapt Dweck's questions for children and ask students to answer them either along with the assignment they are handing in to you or as a follow-up to the assignment once they have received your feedback. The absolute simplest rephrasing would be:

- 'What did you learn from completing this assignment?'
- 'What mistake did you make while completing this assignment that taught you something?'
- 'What did you try hard at while completing this assignment?'

These very short reflections can be worth a few points as an incentive, or you could withhold the students' grades until they have submitted their reflection based on your feedback. They will need *additional* feedback on their reflections, but these can also be brief. These extra reflections will be all the more meaningful for students if you can also preface them with some of Dweck's findings:

- they are more likely to succeed by nurturing an attitude of mind that seeks out the learning to be gained from each experience
- will-power and effort alone do not achieve the same results as a growth mindset

- this mindset needs to be practised daily to become successful
- a growth mindset works best when they set themselves concrete goals each day.

See if you can give your students opportunities to put these ideas into practice in your course.

3. Successful students enjoy reading in the discipline

> I definitely have a subset of students who I know that are, like, 'Oh yeah I've read about such and such. I really want to know what that is.' And then some that pretty much have no idea what I'm talking about.
>
> (US-Constantia-2)

Just as the teachers thought, our research found a correlation between those students who said that they read widely around the subject – not just the required reading for the course – and students who performed well. As anticipated, students who are fully engaged with the course and have a thirst for knowledge will also gain the highest grades.

What we can do

In Chapter 4, we discussed how to encourage students to do the *required* reading for a course. But how do we get more of them to read more widely around the subject when we already know students spend less time per week studying than they used to? The 2010 National Survey of Student Engagement (NSSE) survey found the typical US freshman studied for an average of just 15 hours per week for *all* classes combined; students are also overcommitted with paid work and other obligations – ranging in our survey from 0 to 60 hours per week. Supplementary reading in this context seems a luxury.

Howard Gardner, originator of 'multiple intelligences', wrote that the 'greatest enemy of understanding is coverage' (1993: 24) – the more content teachers cram into their courses, the less students will be able to grasp – and this potentially unpopular principle has influenced our thinking on the topic of further reading. The likelihood for many courses is that you have far more material than can possibly be covered in the time allowed; this provides an opportunity.

A simple graphic, originally from the 1960s (Thomas et al. 1963/2007), can help you decide how to divide your course content between the essential, the recommended and the supplementary (see adaptation in Figure 6.1; you may also have seen a much later, similar graphic for course design in Wiggins and McTighe 1998). We use this exercise so frequently with colleagues that we think it worth including here before examining strategies to encourage students to read around the subject.

For any course you're teaching, you should be able to **separate out the content that students must know** (a threshold requirement to pass the course), from what they **should know** (material they need at their fingertips in order to earn a good grade for the course), from what they **could know** (more detailed content that's likely to lead to the highest grade possible – if not graduate-level work). One difficulty for university teachers is that this third level of content most often includes your own research agenda, the material you love and that motivates you. We usually want our students to take a deep approach to learning (Marton et al. 1997; see Chapter 2), to enjoy the subject, to become absorbed in the topic and to relish reading widely. It's unlikely that all students will take a deep approach all of the time and some students won't be enamoured with your particular pet project. Dividing the course material by these three circles helps you decide which topics are best dropped from the central course content to allow

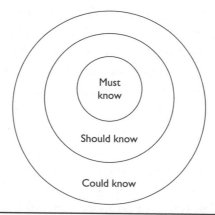

Figure 6.1 Prioritizing course content by degree of importance (adapted from Thomas et al. 1963/2007: 42)

time to ensure students have grasped the key concepts. After that, you can explore how to entice students to delve more deeply into particular sub-topics.

Already, many teachers separate 'essential reading' from 'recommended reading' in their syllabi. It's less common, but very useful, to **break down your recommended (non-essential) reading list by topic** to make it more focused and manageable for students. So, for instance, in a linguistics class that covers phonology, syntax, semantics and sociolinguistics, providing supplementary reading lists for each of these topics (and, if appropriate, sub-topics in each of those areas) enables students to follow their interests, rather than overwhelming them with an alphabetical list of undifferentiated sources. For recommended books, **list specific chapters relevant to each topic** to direct students more clearly. While this might sound onerous, remember that it also helps you with your planning and course organization, since you'll then have your own consolidated list of references by topic, ready for when you want to freshen material or try something different.

If you have a lot of additional material (or if you don't have time to put together an extended reading list before the course starts), **compile lists of further reading for specific class sessions**. This level of detail may be too much for a syllabus, but is well-suited to a course website or an email to students after a class. It also means you're prepared for those after-class conversations where a student wants to know more about the topic and wonders where to start. Sometimes we spend so long focusing on struggling students that we forget that these highly engaged students benefit from additional support, too.

And if you're concerned about the time involved in putting together lists of this sort – particularly if you're teaching in an area that's less familiar to you – then you can treat it as a longer-term venture and **set an assignment where students create annotated reading lists that you can use in future years**. Your students pick a topic they find interesting and produce a first draft of a document that you later tidy up or correct as needed.

When thinking about 'reading around the subject,' you might also want to consider interpreting 'reading' more broadly to **include other media,** such as film, video and audio files, and online material.

Providing varied forms of resources should help more students dig a little deeper, even if only on one topic in your course.

Many university teachers already **offer students a choice of topic for assignments**: it allows them to pursue their interests and you can make it a requirement that their reading for these assignments extends beyond the required reading. Research tells us that choice in assignments promotes deeper approaches to learning (Ramsden 2003: 80), so there's a strong rationale for allowing this option. At the same time, we encourage you to consider how manageable these assignments will be for providing feedback in a timely fashion (ideally, 'timely' here means around 10 working days if you're on a semester system, fewer if you're on quarters). If you allow *any* topic connected to the course theme, you might be inundated with requests for suggestions on readings in unfamiliar areas and, once papers have been submitted, you may find yourself swamped as you try to verify how well your students have represented their chosen topics. Some teachers see this as a helpful opportunity (or excuse, if one were needed) to research a new area of study; others feel distracted from the core of their work – both in teaching and in research.

A midway point between open choice and zero choice for assignments is to **devise two or three assignment questions for each area of study**. They could include one or two subjects that you've been hoping to explore yourself, but have not found time to do, or could incorporate areas that you're currently researching so that time spent on student assignments also helps you move your research forward by encouraging you to do more reading, too.

4. Successful students show tenacity when faced with difficulty

The university teachers in our study believed that students who had a positive attitude and showed tenacity would perform better than those who were more negative. This teacher suggested some of the strategies that such students use when faced with difficulty, echoing findings on students who take a deep approach to their learning (Gibbs 1992).

> Some students, they do have good learning strategies, for example they
> can have a good strategy to manage their time.... They never study in

the dorm, they study in the library, which is quiet – that is a good one. And if they cannot solve the problem they can find another way to do that, not just keep trying the same method again and again.

(US-Delphin-12)

To gauge tenacity, we asked students to describe their approach to their studies, offering five choices from 'Often do less than I should/ less than others do' to 'Frequently do more than I'm told to do'. Our findings indicate that the teachers' presumptions were right: students who show tenacity when faced with a problem did perform better than their less tenacious peers.

What we can do

Students who persevered through problems in their learning per-formed better in our study. The notion of 'mindful tenacity' (Ford and Smith 2007) provides a frame that gives both students and their university teachers a degree of agency in enhancing students' ability to persist. In Ford and Smith's model, tenacity relates to finding creative, imaginative solutions to problems; meanwhile, mindfulness means the ability to check the contextual or personal constraints in a situation so that unrealistic expectations don't thwart your creativity. To put that in more concrete terms, most of us in a university setting have experienced being encouraged to 'think big' about an institutional initiative, only to be dismayed to see that financial or physical resources cannot meet our aspirations. We come away feeling despondent because the institution has over-promised and under-delivered. If, however, we know the constraints in advance, we are just as imagina-tive in our suggestions, but with one pragmatic eye on the limits of the possible, leading to ideas that *can* be achieved. The first situation demotivates us, the second buoys us. How does this translate into the classroom?

When you come across a difficulty in your discipline, how do you work through it? If you **model your own strategies for overcoming disciplinary problems**, your students see an example of an expert's techniques and tenacity, and they'll also notice that no matter what our level of experience in a field, we all face obstacles. Part of the creative problem-solving process will **include practical reasons why you would dismiss some of your ideas**, thereby demonstrating that you are mindful of constraints. Where standard analytical methods exist, **show your students your discipline's problem-solving processes and ask them to use them to analyse a difficult question** as part of the class. In this way, students see that effort and structured thinking can lead to breakthroughs in their understanding of the subject. (These strategies loosely connect with the 'worked example effect' of cognitive load theory [Sweller 2006].) If students are still struggling with an issue, Ford and Smith (2007: 167) suggest teachers should **help students recognize their difficulty and offer an alternative approach** to the problem to 'unstick' them and re-energize their creativity.

On the programmatic level, think about the concepts that you found difficult as an undergraduate and the ones your recent students have struggled to grasp. This gives you insight into student comprehension and misapprehension and enables you to **restructure your syllabus so that you spend longer on the difficult topics**, rather than finding them rushed because you allocated equal time for each topic. If you remember how you managed to master a counterintuitive or complex issue, **share your strategy**: a mnemonic, acronym, anecdote, example, image – whatever your technique, no matter how absurd it may sound. (In fact, absurd imagery is often the easiest to remember and has been recommended since Roman times; see, for instance, Higbee [1979: 615–16].) Shortcuts to correctly retaining an idea help your classes run more smoothly and provide students examples of how to devise their own memory strategies.

If you're unsure which topics in your field are most problematic for students, you could **undertake some action research on 'threshold concepts' in your discipline** (Meyer and Land 2006a), if none has already been published. As we discussed in Chapter 2, Meyer and Land define threshold concepts as being troublesome, transformative, irreversible, integrative and bounded. Knowing the threshold concepts for your field enables you to reorganize your courses and **focus your energies on the trickiest topics**, helping students chip away at them tenaciously until they understand. If you're interested in conducting this sort of research, Glynis Cousin (2009) devotes an entire chapter to the necessary research method in her authoritative book on researching higher education.

5. Successful students spend a limited amount of time using social technologies

Several teachers commented on how much time some students invested in social networking, with the belief that those who spent excessive amounts of time on it performed less well. One teacher went further to suggest a gender difference, believing women spent more time on such sites than men.

> I'm also really interested in the phenomenon of Facebook and MySpace and things like that. Again – generalization – but it seems like there's more investment on the part of women in kind of the social aspect of that. It seems [...] – just my impression, this is very impressionistic – that they're spending more time there. And the boys seem less invested there. And that could account for more engagement on the part of the boys.
>
> (US-Constantia-4)

We asked students to rate their usage of social networking activities, on a four-point scale from 'never use' to 'heavy use'. As expected, those who said they made heavy use of them were least likely to perform well. As well as connecting social networking with lower grades, we discovered teachers correctly observed gender differences: women were far more likely than men to admit to heavy use, as shown in Table 6.2.

What we can do

Our finding that higher social media usage equates with lower grades could be an eye-opener to students, even if unsurprising to their university teachers. So what can you do with this new information? Share it with students, by all means, but we recommend you frame it carefully so that it won't be construed as accusatory. If you have your own social network accounts, you may be able to **draw on your own**

Table 6.2 Student responses in percentages to 'I would gauge my use of social networking (such as text-messaging, Facebook, Twitter, etc.) as...'

	HEAVY USE	SOME USE	LIGHT USE	NEVER USE
Women	42	44	13	1
Men	25	43	27	4

practice to empathize with students about the difficulties of managing social media. We're going to present two sides of the coin for social media here: see which fits most comfortably for you or whether you're a blend of the two.

First, some thoughts on reducing or managing your students' social media usage. If you can relate it to your subject, **ask your students to track the time they spend on social media** for just a few days: it could lead to a productive discussion about how students manage their time and their studies. (We suggest you track your own time using these media over the same period so that your subsequent discussion is more inclusive. In Chapter 7, we discuss time management further.) If you frame this tracking as a means of helping new students quantify their time and become more intentional and successful in their studies, more of them will be receptive to the idea. Once you have some personal data, you'll be at a point where you can **share our findings about social media as well as other research debunking the notion of multitasking**. For instance, in *Distracted*, Maggie Jackson tells of a study by Gloria Mark where workers were found to switch tasks every three minutes, with half those distractions being self-instigated by voluntarily jumping between tasks, leaving email open while working on other tasks, checking for updates, and so on (Jackson 2008: 84–5). While many people can switch easily from one task to the next, their brains only work on one task at a time; returning to a prior task leads to a loss in concentration, so toggling back and forth is inefficient and counterproductive – to the point where US workers were estimated to waste up to 2.1 hours per day on interruptions (Jackson 2008: 85). Our students probably won't want to hear this research, but it's better for them to know as early in their university careers as possible and to devise strategies that enable them to stay connected to their friends and family while managing to complete study tasks efficiently.

Some of you may be of a mind to ban technology use in class altogether. We understand the rationales for that, particularly if students' use of technology distracts *you* as the teacher, which affects your ability to run your course effectively, but we do encourage you to **add nuance to any technology policy in your syllabi**. Some students may need to use technologies to support their studies due to a physical or learning disability; others may have bought an electronic version of the texts for your course and will need to access those in class. Distinguishing – and agreeing upon – appropriate and inappropriate technology usage with your students upfront will help students see how you are aiding their learning and promoting a positive learning environment.

Notwithstanding those caveats above, some university teachers have found constructive ways to curtail social networking in class time. Through conversation at the start of her course on solitude and distraction, communication teacher Mara Adelman reaches an agreement with her students that they won't use *any* technology at all during class, not even during breaks. She has achieved this by using the notion of 'lost conversations,' evoking powerful memories of those life-changing exchanges between students in the queue for coffee or walking between buildings, and lamenting the missed opportunity to foster some of the closest friendships you'll ever have. So enthused are her students that they willingly forego technology for a few hours each week.

A view we have encountered while presenting this research to US educational developers argues that denying use of technology or seeking to dissuade students from using it is authoritarian and fails to treat students as adults who can make up their own minds about how to manage their time. We believe that with a carefully framed conversation, and establishing guidelines for the entire course during the first class, you can set a tone that leads to smart decisions about technology use. At the same time, we tend not to see the classroom as an egalitarian, neutral zone: when one party (teachers) have to give the other (students) grades, an imbalance of power inevitably exists, though that power must be used thoughtfully and constructively. Ultimately, the teacher will have the final say.

The more proactive approach finds university teachers who **effectively incorporate social media into courses**: this merits consideration if you're keen to maximize students' comfort with technology to produce educational gains. At Vanderbilt University, for instance, Derek Bruff created a course blog for his linear algebra class where he posts announcements. Students can bookmark the blog, subscribe to an RSS feed to be sure to receive announcements, or can 'like' a Facebook page for the course so that they receive the same announcements in their own Facebook live feeds if they want them.

Offering these options (which Derek has cleverly set up so that he only has to post to the blog and the Facebook page updates automatically) allows students to choose whichever technology suits them best. In his course on cryptography, Derek also asks his students to **post responses to readings on a blog**, rather than using private online discussion forums. One argument for this is that a blog, with the possibility of a genuine public audience, can boost students' motivation to write clearly and with insight, and also allows for the possibility that peers, members of the public and even authors of the readings might respond. For further ideas on these strategies, we recommend you read Derek's blog at www.derekbruff.com.

So, clearly, there are smart ways we can use social media to promote student learning and tap into students' interests and habits. We do caution, though, not to allow students to become your friends on your personal Facebook accounts, though a small number of teachers permit this. There are myriad legal ramifications to such decisions, so we suggest you limit your list of friends, set your privacy settings as high as you can, and perhaps most importantly, refrain from posting work-related messages on your own sites. Your university's counsel can give you further advice on this growing legal minefield, including what happens when you set your own privacy settings very high, but friends repost your messages on their own, less private sites. Successful strategies here include excluding *all* colleagues from your Facebook account, or setting an 'exclusion zone' so that anyone living within a certain radius of campus cannot be a Facebook friend since you can see them in person anyway. It may sound Draconian, but your colleagues will understand why you do this.

6. Successful students are not in their first year of study

Teachers recognized the transition that occurs from the first year (freshman) to later years (sophomore, junior, senior). Students mature over time, and possibly more importantly, they learn what is expected of them: how to be a student. Unlike the UK, where a cohort model prevails in most programmes, it is not uncommon for students from different years to take the same course at the same time in the USA, allowing teachers to compare students at different stages of their studies. This most often occurs in required courses as part of the general education portion of US undergraduate degrees. Our teachers observed that a lack of knowledge among freshmen about how to study and their unfamiliarity with university-level expectations affected their performance.

> Our students, by and large are well prepared, but when they are not well prepared, it is immediately obvious. I mean, I can see it in freshman year and there is very little we can do.
>
> (US-Delphin-10)

> However I would say that the sophomores or juniors or seniors tend to do better versus the freshmen. [...] I think the maturing [that] would happen between 18 and 22 is pretty impressive, so I wouldn't be surprised if it wasn't that as much as anything else.
>
> (US-Constantia-2)

Our research showed that the teachers were justified in these beliefs as first-year students tended to score less well than sophomores, juniors and seniors. Furthermore, we found that the more advanced students were in their university career, the better they performed.

What we can do

If performance in these 100-level (first-year) courses is lower for freshmen, then addressing those disparities head-on by discussing them with students will be key. As newcomers, freshmen may be unaccustomed to the intellectual demands of higher education. As we discussed in Chapter 4, the learning strategies that worked for them in secondary school won't typically suffice for the new challenges they face. At the same time, they may be grappling with disciplinary cultures that require different skills and follow different norms, leaving them baffled as to how to respond: their successful strategies in history may not translate to the chemistry class they are taking in the same semester, yet they may be unaware of the cultural differences in disciplinary expectations.

One strategy that will immediately benefit all your students is to **explain your disciplinary culture**, though it's more difficult to fathom than it sounds. Disciplines tend to be less homogeneous than they appear from the outside (Becher and Trowler 2001; Wareing 2009); identifying the disciplinary culture in your own institution may be the most you can achieve. Questions you can ask yourself to illuminate the culture include:

- What counts as evidence in my discipline?
- How does my discipline construct an argument?
- What linguistic and stylistic norms exist when writing in my discipline?
- What really *matters* in my discipline?

If you're able to answer these questions, you can help students understand them by creating exercises where they analyse examples. You can **share good and poor course work from past students** (anonymized and with final grades removed), and ask students to judge which are superior and why; or with the same course work, **ask students to use your grading criteria** (rubric), after which you compare their scores with your own and discuss them. Such activities help contextualize courses and mean that students are less likely to see your methods and grading as random or vindictive.

US-specific preconceptions that were not upheld

US university teachers wrongly presumed that successful students shared the 12 characteristics we address in the next section of the chapter. We identified students with those characteristics and cross-referenced them with their end-of-course grades. While the preconceptions were unfounded in our study, they merit consideration both to learn what the teachers meant and to understand how we can better support our students. If we harbour preconceptions – which may be hard to dispel even when we discover they are unfounded in the data – then we risk disadvantaging students who we believe fit certain categories. Instead, we can build in measures to pre-empt the perceived drawbacks of those categories: not only will this help us counteract our preconceptions, but also the strategies we incorporate could aid a far wider group of students.

7. **Teachers believed that successful students use the learning centre or writing centre**

The findings for this preconception are less clear-cut than for others, so we're addressing it first in this section. Most universities in the USA and the UK now have learning centres, writing centres or other resource centres dedicated to supporting students as emergent academics, independent of individual disciplines. Students were asked to indicate their level of agreement with the statement 'I have taken action to improve my learning skills'. There was no overall correlation between the response to this statement and subsequent performance. However, when examining the student data (divided into quartiles based on end-of-course grades), we found that students in the second and third quartiles *were* more likely to agree with the statement. We interpret these data to mean that the efficacy of study skill centres is masked by the strong performance of students who already display good learning skills – those in the upper quartile – and who do not feel they need support. In contrast, students who have taken steps to improve their weaker study skills perform better (second and third quartiles) than those who took no initiative at all (bottom quartile). This suggests that learning and writing centres particularly address the needs of motivated students whose schooling has not prepared them for university-level work: they may help redress inequities in the education system. It also suggests that the teachers were *partly* right in their assumption: some students who use the learning centres will perform better than if they did not use them, but the best students may not use the centres at all. So what did the university teachers say about these centres?

> Well, I tell them, actually on the first day – because I'm a big proponent of the writing centre here – that this is the one skill that will get them the most grade for their time in any class. Because I figure if *I'm* grading it that heavily [...,then] any other class is going to be even more significant – a non-science class. So if they can learn to communicate clearly and logically and well, and spend the time doing it and proofread and all that stuff, they're going to do better in my course, but *way* better in other people's courses probably.
>
> (US-Constantia-2)

To recap: while the highest-performing students skewed the results such that there was no overall link between visiting a learning or writing centre and student performance, remember that students in the second and third quartiles in this study *did* take steps to improve their study skills. This suggests that learning and writing centres particularly aid academically underprepared students close the gap in their abilities – provided they take the initiative.

Since the findings for this preconception are more nuanced than many others in our study, we'll provide some further background research before suggesting actions. The 2010 NSSE survey addresses the bottom quartile of our survey when it reports that 'students who were likely to need the most help [with academic skills] were the least likely to appreciate that help or seek it out' (NSSE 2010: 15). Likewise, other studies demonstrated a link between student success and use of central learning resources, particularly in Peer-Assisted Learning, when students are paired with trained student tutors (see for example, Parkinson 2009 for mathematics and chemistry tutoring; Rheinheimer et al. 2010 for at-risk students; Cooper 2010 on drop-in centres). How can university teachers encourage students to visit these centres and attend their events?

What we can do

Be upfront about these findings. Students may feel embarrassed about seeking help to improve their study skills (just as university teachers may do when required to use a new piece of software). Be sure to **depersonalize the data by emphasizing that this is about students' schooling, not their capabilities**. Whether we take the view that the school system has inadequately prepared students for higher education or that the role of schools is solely to enable pupils to complete secondary education, we can talk with our students about writing and learning centres as places where the university has recognized the increase in academic demand and provides the tools to help students succeed. If you can **refer to any experience you have had with a centre like this** – either when you were a student, or if consulting with them in your role as a teacher, as we suggest below – then you also help diminish any stigma associated with attending study skills events and appointments.

Get to know the professional staff in your universities' writing and learning centres so that you know what they offer and can refer students accordingly. Often, writing centres, for example, work with students on higher-level questions of how to organize ideas, rather than only lower-order language and grammar issues, so it's important to know who provides support in particular areas; there may be specific elements of centres' offerings that relate to aspects of your courses.

You'll also learn a great deal if you **take your assignments to the writing centre for feedback before the start of term**. Writing centre staff can suggest how students will interpret your assignments and help you rephrase them for clarity and consistency – something that colleagues in our own disciplines may miss, since they're reading your assignments as subject experts, not novice learners. **Ask for feedback on your grading criteria**, too. This can save you considerable time both in the run-up to deadlines, when you face a barrage of enquiries about unclear statements, and in the marking, when you realize your criteria don't quite work. And remember to **let your students know you took your assignments to the writing centre** for feedback: it shows you care, that you're willing to learn and that a place like the writing centre is a recommended resource, not a remedial crutch. This helps normalize using a writing or learning centre. Depending on availability of centre consultants and the timing of your assignments, you might also *require* **that students discuss a paper with a writing centre colleague**. Similarly, **announce upcoming study skills workshops** and **forward the announcements to specific students** if you notice a topic that will benefit them, based on their performance to date.

8. Teachers believed that successful students regularly attend religious services

As we explained in Chapter 3, a high proportion of Delphin students are members of the Church of Jesus Christ of Latter-day Saints (LDS). In response to the statement 'I regularly attend religious services', 65 per cent of Delphin respondents strongly agreed and a further 16 per cent agreed. (In contrast, at Constantia – a religiously affiliated university – 18 per cent strongly agreed and 4 per cent agreed.) Some teachers (particularly those at Delphin) believed that students who regularly attended religious services were more likely to have a strong work ethic which they would apply to course work, as well as in every other area of their lives, and therefore would perform better than their more secular peers:

> If they are, as undergraduates, attending church regularly, it means they are deeply imbued with those values and one component of which is this work ethic.

(US-Delphin-10)

A striking feature of this expectation is that most teachers who voiced it said they were not religious themselves; in other words, they were commenting on a group that was to some extent unfamiliar. Our study did not show a correlation between those students who said that they regularly attended religious services and performance.

What we can do

A bias related to belief system, albeit a positive bias, is another form of stereotype threat (see Chapter 2): a teacher's off-the-cuff remark could produce two negative outcomes: on the one hand, it could trigger performance anxiety among religious students who then feel additional pressure to live up to an expectation; on the other, it could undermine those who don't consider themselves religious. Furthermore, exceptional performance by students who are regarded as religious may be undervalued by teachers who hold this belief; the same performance by a non-religious student may be valued more highly, because the non-religious student is regarded as being disadvantaged by his absence of faith.

Importantly, though, the issue underlying this preconception was work ethic, rather than religious belief. The fact that university teachers in this study – most of them describing themselves as not religious – expected students with a faith to perform better deserves our attention, particularly since the notion of the Protestant work ethic is prevalent in the USA, even if it's less commonly mentioned in academia.

Max Weber (1904–05/2009) argued that individuals' religious belief systems influenced economics and spurred on capitalism, and one core value of the Protestant work ethic (PWE) particularly resonates in an educational setting: the belief that effort and hard work lead to success. Various studies have examined how PWE values manifest themselves in students, noting highly complex interactions that defy easy pigeon-holing: in the USA, Wentworth and Chell (1997) found higher PWE scores among younger, undergraduate and *non*-American students; similarly, Aygün, Arslan and Güney (2008) report that students with a faith system in both the USA and Turkey scored higher PWE values, showing that this work ethic is reserved for neither Protestants, nor Christians; in a study where Taiwanese students had to complete anagrams, those with low PWE scores who were given negative feedback partway through the task allocated more time to solving problems than those with high PWE scores, suggesting that the introduction of challenge – and the fear of failure – led low-PWE students to exert greater effort (Tang 1990); studying the academic performance of high school pupils, Warner (1999) reported that endorsement of PWE factors cannot predict success or failure in academic settings. And in a study examining the intersection of social class, ethnic identity and PWE, Cokley et al. (2007) found that among white students, PWE values were strongest in those from higher social classes, while social class did not significantly correlate with PWE scores among black students; one inference to draw from this research is that students are less likely to believe in the Protestant work ethic if they have witnessed occasions when effort has *not* been rewarded by success.

We've provided this background to highlight the pitfalls of believing in a causal relationship between the Protestant work ethic and academic achievement. Further troubles arise when we equate effort alone with success, since the level of effort a student exerts in a course may bear little resemblance to the grade she earns: as we discussed earlier, in most university courses, teachers grade students' work according to academic outcomes – the amount of time and concentration required of students to complete the same task can vary greatly.

Rather than focusing on perceived work ethic among your students, **seek evidence before deciding to act**:

- How engaged are your students in class?
- Do they demonstrate familiarity with the readings?
- What indications do you see of good note-taking?
- How well do they perform early tasks (whether graded or not)?

If you detect signs that students aren't exerting sufficient effort, then Tang's (1990) finding about negative feedback may prove helpful. For some students, brief feedback on their underperformance may be enough to spur them to work harder; in accordance with our earlier comments in this chapter about using edifying language, we suggest you keep it more positive and **take students to one side to let them know you had been expecting more from them and want to find ways to help them rise to the challenge**. This doesn't imply that you'll be doing the work for them, but that you'll briefly work on strategies together. You may discover, for instance, that they know they perform better when they might be called on individually in class, or you might both agree that they will make a certain number of contributions per class to motivate them to keep up. Ask these students what pushes them to produce their best work and see whether you can find low-maintenance ways to support that effort in your classes. We provide further strategies to boost students' diligence in Chapter 7.

As a final reminder, be cautious about conflating behaviours or characteristics that may be unrelated. In our study, teachers equated attending religious services with work ethic, and then work ethic with academic achievement. Their beliefs were not upheld.

9. Teachers believed that successful students are independent thinkers whose parents encouraged debate

Our university teachers believed that students who were encouraged by their parents and schoolteachers to debate issues were likely to perform better than those who were raised to be more conformist.

> I guess the bottom line identification for me are those – and this may sound obvious – but they seem to be the independent thinkers [...], they seem to have come from households or families where there's been maybe less – [*sighs*] how would I put this? – sort of conformity of thoughts [...]. And it often seems to be that [successful students'] parents have pushed them in interesting ways or they've talked. I mean, I have some students who say they just don't talk to their parents about their academic lives or about politics – that seems to be the big one.
>
> (US-Constantia-4)

However, our study revealed no connection between those students who said their parents encouraged them to debate and subsequent performance. As we discussed earlier, when seeking explanations for student behaviour, teachers often look to models of learning that resonate for them personally. Students who question and engage with the discipline, and who don't take evidence at face value, may well perform better in class and be more stimulating and rewarding to teach. However, they do not appear to earn higher grades than their more quiescent peers. It's also possible, of course, that students who didn't engage in debate with their parents *did* debate with other people, such as teachers and peers.

What we can do

We'll start this section with a couple of caveats. First, not only parents influence their children's thinking, so perhaps our question – based on our teachers' comments – didn't capture a broader environment of debate and discussion with peers and schoolteachers, in school or in leisure activities. And, second, we expect that some students will be independent thinkers who keep their opinions to themselves for a variety of reasons: not wanting to attract attention, a desire to maintain politeness at all costs, not knowing how to debate without it turning into the polarizing slanging matches they've seen on TV, conscious that their views put them in a minority, or playing along with groupthink (Janis 1972) to fit in with the majority. (Irving Janis coined the term 'groupthink' to sound like newspeak from George Orwell's *Nineteen Eighty-Four* (1949); we see this phenomenon in university classes, too, where conflict-avoidance and the desire for consensus lead groups of students to reach decisions despite insufficient probing and analysis.)

Notwithstanding those caveats about our findings, we know that independent thinking is one of the intellectual skills demanded of graduates. University teachers can take action both to promote independent thinking in their classes and to create a climate that welcomes diversity of opinion and discourages unreflected uniformity.

In each class session where you seek debate and discussion, **allocate one group of students the task of playing devil's advocate**. Give this group clear rules about its purpose – offering alternatives, demanding deeper analysis of the issues, sharpening everyone's thinking and putting themselves in the shoes of minority viewpoints – so that everyone in the discussion can develop the attitude of mind where opinions and feelings are separated from evidence and analysis – in other words, taking the personal out of the intellectual for the duration of the debate. **Rotate the devil's advocates in each discussion class.**

Though our experience tells us that few students naturally play devil's advocate, you could sound out your group early in a course.

Use Sylvia Hurtado's 'Take a Stand' activity (see Huston 2009: 185–7), **where students explain how they tend to behave during class discussions**. Hurtado suggests four categories, and, after a few of us experimented with these, Therese Huston now suggests the following four: (a) I talk a lot; (b) I mostly listen; (c) I rehearse my comments in my head before speaking; and (d) I play devil's advocate. You may prefer to create your own headings based on your observations of in-class dynamics. Students, subsequently, describe how they regard the other groups' behaviours (for instance, 'I get irritated at others' silence or over-talking', 'I feel anxious that I can't keep up with the discussion'). Once you've discussed these roles and their impact, you can use them for the rest of the term as hooks to bring in new voices or as dampeners to quieten your most verbose discussants:

> Now I'd like to hear ideas from people in the 'rehearsing' group.
> The 'talk-a-lots' have done a great job getting this debate going, so I'd like them to take a break and other groups to join in.
> Could someone from the 'mostly listens' group give us a quick summary of the points so far?
> Who would like to play devil's advocate on this one?

As well as encouraging independent thinking, this simultaneously creates a more democratic classroom environment.

It can also help to **let students know about education research on critical thinking** so that you all have a shared framework for discussing metacognition – thinking about thinking. In Chapter 2, we discussed Perry's scheme of intellectual and ethical development (1970), a metacognitive model that's relatively easy to explain to students.

We see it as helpful for your students to understand Perry's scheme to raise their metacognitive awareness and we have permission to share with you the 'Perry Game' devised by Christine Reimers and William Roberson (2004). The game engages students through a series of statements representing the three lower levels of Perry's model – namely, dualism, multiplicity and relativism – and we provide examples in Table 6.3.

The statements are distributed to the participants, who have to find 'kindred spirits' whose statements are similar. They may need help from facilitators to persist in finding links, as this is not an easy exercise. Essentially, the statements lead to three groups, but it is likely that

Table 6.3 Example statements related to Perry's scheme of ethical and intellectual development, from Reimers and Roberson (2004)

LEVEL	EXAMPLE STATEMENTS
Dualism	I like True-False and Multiple choice tests best because there's always one right answer.
	Discussion classes don't make any sense to me. How am I supposed to say something correct if the teacher won't tell us the answers?
Multiplicity	If my teacher doesn't have an answer to my question, it is because there's no right or wrong answer and whatever anyone thinks on the subject is ok.
	It doesn't matter what you think – one person's opinion is usually as good as another's when it comes to discussing politics.
Relativism	Listening to different points of view on topics allows me to weigh different kinds of evidence and helps me to formulate my own opinion.
	Determining a good course of action in a given situation depends more on understanding the situation than relying on a standard response.

more than one parallel group will be formed. Once the students feel they have found all their kindred spirits (and it is vital to stress students are representing the statement, not their own stance), you ask them to summarize the statements' ideas on flipcharts. A debriefing should then uncover the assumptions of the statements and can explore the participants' emotional responses to the statements, since emotion can be so significant when challenging or clarifying deep-seated assumptions. Follow this exploration with a review of Perry's research and its implications while being careful not to create the impression that you are pigeon-holing or typecasting individuals. Students can come away with the idea they are 'dualist', as though that were a permanent feature. Explain that attitudes depend on a person's level of familiarity with different topics, and people change over time. Part of the power of the game is in giving students insight into their own learning. Some may recognize their dualism in one subject, but signs of multiplicity or relativism in another. This may lead to their understanding why a teacher may answer their questions with further questions, for example.

Explaining a scheme like Perry's means you can also use it to **debrief your class discussions and challenge students in their independent thinking**. Though the model sounds neatly structured, actual intellectual development comprises a jumble of forward and backward steps, rather than a tidy, linear sequence. So, in class, you could point out,

> Earlier it felt like we were talking at the level of multiplicity, but by the end, I heard dualism resurfacing, so keep thinking about our discussion after class and let's see if next time, we can all move our understanding forward toward a more relativistic view of the topic.

As well as encouraging students to think more critically, you also demonstrate to them that you are taking a research-based approach to your class, rather than being mean, awkward, or unreasonably demanding.

10. Teachers believed that successful students show an interest in current events and politics

Teachers who felt that independent thinkers would perform well also tended to believe that students who showed an interest in current events and politics would excel.

> And so people who are also interested in current events and keeping up with reading and they're just interested in political things, they might have heard of these things and they just have a little bit more interest in them.
>
> (US-Constantia-2)

Wouldn't it be wonderful if all our students *were* interested in current affairs? If they were engaged in the world and thinking critically about it – and about how they could make a difference? Such aspirations materialize in many universities' mission statements, including some of the institutions in our study, yet we didn't find a link between political engagement and student performance. In some cases, current affairs may not pertain directly to the course, but often they do. If that was true in the courses we examined for this study, the students didn't demonstrate an awareness of it, or a habit of mind that promotes broader general knowledge.

What we can do

Connecting awareness of current issues to grades should motivate many students to keep abreast of developments. **Consider whether your assignments can incorporate a current political context or ongoing issue**. Examples here are an exam that asks students to work out the economic impact of the 2010 US healthcare reforms (which is positive, incidentally), an international studies class where students role-play negotiations between nation-states on contested issues (or long-standing disputes), and a communication course where all assignments revolve around a case in which students advise a client on how to remodel an old home using environmentally sustainable techniques and materials. This last case shows how a topic that isn't directly related to the content may be used as a framework for the theoretical and practical aspects of the field.

Many other small-scale measures can help your students develop a habit of following the news. The University of Southampton offers a comprehensive range of resources to assist in teaching citizenship that can be used for anything from minor interventions to a complete course (University of Southampton School of Sciences 2008). **Make repeated reference to current events** in your classes to reinforce how your topic connects with the outside world or how it can help inform people on models that could contribute to a deeper understanding of the issues involved. **Put news sources in your syllabus** and **add RSS feeds for relevant news sources to your VLE** (CMS), including discipline-specific ones and more general newspapers, magazines, broadcasts and websites. Where possible, include sources from other countries, too, to encourage students to compare reporting from different perspectives. Before class starts, **chat with your students about today's latest news,** even if it's not directly related to your class. Set up the norm that smart people engage with the wider world and follow what's happening in areas other than entertainment and sports, though those still have their place.

11. Teachers believed that successful students have at least one parent who attended university

The next two preconceptions in our study are interrelated, so we suggest you read them together. Contrary to the teachers' expectations, we did not find a correlation between performance and whether students' parents attended university. The rationale behind this belief relates to the expectation that the more prepared a student is for higher education, the better he will perform: if one or both of your parents have attended university, you are more likely to appreciate what is expected of you. Evidence in both the USA and UK suggests that students who are from the first generation in their family to attend higher education are disadvantaged compared with their peers (Gorard et al. 2006; Gupton et al. 2009). Yet the reason for their disadvantage isn't necessarily because they are first generation, but because of the contributory factors that led to that position. First-generation university students are likely also to come from less socially affluent backgrounds, and this lack of affluence, rather than parental experience, has the greater effect on subsequent performance. In the case of students in the USA, we specifically asked if both or either parent had *attended* college, not whether both or either had *completed* college, so in fact the bar was lower than in many studies that focused on graduation. Nevertheless, parental experience of higher education – successful or not – did not affect levels of student success. Our findings are counter to those of Chen (2005), who found that first-generation students in the USA were disadvantaged compared to non-first-generation students at every stage – from access to HE, to persistence once there, to final attainment. However, the Higher Education Research Institute (HERI) briefing on first-generation students (HERI 2007) looked at a breadth of factors, concluding that for both first-generation students and their peers, parental *support* is more important than whether their parents attended or completed university themselves. For example, first-generation students were more likely than their peers to work long hours (20 or more in the final year) and to have financial concerns, both factors being more significant in disadvantaging students than their parents' educational attainment.

What we can do

Naturally, parents' prior educational experiences are immutable facts, so we can't offer 'strategies' to overcome them. But we can offer thoughts on students' relationships with parents in general. Though our results didn't show a link to student performance, there is plenty of advice for the parents of students on how best to support their children as they learn to become independent, forge their identities as adults and undergo the upheaval of questioning prior assumptions and beliefs. Counselling centres at many universities provide guidance for parents on their websites and links to additional resources that will help parents help their children – without meddling.

Counsellors also recommend that students build a support network of trustworthy adults they can turn to. When students come to see you to discuss any difficulties they are facing – whether academic, personal or financial – **ask whether there are people at home to advise them**. These might be relatives or family friends who understand what it means to be a student and how to cope with competing demands during a period of potentially disorienting personal development. Such a support network plays a role not only in helping the student but also in situations where parents are worried about their children's studies or the debt they will incur: if parents can turn to their own peers for reassurance, that should take pressure off students, allowing them to focus on their studies.

Helping your students manage so-called 'helicopter parents' is problematic. These parents hover above their children and intervene at the slightest sign of difficulty, often by approaching senior university figures and demanding immediate action. A characteristic of the current generation of students is said to be that they often see their parents as best friends and heroes, which may make it difficult for them to take responsibility for their own development. Prompts that **encourage students to solve problems for themselves and give them opportunity to demonstrate their independence in decision-making** could help loosen the ties that constrain students from becoming autonomous adults.

As teachers, you can also help your students develop a better understanding of their parents by **offering personal anecdotes, reassurance, and sharing your own perspectives**. As an example, the late Bernard Standring, a kindly and gentle professor of Old Icelandic and Old High German in the UK, always told his first-year students of the emotional roller-coaster they should expect, and encouraged them to tell their parents and families, too. He explained that the first term was a high of excitement, meeting new people and exercising control over your life; the second term was a low when you realized the friends you made in first term weren't so brilliant; the third term was the upbeat time when you made plans to move in with new friends who were a better fit; and the start of year two was the disappointing realization that even those new friends weren't necessarily much easier to live with than the crowd you dropped in the second term. That one-minute pep-talk – an aside in the middle of a translation class – helped many students manage their own expectations and reassure their parents of the predictable bumps and upsets in student life.

12. Teachers believed that successful students' families encouraged them to attend university

The US university teachers in our study believed that students who had the support of their families would perform better than those who did not. Once again, however, this proved not to be true in our study, a finding mirroring that of Eggens et al. (2008). In the example below, the teacher was discussing women engineering students, who make up only 10 per cent of the cohort:

> It's best if I can tell that confidence comes from family support; it may be a mom or a dad or both, but it seems that the very successful ones – because they're doing something that's very non-traditional – seem like they always have that real strong support network to fall back on. And I would say those that were less successful and more full of doubt, they had no support group backing them up.
>
> (US-Delphin-17)

So although the raw data in our study did not support this belief, the measure may well have been too blunt to pick up the subtleties of individual cases such as this.

What we can do

A lack of family support will certainly not help students achieve their full potential. If you have children at university, or friends' or relatives' children, **let your students know what ideas and concerns are most likely going through family members' minds**. Are students phoning home so frequently that parents worry their children can't cope with the pressure or independence? Or so infrequently that parents fear their children are constantly high on drugs or alcohol and unable to call? Helping students maintain a healthy relationship with families can be achieved by occasional prompts in class:

> This is an assignment grade to phone home about!

It's three weeks to Thanksgiving, and if you're going home, have you started negotiating plans with family so that they get enough time with you, but you see your own friends, too?

What changes have you noticed in your relationships with siblings now that you're at university?

Some families are simply unhappy that relatives are attending university. Worries about graduate debt, a desire to see their children earning a living sooner and a lack of understanding about what university life means can lead to obstructive behaviours that distract students' attention from their studies. Some undergraduates find themselves pressured to skip classes for non-essential family events, to assist relatives when other family members could do so, or to return home more often than is advisable if they have moved away. **Refer students to your counselling service** rather than trying to help them with these larger family issues – you're not expected to be a qualified counsellor as well as a fantastic teacher and researcher. We discussed how to do this in Chapter 5 on the topic of 'anxiety.'

13. Teachers believed that successful students are not married

The number of students at Delphin who are married – 13.3 per cent of those in the survey – is higher than the national average, which is less than 2 per cent of 18 to 19 year olds and 12 per cent of 20 to 24 year olds (US Census Bureau 2009). Figures were not available for specific marriage rates among US university undergraduates, but we can assume that they are lower than among the general population since college students tend to marry later (Witte 1990). Teachers commented on the high rate of marriage among undergraduates at Delphin and believed that those who were married, particularly those who had children, were less likely to perform well. They also acknowledge the complexity of their students' family situations.

> And a lot of them, like the one mother I was telling you about, they're carrying a large debt load, you know, so they get all the grants they can, but then they borrow the rest and that's kind of worrisome to me, but it's pretty common.

> (US-Delphin-9)

My very first year that I taught here, actually, I had a class (a freshman class) and the very best student in that class, who was the very best by a wide margin, dropped out of school the following semester because she had – she and her husband, both of whom were undergraduates – already had four children. And they decided when she had her fifth – she is not out of her 20s – [...] that she really needed to stay at home, even though her GPA was 4.0 and his was only 2.7.

(US-Delphin-10)

As this last excerpt shows, the issues can be very complicated, particularly where two students are married to each other and they have children, which was not an uncommon situation at Delphin. Undoubtedly some students – married or not – face challenges from their circumstances that may interfere with their studies and we don't want to diminish the impact of their difficulties. But despite the compelling stories we've heard, overall our study did *not* show a correlation between those who were married and those who performed less well than their peers.

What we can do

Access to university continues to widen and the student population diversifies, meaning that, increasingly, courses are attended by students with a variety of home commitments to juggle, whether as parents, partners or care-givers.

Check your courses to **ensure you have humane policies that recognize students' home lives**. There's probably little you can do about the class schedule, but what other activities or requirements do you have, and how will these work for your students with additional outside commitments? For example, do you distribute assignments in a Friday class that are due on Monday? Not easily doable for students with dependants unless given plenty of warning. Does your course schedule list the dates when you will distribute assignments as well as when they're due? That enables students to plan in advance, though it's still helpful to be sure the turnaround time for papers isn't too tight. Is all the reading listed clearly for each class? An effective course schedule will **list preparation to be completed ahead of class (including reading), assignments to be completed and general**

content for each session (see Table 6.4 as an example). Your students will appreciate this level of detail and, during the planning stage before term starts, you'll benefit from seeing this overview to be confident that *you* can manage the workload, too.

This next point may be a little contentious. Many university teachers in the USA include chances for students to earn additional points toward their final grade – something you tend not to see in the UK. These might include optional service-learning opportunities (as discussed in Chapter 4) or outings to exhibitions or performances related to the class content. **Are opportunities for extra points in your course fair to students with outside commitments?** If some of your students can't earn these points because they don't have the luxury of free time enjoyed by single students or by wealthy students who don't need paid work, then your course disadvantages those who are already at a disadvantage. We're being unusually blunt and directive here: please **be sure that yours is an equitable classroom** where students have an equal chance of success if they put in the work and rise to the intellectual challenge.

14. Teachers believed that successful students are not student athletes

Teachers at both universities were concerned about student athletes. Most teachers believed that student athletes, particularly those playing team sports, would underperform. They cited both a lack of focus among students who prioritize sport over studies and a negative attitude displayed by many student athletes. Our teachers weren't

Table 6.4   Example excerpt of course schedule

Tu, Oct 18	PREPARATION:	Read Pitt (2006) 'Downlow Mountain?'
Session 9	ASSIGNMENTS:	Hand in short paper 3 to instructor & peer group
	TOPICS:	**Differential treatment I Mid-term evaluations I Paper 4 briefing**
Th, Oct 20	PREPARATION:	Read Norton et al. (2006) 'Color blindness & interracial interaction'
Session 10	ASSIGNMENTS:	—
	TOPICS:	**Political correctness I Intergroup dialogue**

unanimous, however: a minority thought student athletes performed as well as non-athletes, while others believed athletes performed even better. Those who held this latter view tended to expect students who took part in individual sports (such as running) would perform the best.

> The basketball players are definitely not doing as well as the track and field sports; softball, soccer, football – they're […] a little bit better than basketball.
>
> (US-Constantia-3)

> But I think about running as this independent, very self-motivated [sport]. Some of the team sports they just – soccer players, particularly soccer-playing men – I am afraid that I have already a preconceived notion of what's going to happen.
>
> (US-Constantia-4)

What we can do

Like students with dependants, student athletes bear additional responsibilities outside class, so expect a few parallels between the two groups; athletes also need to maintain their grades so that they can stay off the bench, so you have plenty of opportunity to treat them as potential allies in the classroom, rather than 'problems in waiting'. Ideally, your student athletes will be well-organized individuals who plan their schedules and discuss what they need to do to keep on top of the work when they miss classes for sporting events. Be sure to familiarize yourself with your university's athletics policies: it's most unlikely that *you* will be responsible for keeping students up-to-date on material they've missed, so you can help them plan where they will get notes, when they will submit assignments, and so on. If you see any of your athletes' work slipping, **speak to both the faculty athletic representative and to the advisor in student athletics**: despite the culture in some areas, these are student athletes, not athlete students, and as their teacher, your key responsibility is to uphold the quality of the university's degree, not the number of trophies. We know this is obvious, but teachers do feel pressured to bend rules in a way that's detrimental to learning. We encourage you to hold firm.

Student athletes' motivation to study your subject may suffer in comparison with their drive to perform well in sports, so you may need to **work differently to demonstrate the relevance of your field to them, their futures and their thinking**. Earlier in this chapter, we discussed motivation as a combination of a supportive learning environment, value (relevance) and an expectation of success, and you might want to highlight these even more if athletes attend your courses.

Sporting metaphors and analogies can help *all* students understand the work involved in their academic progress and here you can **capitalize on the presence of your student athletes**. We have three analogies for you as examples. The first is in response to consumerist attitudes, where students say they 'paid' for the course and so should receive high grades. (We've heard of situations where students have told teachers: 'I pay your salary, so give me an A'.) Paying university tuition fees is like paying for gym membership: you pay to use the equipment, to be coached by a trainer and receive feedback on how you're doing. But if you don't do the exercise, you won't get the results. Equally, if you do the wrong exercise – such as hours of weightlifting when you really need a cardio workout – you'll see little return for your investment. So it's important for students to listen to the trainer, invest effort on the right exercises, and then they're *more likely* to get results, though that's still not guaranteed.

The next two analogies address the issue of 'grade inflation' and students' unrealistic expectations that they will all get A's. At high school, our students were probably seen as the 'most valuable players' (MVPs) in their class: they did well academically and so they were admitted to university. Now they find themselves in a room of MVPs and they'll need to work harder to retain that MVP title; not everyone can stay MVPs in this new environment. In contrast to some high-school experiences, students will also find that completing an assignment does not mean an automatic A: completion is more likely a threshold grade of 'adequate' (C in most universities), not the 'superior' work expected of an A. The comparison to draw here – borrowed from historian Theresa Earenfight at Seattle University – is running a marathon: you may finish the marathon, but if there are 3,000 people ahead of you, you won't get the top prize. Likewise, completion of an assignment to a lower, but acceptable, standard will not be an A.

Our reason for sharing these three analogies with you is that they will resonate with your student athletes in particular, while the entire class will understand them readily. Your athletes may also be able to provide personal examples that encourage them to find more intrinsic motivation to rise to the challenge and excel, just as they do in their sporting roles.

15. Teachers believed that successful students speak english at home

I have noticed international students struggle with the language.

(US-Constantia-7)

But there's just a pace, there's a certain diction that you can tell – it's not quite capturing who they are.

(US-Constantia-9)

While it may seem self-evident that students who study in a second language will perform less well than those who are working in their mother tongue, the evidence in our study did not support this assumption. In individual cases it is undoubtedly true that some students who speak a language other than English at home will struggle more than their peers, yet in our study overall this was not the case. That university teachers raised English-language issues indicates, on the one hand, that students' language abilities in general cause concern, and on the other, that teachers' attitudes may be an additional obstacle to non-native speakers (see, for example, Robertson et al. 2000; Schmitt 2005).

What we can do

Working out which of your students are non-native speakers is highly problematic. Asian-Americans, for instance, are often presumed to be international students, no matter how many generations of ancestors have been living in the USA; to be a born-and-bred citizen and then complimented on your English by your teacher constitutes a micro-aggression (Sue 2010a; see Chapter 2) that could negatively affect engagement in a class. Similarly, students' names may not illuminate. If you want to know your non-native speakers so that you can point them to additional support on campus, simply **ask them to stay behind after the first class for a brief chat**.

Data from employers of graduates support the notion that students' language skills warrant additional work: in *The Ill-Prepared U.S. Workforce*, Casner-Lotto et al. (2009: 9) report that 'writing in English' is the highest-priority basic training programme needed for new employees, with 55.9 per cent of surveyed employers considering it a 'high need' training issue. In other words, universities don't provide the kinds of linguistic finesse that employers look for in graduates. So what can teachers do to enhance students' English-language performance, while remembering that it's not about the students' home language?

To signal that accuracy and style in English are important to you, the simplest route is to **allocate a percentage for each assignment to the quality of the English**, perhaps around 10 per cent so that it looks significant enough to attend to, but doesn't outweigh the intellectual skills you expect. (Bear with us on this if you're concerned that yours isn't a writing course and you don't feel qualified to grade English.) Ideally, your 'quality of English' criterion would appear in a rubric – a grid showing the criteria you use to assign marks, with short statements to explain what you consider an A, B, C, D or F grade in language (see Table 6.5). This both highlights to students that you value the quality of their communication skills and gives them an idea of what they need to do to perform well under this criterion. In Table 6.5, for instance, errors in grammar and spelling lead to a maximum of a C+ for this criterion. That may sound severe; however, when used throughout a course, starting with short assignments worth only a small proportion of the final grade, students quickly see how firmly the teacher applies the rubric and it encourages them to proofread from early in the course.

While your own classes may not be specifically about academic or professional writing, we know how frustrated teachers become when they read incomprehensible or poorly expressed student work in any discipline. So for a moment, compare stylistics and grammar with eating: you don't need to be a chef to know when something tastes wrong; you can send a dish back without having to explain there's too much nutmeg in the moussaka or that the tiramisu was made with coffee, rather than espresso. Similarly, you don't need to know a

Table 6.5   Example of rubric (grading criteria) for quality of English

	A SUPERIOR 90–100	B GOOD 80–90	C ADEQUATE 70–80	D POOR 60–70	F FAILING <59
Quality of formal, written English: style and mechanics	Clear, concise, precise style; flawless grammar, spelling and punctuation	Minor blemishes of style; flawless grammar, spelling and punctuation	Clear, but at times lacking in conciseness, or precision; a few errors in grammar, spelling or punctuation	Ambiguous sentences, or clumsy phrasing; some errors in grammar, spelling or punctuation	Meaningless sentences, clumsy phrasing; many errors in grammar, spelling and punctuation

student misuses the progressive aspect or omits definite articles to be able to identify a problem sentence. Your role is not to correct the English, but to point out problem areas. Students can then go to the writing centre or consult handbooks of English usage to work out how to remedy their errors.

A second step is to **ask students to read and grade the quality of English on anonymized examples of past students' work** (say, one paragraph from four students). They do this in groups and use your rubric. The whole class then discusses their grading and rationale with you and you tell them how you would grade the pieces. If possible, be sure that the highest-scoring example you use came from a non-native speaker. This boosts non-native students' confidence that they *can* succeed despite working in a second language and reminds native speakers that they can't be complacent.

When grading assignments, we suggest you **try Haswell's 'minimal marking' technique for noting language errors** (1983). Haswell found that students could identify 60–70 per cent of their own mistakes, indicating that the cause was carelessness, rather than ignorance. Instead of correcting errors in full or underlining them, you put a vertical bar in the margin alongside the line for each error. Return assignments *without* a final percentage or grade (be sure to keep a note of the grade separately) and require students to correct their errors before you let them know how they performed. You still leave the grade exactly as it was, but students will realize how much better they would have performed if they'd paid more attention originally. And you save yourself unnecessary work.

16. Teachers believed that successful students come from specific US states

Most of our teachers said they didn't notice a difference in students from particular states, but a significant minority did raise it as an issue. In general, teachers thought that students who came from outside the university's state performed better, unless they came from either Hawaii or Orange County in California. Teachers reasoned that Hawaiian students' schooling prepared them less well for university work, whereas students from Orange County were perceived as highly privileged and less likely to work hard. It's worth mentioning these preconceptions as they may have an impact on the way that some teachers interact with their students. Although the number of students from those particular locations was small in this study (5 per cent from California and 1 per cent from Hawaii), we found no correlation between home state and underperformance.

What we can do

As with gender and ethnicity in Chapter 4, this presumption reminds us that we all have internal biases that may not be apparent to us. People in many countries and cities can tell you which places are the butt of local jokes. For Seattleites, it's mostly nearby Tacoma and Spokane, for instance, while for Brummies in the UK, it's neighbouring Wolverhampton and the Black Country. Those tacit, pejorative views may colour our attitudes towards students from those places, even when we regard it only as mild ribbing. Voicing our geographical prejudices activates stereotype threat just as much as our other biases: Clark, Eno and Guadagno (2011) found students who identified as US Southerners underperformed when stereotypes about the South were triggered. Our comments, tone and body language may all betray unconscious negativity that could affect students' performance.

While it wasn't true in this study that students from specific counties or states would underperform, we can still think about the difficulties we see students face when they come from a particular background.

If, for example, you notice students from one state tend to struggle in your classes, you *might* want to **let them know what factors have helped their predecessors succeed**, such as using the mathematics centre for extra tutoring, creating study groups to discuss readings in advance, and so on. Rather than seeing students in terms of a deficit model, consider what support you can offer (or refer students to) so that they have a better chance of succeeding.

Equally, if you've noticed some students coasting in your classes and ultimately underachieving, can you **build an early assignment into the course to provide an incentivizing shock** (whether graded or not) that will help them avoid complacency? Comments on developing new study skills in Chapter 4 might help you work out how to respond after students underperform in an early, formative quiz or test. Instead of being a potentially undermining onlooker, your role becomes that of supportive, challenging coach.

17. Teachers believed that successful students attend a high school where most of their peers expected to go to university

Several teachers believed a student's high school culture was a key factor in subsequent performance. One teacher in particular described the difference between a high school that values academic competition and another where sport is favoured. She mentioned a school in the town where her sister lives:

> They've cut the [high] school way back to four days a week because the sports teams have to travel so far to compete with their peer institutions. And I had this huge reaction to that. And it made me so upset and [my sister] said, 'Well that's the culture here. The culture is athletics'.

> (US-Constantia-4)

Teachers' views about high schools tend to boil down to whether students attended a school where academic work was valued or where sports were privileged, with the former likely to result in students who perform more strongly than those from the latter. Despite this perceived distinction, we didn't find a correlation between students who said that most of their peers expected to go to university and subsequent performance. We did, however, find that over half of our students (58 per cent) said that academic achievement was valued most at their school, with most of the rest citing sporting prowess, being cool or musical ability as the most important values.

What we can do

While we found no link between high school culture (academics, athletics, socializing) and success, we do know that some students come to university less prepared for study than others. If students in your class came from schools that you know prepare students poorly for higher education, **encourage them to make use of any service offered on campus**: attending learning and writing centre workshops and consultations, forming study groups, seeking extra tutoring where it is offered, and talking through the difficulties of a culture shift with student counsellors or supportive staff in student development or student services. Wherever possible, **reinforce the distinction between your students' intellectual capabilities and their level of preparedness for higher education**. Many of the 'traits' identified by university teachers are the product of the secondary school system, not innate qualities of the students.

18. Teachers believed that successful students are not in their final year of study

In our final preconception, we found some teachers believing that seniors (fourth-year students) sometimes do not perform as well as second- and third-year students:

> Some of the seniors, when they take my course, they put it off, and so they're sort of in that eye-rolling phase.
>
> (US-Constantia-8)

Anecdotes abound about seniors who have dropped the ball academically, with two seemingly sound rationales: some students wait until the very end of the studies before taking a subject they find daunting, be that the squeamish student taking biology as the only available lab science or the tone-deaf student procrastinating over a music requirement; other students suffer from so-called senioritis – they're so close to finishing their studies that they lose focus and coast along, particularly if they have a job lined up and needn't worry about their final grade.

Our research did not support this belief overall: in our data, the more senior the students, the better they performed, with a gradual improvement from freshmen to sophomore to junior to senior.

What we can do

If your first-year course includes a number of final-year students and you wish to offer further incentive for them to invest in the subject, **emphasize what's coming next in most cases: the world of work**. What transferable skills are these students currently *unable* to demonstrate that they might be able to develop in your course? What evidence do they have of their perseverance, or of their ability to use context-appropriate approaches to problem-solving? Can they finesse their written or oral communication skills, their team-building skills, and so on? If you **highlight and reinforce these future-focused elements**, your seniors may feel encouraged to try harder, become more engaged, and actively seek to fill gaps in their CVs, while maintaining their overall grades in the process. If your class sizes allow, then – once again – requiring each student to meet you for that 15-minute appointment at the start of term will allow you to have this private conversation early to help motivate potentially switched-off students and also to find out what makes them tick. We have additional suggestions on this in response to students' comments in Chapter 7 under 'motivation'.

In these last three chapters, we have explored the 37 preconceptions raised by university teachers in the UK and USA in this study. Only 12 of those presumptions were upheld in responses from our 1,241 students. But what did the students themselves think makes a good learner? Chapter 7 provides us some answers.

7

UNDERSTANDING STUDENTS' BELIEFS

A successful student has two defining properties: they are a student, they are successful. Seriously, there is no magic formula. It's different for each person.

(UK-Arial)

Chapter 7 presents the students' points of view. We asked them what they considered characteristics of a good learner, to which some students gave lengthy replies while others left the question blank. Along with the witty (and sensible) answer above, students' responses varied enormously, with one-off comments including 'Caffeinated beverages' (Delphin), 'Strong personality' (Arial), 'Reflective' (Constantia), 'Imaginative' (Arial) and the demanding expectation that successful students be 'Responsible, just, charismatic, confident' (Constantia). The word cloud in Figure 7.1 gives you an instant snapshot of the students' key ideas after we collated all their comments and sorted them into themes.

We added the question on students' views only after the pilot study, meaning we have responses from Arial, Constantia and Delphin, not from Baskerville. Since students in the USA also gave more voluble responses than their UK counterparts, our data for this chapter are more US-based. As with most textual data, we could organize these comments in a variety of ways around different headings; for the purposes of our discussion here, we chose to group the comments from Table 7.1 under motivation, diligence, time management, attentiveness, homework and preparation, learning strategies, attendance, active engagement in class and natural aptitude.

Figure 7.1 Word cloud of student responses: What are the characteristics of a good learner? (adapted from www.wordle.net)

From belief to action

As you will see in this chapter, we also compared students' responses to our question on the characteristics of successful students with some of their answers on their own behaviours and habits. This enables us to see whether the students put into action the factors they say are significant for learning. So, if students say punctuality is important, do they show up to class on time? If they cite preparation, do they complete their homework before class?

You can probably guess the outcome: many of our student respondents tell us they don't always act in ways that match their beliefs about archetypal 'good' students. But why should that be the case? Research on social desirability helps us answer this question: individuals are more likely to provide answers they regard as culturally more acceptable, even when those answers don't match their own behaviour (see, for instance, Crowne and Marlowe 1960; Nederhof 1985). Based on this theory, we'd expect some students to regurgitate responses that they've heard their teachers espouse repeatedly, rather than telling us what they really think. At the same time, their responses may reveal

Table 7.1 Summary of students' responses to 'what makes a good learner', including numbers and percentages for the institutions

CATEGORY	TOTAL		ARIAL		CONSTANTIA		DELPHIN	
	No.	%	No.	%	No.	%	No.	%
Diligence	184	17	36	20	62	12	86	23
Motivation	179	17	45	25	65	13	69	19
Active engagement	100	9	7	4	72	14	21	6
Homework and preparation	85	8	24	13	37	7	24	7
Learning strategies	81	8	7	4	34	7	40	11
Time management	74	7	3	2	45	9	26	7
Attendance and punctuality	65	6	28	15	21	4	16	4
Asking questions and seeking help	54	5	2	1	40	7	12	3
Natural aptitude	45	4	5	3	18	3	22	6
Listening skills	30	3	3	2	14	3	13	4
Balance	30	3	6	3	16	3	8	2
Focus	29	3	8	4	11	2	10	3
Open mind	22	2	1	0.5	13	3	8	2
Application of knowledge	14	1	0	0	11	2	3	1
Social learning	13	1	4	2	7	1	2	0.5
Teachers' influence	10	1	0	0	7	1	3	1
Critical thinker	6	0.5	0	0	5	1	1	0.2
Teaches others	4	0.3	0	0	1	0.2	3	1
Miscellaneous	3449	4	5	3	40	8	4	1

what they *think* will help a 'regular' student succeed academically, while regarding themselves the exception to whom these truisms do not apply. Yet the students' honesty in other questions makes us want to temper this interpretation a little: in our survey, students have been very upfront about their own shortcomings, such as lack of application or effort, tardiness, boredom and general disengagement. Hopefully, many of them are being honest in this question, too.

Where does this leave university teachers? Well, it tells us we might be wasting our energies if we try to persuade students of the relevance or validity of particular beliefs about learning. What's more likely to be influential, though, is helping students shift their *behaviours*. Another body of research from social cognitive theory provides further insight here: self-efficacy, which Bandura (1997: 3) defines as 'beliefs in one's capabilities to organize and execute the courses of action required to produce given attainments'. In the rest of this chapter, we discuss the key themes from the students' comments on their successful peers and suggest ways in which you can promote constructive learning behaviours to help students help themselves, particularly in relation to their self-efficacy. We do have a caution for you, however. Students need to feel they are in control of their learning to become self-efficacious. If we build too many *compulsory* elements into our courses, we could end up disempowering our students because they will not feel in control (Wlodkowski 2008: 189–90). We're more likely to reach a successful outcome if we can employ a range of non-assessed strategies, activities and techniques that allow students to develop their confidence in their abilities.

Bandura (1997: 240–3) also reports on a range of studies that find teachers' own sense of self-efficacy influences their students' level of success. The more confident you are about your ability to motivate, support, guide and influence your students in a positive atmosphere, the better the academic outcome for your students. So, as you read this chapter, focus on the suggestions that feel most comfortable and appropriate to you to ensure that you can implement them with confidence.

Motivation

Seventeen per cent of students cited motivation as a key factor in student success, suggesting they generally believe in their control over their studies and potential. Students from the USA and the UK used similar terms, indicating they mean intrinsic motivation more than extrinsic: there was agreement that if you 'really want to learn' and you have 'drive', 'desire', and 'care deeply about the material' (all from Constantia), then you can achieve. By implication, these students suggest that a lack of intrinsic motivation could lead to failure. Their teachers shared these sentiments. As we saw in Chapter 6, actively choosing a course and the ability to show tenacity are linked to high performance, suggesting that these students – along with their teachers – are right to value motivation; it's encouraging to see that teachers may be kicking at an open door when trying to boost students' intrinsic interest in the discipline.

What we can do

Of the three components of motivation discussed in Chapter 6 (supportive learning environment, expectation to succeed and value), we propose that you **encourage students to reflect on 'value'**. Explain the three components to students and show how you are working on the first two – how your class is designed to build the positive learning environment and expectation to succeed. Then ask students to write down on their own what they think will motivate them on the course. Direct them to use two columns: the left side captures content-related factors ('I am fascinated with bridge-building,' 'excited to learn about the experiments conducted on people in the 1960s'), including the longer-term relevance of the subject ('I know that as a future marketer, accountants will block my ideas, so I'm keen to learn accounting so that I can understand and persuade them,' 'learning about comparative government will help me when I go on to study law after I graduate'). The right column is for process-related items ('I enjoy presentations, so I'm looking forward to that final assignment,' 'the service-learning component of this course means I'll really feel I can help the wider community'), including current gaps in students' CVs that will be filled ('the last essay assignment is really going to push me to enhance my writing skills,' 'my CV will look great with that final simulated negotiation task, so I'm going to work on developing my abilities in that area'). Give the students a few ideas like these, and then allow them time on their own to put together their thoughts. Once they have completed the exercise, you may wish to meet with each student for a brief personal tutorial. Alternatively, you could group students into triads to share their reflections. Depending on the size of the group you may find it most useful to share thoughts as a whole group.

The aim of the last exercise is for each student to set themselves two challenges for the course: one content-related and one process-related, with a focus on building knowledge and skills that they don't currently have, all the while tapping into the 'growth mindset' we discussed in Chapter 6 (Dweck 2008). In subsequent meetings you can encourage the students to reflect on their challenges and their progress towards achievement. You can strengthen this by pointing out which assignments or activities relate to which challenges, so they can be flagged during class – 'six of you really want to work on this for your CVs – if you'd like further resources on it, let me know'.

Diligence

Students in our survey mentioned diligence marginally more frequently than motivation (though both stand at 17 per cent), with the same students often citing both. They put great value on the need for, and the efficacy of, hard work in order to succeed:

> Hardworking, willing to put up with non-productive tasks.
>
> > (US-Delphin)
>
> Devotes themselves to studying
>
> > (UK-Arial)
>
> Committed to hard work, being on top of things.
>
> > (US-Constantia)

Later, we'll discuss both how students manage their time and what types of work they do in that time, but here, diligence specifically means regular, sustained effort, rather than occasional bursts of study followed by periods of inactivity. It shouldn't surprise us to see diligence (which UK students simply called 'hard work') appearing on the students' radar: As long ago as 1955, Yourglich found that both students and teachers agreed on the importance of diligence for academic success. Potentially more surprising, though, is that some students viewed diligence more negatively, commenting that a successful student is 'someone with no social life' or who has 'less [sic] friends' (Delphin). Divergent opinions like this accord with findings by Covington et al. (1980), who suggested that in a culture that equates grades with self-worth, some students may decide it's in their best interests to reject the system by not studying, thereby providing an excuse for academic failure. Wlodkowski (2008: 201) similarly notes that 'when their expectancy for success is low, adults tend to protect their well-being by remaining withdrawn or negative'. So students can save face by claiming their failure is due to lack of effort, not lack of ability. This may help explain why, despite the general agreement that diligence leads to reward, not all students exert maximum effort at all times.

What we can do

At an early stage in the course, **engage students in an activity about the amount of studying they expect to do**. Ask them to track how much time they spend on out-of-class study for one week (we suggest they work in 15-minute increments), noting which activities they were working on, such as reading, writing up class notes or rote-learning. Explain that this is an exercise for them, and not in any way related to their grades. One week later, ask them to write their total number of study-hours anonymously on a scrap of paper, collect these responses and sort them into three groups of equal size (from the most to the least amount of time worked) for the first stage of a cross-over (also called a jigsaw) activity. Tell the students the thresholds for the three groups (for example, [A] the 'most' category may be over 10 hours, [B] 'medium' is 5 to 10 hours and [C] 'least' is less than 5 hours) and ask them to organize themselves accordingly. In their groups, students then discuss how they spent their time. They should specifically focus on their use of time (reading, searching databases, writing), not on the learning strategies they employed – those come later. As this is a group activity, individual students need not feel exposed about their personal study habits. In the second stage of the cross-over activity, create new groups with representatives from each of the original groups (A + B + C) to share the strategies they discussed. Finally, encourage the students to report back to class anything that they have learnt. It may be that some of those spending excessive hours are surprised to learn that they might not have to spend quite so long on an aspect. On the whole, though, we expect this exercise will encourage those who aren't putting in much effort to realize what they could and should be doing if they hope to succeed.

If you are concerned that students might be reluctant to admit to spending less time than their peers on their studies, **engage students from a previous year to facilitate the session**. Students may feel more comfortable 'admitting' to certain study habits in front of them than in your presence.

Time management

While 'diligence' was about devoting hours to study, another batch of comments clustered around how students organize that time.

We grouped together comments on time management (7 per cent) with those on the need for balance between studying and other activities (3 per cent). The following three examples provide a flavour of the students' opinions on time:

> Most successful learner[s], however, I believe, can study more in less time – time management may be key.
>
> (US-Delphin)

> When studying, don't study all at once, instead try to plan ahead.
>
> (US-Delphin)

> A lot of people I know have the ability to time-manage but not the motivation – there is an idea that stress is the only way to get yourself working.
>
> (US-Constantia)

A different angle to time management arises in comments focused on the need for a blend of time devoted to study and time for leisure and pleasure. Students expressed the need to 'put homework/studying before hanging out and partying' (Delphin), while several talked about getting enough sleep and the self-awareness to 'Know the balance between "work" and "play"' (Arial). Somewhat more facetiously (we hope), one Arial student cited 'Drinking alcohol, eating a poor diet, spending time in library, late nights/lack of sleep' (Arial).

What we can do

You can **provide your students specific guidance on how to make best use of their time**. For example, at Baskerville, medical students faced with several hours of lectures each day did not think they had time to study in between. However, their teachers made a list of tasks that could be completed in 15 minutes, 30 minutes or an hour. This demonstrated to students that it was possible to use their time more efficiently than was currently the case for many of them. Suggest that they avoid going to the library at busy times if checking out books and that they group tasks to avoid multiple, time-consuming trips if certain facilities are on one part of campus or at a different site altogether. Although this will sound blindingly obvious to you, it's less so for students who are increasingly accustomed to 24/7 access and have therefore not needed to plan ahead in the same way that you may have done as a student.

To make this more interactive, **set a few small tasks for groups of students to complete while timing themselves**. Both you and your students estimate how long you would expect each task to take; then, in small groups, students record and report back the time taken to perform each task. You can post the findings – as well as the estimates – on the VLE (CMS) to help students' future planning. In addition to developing a better sense of the time required for specific activities, students should also start to notice the sense of accomplishment they gain from being able to cross tasks off their to-do lists.

We mention to-do lists here with purpose: many students still don't keep a calendar of commitments or a list of tasks to be completed (beyond a scribbled line at the end of notes from class), so see if you can surreptitiously **promote the notion of keeping an electronic or paper-based organizer** to stay on top of required work and commitments. For an extra sense of progress and achievement, suggest to students that they mark each task with a box in the margin (rather than, say, a dash or an asterisk) so that when they have finished the task, they can put a tick (check) mark in the box. Having picked up this tactic from Therese Huston, we have found it curiously rewarding and motivating.

Encourage students to keep a study diary for a week or require them to do this by making it a reflective assignment:

- How were they using their time?
- When did they find the work straightforward and when was it heavy going?
- What environments helped them to be more focused?

At a later session, review the diaries, so that students can identify their own personal weak spots – and discuss support. Help them to work out what times of day they can best engage in higher-order thinking, as we mentioned in Chapter 4.

Our next suggestion addresses an issue that may be less apparent to your students: **help students identify and strategize around 'time-bandit friends'** – those people who somehow manage to eat up all your out-of-class time and leave you both behind in your tasks and potentially drained. That realization alone could be enough to prompt some of your students to change their behaviours, but further advice and guidance about how to limit or control interaction with those friends would aid them in using their time better. Suggestions might include meeting these friends directly before a class or another appointment so that you can't talk for long or always trying to see them at their base location so that you control when to leave.

Many time management books (for instance, Green 2004) recommend taking a startline-focused approach, rather than being deadline-focused. In other words, when a task is set, you establish what work is required to complete the task and set yourself smaller deadlines – 'proximal subgoals' (Bandura and Schunk 1981) – en route to achieving the final goal. While the adrenaline rush of last-minute work will be missing, the quality of work is typically higher because students have a chance to review their work and correct any errors in style or content before handing it in. **As an activity when you hand out an assignment, ask your students to work out what they will need to do to complete the task and to set mini-deadlines for achieving each**. If you do this one activity early in your course, students have a template from which to work for future assignments. Bandura (1997) notes that self-set goals influence self-efficacy more strongly, particularly if students receive ongoing feedback.

You can also adapt the mini-deadline activity to **engage the students in an exercise to identify both academic and personal goals**. As well as approaching individual assignments from a startline basis, encourage them to take a similar approach to their life as a whole. Ask students to list all their medium- and long-term academic and personal goals. Where do they want to be in 2 years, in 5 years, in 10 years? This will encourage them to identify what they're aiming for. Next, they reflect on what they will need to do to achieve these goals and how they might break down the goals into a series of 'staging posts' to track their progress. Once they have mapped out these mini-goals, encourage your students to allocate sufficient time with realistic timelines for each element so that they do not feel overwhelmed by their own ambitions. At this point, it's useful for them to consider whether their various goals conflict with one another, as they might, for instance, if a student aims to secure the highest possible grades while devoting extensive time to the university rowing team and working 10 hours a week in a hospice. In the final stage of the goal-setting process, ask your students to **prioritize their mini-tasks and decide on how to reward themselves** for each completed task, so that they remember to aim for balance along with all their other ambitions.

Attentiveness

An extension to both diligence and time management is the question of attentiveness, which we classify as concentration and focus on the one hand, and active listening on the other, each of which was raised in another 3 per cent of students' comments, approached from various angles:

Pay attention in class.

(Several students from all universities)

Doesn't get distracted.

(UK-Arial)

It's important to stay focused and place yourself in an area you won't be distracted.

(US-Delphin)

Doesn't get caught up in what other people say/the hysteria of other students.

(US-Constantia)

Active listening in class.

(US-Delphin)

Someone who LISTENS, not just someone who hears things.

(US-Constantia)

Merely putting in hours of study and showing up to class may not be an indicator of productive work if that time is actually taken up with multitasking, when students are also social networking or texting, or are simply zoned out (as we discussed in Chapter 6). In addition, the comment on hysteria reminds us that distractions are not only techno-logical but also can arise from a climate of anxiety, particularly in high-pressure and competitive courses, sapping students' energies on topics outside their control.

What we can do

One means of turning down the heat in a course is to **help the students think pragmatically about how much they can achieve when they are focused**. The activities we suggested above under time management can facilitate this and you can also recommend that students try the Pomodoro Technique (www.pomodorotechnique.com), which asks you to choose a task, set a timer for 25 minutes, and work solely on that activity until the timer goes, after which you get a 5-minute break. A key feature here is to **remind students to work on only one thing at a time**, and that if other items pop into their heads ('need to check that reference', 'my cousin expects me to phone'), they should write them on a piece of paper and wait until their devoted time is finished.

Even diligent students may come to find that they're spending their time unproductively: reading without absorbing information, creating endless study plans with coloured pens and mountains of paper. (We have been there ourselves!) The intention of the group discussions in the previous two sections is to elicit *efficient* approaches to studying. Sound learning strategies are, of course vital, as we discuss later in this chapter.

To develop active listening, try to **find a hook that makes the next topic real for students**, as your own contribution to creating a sense of value. In a management class, for example, you might ask students to remember the last time they had difficulties in group work before going on to look at research into teams; in mathematics, you could show footage of a tsunami before studying the mathematics of waves. When students see that the topic has immediate applicability or somehow informs their actions, they are more likely to listen closely to the subject. Similarly, you can **foreground an anecdote or lecture segment with a comment that students will be analysing the material in the next activity**. When students know they will work with your story or mini-lecture immediately after they hear it, there's an incentive to pay attention.

Philippa Tipper, a professional storyteller in the UK, tells tales to which students will later apply theories. She lets students in on a technique storytellers use to recall even long fables: the seven-word summary. You can apply this in your own setting: after a lecture segment or an example, **ask students in groups to summarize the segment in seven words** and then record the groups' words on the board.

You'll most likely see a mixture of concrete and abstract words ('Parthenon, optical illusion, perfection, frieze, theft, anger') and can highlight how some will trigger clear associations that help students retain material and retrieve it, while others might be weaker words that could be discarded in favour of more evocative ones. Once students are primed with this technique, Philippa takes it further by asking them to **summarize the next tale in only three words or in a full sentence**. By now, students are actively listening for strong words, associations or emotions that will help them piece together potentially complex material.

Homework and preparation

Completing homework and doing any preparatory work arose in 8 per cent of comments, including general remarks on studying outside of class time. Students made clear links between this preparation and successful studying: 'Studies beforehand' (Delphin), 'Doing course work well on time' (Arial), 'Studying material before class' (Delphin).

We asked all students to let us know how much studying they do in preparation for class, giving them the five options shown in Table 7.2, where we summarize the responses of all students who gave an answer and of the subset of students who identified homework and preparation as characteristic of successful learners. The responses tell us this latter group of students is more conscientious than those who don't identify being prepared as important, though only by a small margin.

Table 7.2 Students' responses on homework and preparation

WHICH OF THE FOLLOWING MOST CLOSELY DESCRIBES YOUR APPROACH TO YOUR STUDIES?	RESPONSES OF ALL STUDENTS (%)	RESPONSES OF STUDENTS WHO ATTRIBUTE HOMEWORK AND PREPARATION TO SUCCESS (%)
Often do less than I should/than others	10	8
I only do work that is going to be assessed	11	12
I do just enough to get by	21	16
I usually do everything my teacher suggests	48	51
I frequently do more than I am told to do, e.g. read around a subject, complete optional exercises	10	13

And while just over half of this same group said that they usually do everything the teacher suggests, over one-third of them still do *less* than is required. This tells us that even among students who recognize the importance of being prepared for class, a sizeable group remains underprepared. So how can we encourage students to increase their awareness of how to improve their performance in class and to act on it?

What we can do

If time allows, you may wish to **conduct your own class survey** so that students reflect on their actual, not just their espoused, level of preparation. Anonymity is essential, so that students aren't reluctant to be honest with themselves and with you. If you survey students about halfway through the course – when they can include grades on assignments to date – you can compare their level of preparation with achievement in your summative assessments. Presenting your findings in the next class allows students the chance to remedy any counterproductive habits swiftly. If you repeat this exercise at the end of the course, you can share the results with subsequent classes to help them gauge the level of preparedness required to succeed. Should you discover that students doing minimal homework and preparation perform exceptionally well in your class (such as the Constantia student who noted 'There are some classes you can sleep through and still excel in'), that's typically a cue to overhaul the syllabus, assignments and your grading rubrics, so this potentially labour-intensive activity provides useful feedback to you, as well as to your students.

If you **establish ground rules** at the start of the course (see 'agreements' in Chapter 4), include a discussion about reading materials or doing exercises in advance of class. Help the students to realize not only that preparation will help them succeed but also that they owe it to rest of class to prepare. As talk of tuition fees and the cost of higher education escalates, it behoves students to consider that they are shortchanging one another, not only themselves, when they come to class unprepared; a little peer pressure here may prove beneficial.

We found in our research that students know what they should do, and often want to do their best, but somehow other things get in the way. You may wish to **explore the factors that ambush students** and thwart their plans. Ask students to write down what prevents them from spending time on their studies outside of class, providing prompts such as paid work, social life or caring for dependants. Students should list as many reasons as possible, and then pick one top obstacle. Ask them to call out their top issue and then take votes on how many people wrote the same item in their list. (If you are concerned about anonymity, ask the students to rotate their sheets in groups, so they're reading other people's barriers.) Write each idea on the board, along with the numbers of students who listed it. This can lead to a group discussion on these top barriers and (a) whether they *want* to overcome them and (b) how to overcome them. You may not want to entertain (a), fearing that it might lead your students to slack off and decide they don't need to work in your course. We'd argue, however, that by reminding students they have a choice *not* to study, you enable them to see that they have a degree of control over their likely success in your course. They'll also realize that if they choose not to overcome barriers and devote time to your course, then they are unlikely to perform well.

For the question of overcoming barriers themselves, we suggest you **relate questions of student effort and preparation to studies on how university teachers can become more productive scholars** (for instance, Boice 2000; Rockquemore and Laszloffy 2008). Key advice suggests that the most effective strategies for researchers include short bursts of daily writing (which you'd translate for students into working consistently on assignments and readings, rather than cramming), along with keeping a record of how much time is spent on each project (an activity we suggested under time management), and being accountable to others – either through daily phone calls or regular meetings (in the students' case, through study groups) to keep everyone on track. When students see their teachers modelling these practices, they'll realize it's normal to experience barriers to productivity, but also that they can employ strategies to overcome difficulties and achieve more. In addition, they may identify more with university life, seeing themselves as trainee scholars.

Learning strategies

In total, 8 per cent of students commented on the importance of learning strategies for their academic success. Students at Delphin, in particular, were explicit about the nature of desirable study skills:

> Someone who is proactive at note-taking.
>
> (US-Delphin)

> Someone who is open to different learning styles and acquiring better study habits.
>
> (US-Delphin)

> Learning how to study for each class
>
> (US-Delphin)

> A flexible approach to learning.
>
> (UK-Arial)

The last two students' realization that there is more than one way to study strikes us as particularly promising and echoes this student's observation: 'That's hard to say. Everyone has a different way of learning' (Constantia).

What we can do

In Chapter 4, we recommended you **embed short segments on learning strategies in your class-contact time**. Most students benefit from these reviews, where you share students' ideas, relevant research and your own tactics to reap dividends in student performance. We'll take the example of *note-taking while reading* to walk you through the kinds of short classroom activity we mean.

First, **consider the types of reading you require of your students in each course**: do the genres demand different approaches and what reading practices are common in your field for each type of text? Working this out first enables you to plan a successful class segment. We have a couple of examples to help you think about it. On the one hand, if you ask your students to read discursive articles, you might find that the norm in your discipline is to read in the following sequence: abstract; headings and subheadings; tables and figures; first and last sentences of each paragraph; only if the first and last lines are unclear do you read the entire paragraph. On the other, a key genre in your field may be experimental articles, where the typical reading pattern may be: abstract; discussion and conclusions; findings, if needed; method, if needed; introduction, if needed.

Once you have worked out the key genres for your course, you can **structure the class activity by posing the simple question 'How many of you...?'**, along with a range of productive and unproductive learning strategies for that genre, leading to discussion and sharing of ideas. By including unhelpful strategies, you can caution students whose current approaches are likely to waste their energies. In Table 7.3, we take the example of the discursive article from above, and suggest a range of relevant strategies you could discuss. Depending on the amount of time you wish to devote to this activity, you can whittle this list down to a few key strategies that you know tend to work well in your particular field for the specific genre your students are reading. Each question in Table 7.3 – some of which are our own, while others derive Bean (2011), Boyd (n.d., cited in Weimer 2002) and Mulcahy-Ernt and Caverly (2009) – leads to a quick show of hands and a brief discussion of pros and cons. If, as part of the activity, you can **show your students your *own* methods for note-taking and reading** (either as you do it now or as you did when you were a student), that provides added evidence and concrete examples.

In previous chapters, we discussed collaborating with colleagues from your university's learning centre or writing centre, and we hope you'll encourage students to make use of the academic support available. **Invite learning centre colleagues to come to class to discuss a particular learning strategy at a point when it is going to be immediately useful to the students**. The applicability of these skills helps sceptical students reframe their perception of learning centres as a resource suitable to all learners, rather than the preserve of those who need remedial support. Your learning centre colleagues can also use the opportunity to précis the other services they offer. To be more persuasive yet, **harness the support of former students who have used learning centre resources or who have developed exceptional learning strategies** by inviting them to class to discuss what worked especially well or uploading their comments to your VLE as podcasts.

Table 7.3   Examples of questions to pose when discussing students' reading and note-taking strategies

HOW MANY OF YOU...?
Skim each chapter first?
Work out timing so you know whether you can reach a convenient break in the text in the time available?
Check section headings to identify structure?
Check for tables and figures to see what information they summarize?
Read only the first and last sentence of each paragraph, unless the meaning is unclear?
Look up new words (particularly if you read them three times or more)?
Re-read troublesome sections?
Take brief notes in your own words?
Keep page references in your notes so you can find original passages?
Underline key points?*
'Nutshell' the gist of complex sections?
Create written summaries of sections?
Connect the text to prior reading?
Write down the questions that arise from the text – whether due to confusion or new ideas?
Focus on the 'Why' questions that the text answers[†]
Discuss your readings and questions with friends?
Look at supplemental texts to check whether you have understood an idea?
Bring outstanding questions to class for clarification?
Review your notes later?
Test your own comprehension?
Create concept maps instead of linear notes?

* Underlining is only helpful when students are already able to identify main ideas in texts, and even for those students, it is often ineffective, depending on the task at hand (Mulcahy-Ernt and Caverly 2009: 184–5).
† 'Why' questions (requiring higher-order thinking) have been found to be especially successful for recall, drawing inferences and coherent understanding of texts (Mulcahy-Ernt and Caverly 2009: 186–7).

Attendance

Students identified the need for attendance and punctuality to succeed. UK students were more likely to mention punctuality, while US students mostly focused on attendance – an item that more often earns points in the USA. Students' views here mirror those of our teachers, who said turning up for class was a good start and that students who are punctual are more likely to do well than those who are habitually late – a belief that was upheld by our research (see Chapter 4):

Go to class every day, study at least 2 hours every day.

(US-Delphin)

Someone who makes it to class on time.

(US-Constantia)

Turning up on time for lectures.

(UK-Arial)

When we analysed students' responses (Table 7.4), we discovered that students who (correctly) said punctuality affected performance were *less* likely to report that they always attended on time than respondents as a whole (48 per cent/59 per cent), and *more* likely to say they were occasionally a little late (49 per cent/38 per cent). Again, the students who realize that a particular behaviour will help them succeed say they don't necessarily put that behaviour into practice themselves. This raises questions about whether these individuals are harder on themselves, believe the punctuality principle only applies to others, are more honest in their responses and simply less punctual, or whether the desirability of punctuality – regardless of their own actions – prompted their initial comment.

What we can do

First, **share our research findings about the link between attendance and performance with your students**. A concrete reminder of the

Table 7.4 Students' responses on punctuality

HOW PUNCTUAL ARE YOU FOR THIS CLASS?	RESPONSES OF ALL STUDENTS (%)	RESPONSES AMONG STUDENTS WHO ATTRIBUTE PUNCTUALITY TO SUCCESS (%)
Always on time	59	48
Occasionally a little late	38	49
Often late	2	3
Always late	1	0
Frequently do not attend (in other words, attend less than 50% of classes)	0.5	0

connection between attendance or punctuality and performance may be all it takes to motivate some students into organizing themselves better. Secondly, if you use agreements in your class (as we recommended in Chapter 4), we strongly suggest you ensure punctuality is one of them. As part of the agreement-forming process, **discuss the detrimental effect of late-comers on the punctual majority**.

For your persistent late-comers, we suggest you **meet privately and conduct a modified 'barriers' exercise** with them (as explained earlier in this chapter under 'homework and preparation'), where you explore the factors that stop them from being punctual and agree strategies to deal with them. You may find at this point that you need to take a firmer line with students than you'd wish. One of us once taught a student who confessed that his daily late arrival was a passive-aggressive form of rebellion against the power structures of universities. We had to point out that any system where one person assigns grades to the work of another is bound to involve power relations, and that arriving late did nothing to rebel, only to lower the chances that the student – and his peers – would do as well, since class was regularly disrupted. Punctuality did improve, though only for a few weeks.

Active engagement

The next cluster of comments relates to how students provide evidence of their attentiveness by engaging with their peers and teachers, seen in 5 per cent of comments, including 'Someone who actively tries to learn' (Delphin) and 'not afraid to put themselves forward'(Arial). One aspect of this active engagement is question-asking, which, as we discussed in Chapter 4, was not linked to successful students in our analysis, though we see differences in teachers' and students' interpretations of asking questions. In interviews, teachers highlighted students who were interested in the topic and who wanted to extend their knowledge beyond the class material; when students talked about asking questions, in contrast, they emphasized seeking help or clarification:

> Ability to ask questions, and not feel anxious or embarrassed about asking.
>
> (US-Delphin)

Willingness to ask questions and not be afraid to fail in something.

(US-Constantia)

Creates opportunities to ask questions and get clarification when needed.

(US-Delphin)

Ask tutors where things are not clear.

(UK-Arial)

Asks the professor for extra time to talk about the subject matter.

(US-Constantia)

Someone who is not afraid to ask questions about the subject and challenge the answers received if they believe otherwise.

(US-Constantia)

This last comment illustrates a phenomenon known in the USA as 'push-back'. Teachers report instances where students resist an argument, particularly on a contentious issue: they refute evidence based on their feelings or their (often limited) experience. Teachers report difficulty in getting such students to separate opinion from evidence and to take a more dispassionate view of topics that are uncomfortable. The challenge for teachers lies in distinguishing students' unreasonable push-back from their intellectual engagement. If you can presume your students' questions demonstrate engagement, rather than conflict or denial, it's easier to maintain a positive atmosphere. You also move students' thinking forward through an emphasis on evidence over emotion. It is worth bearing in mind, too, that a willingness to ask questions and to engage in debate does not depend wholly on the student, as this student states with some vehemence:

The teacher must be approachable and willing to be helpful! THAT IS THEIR JOB!

(US-Constantia)

Two questions in our survey related to active engagement through dialogue: 'I am willing to ask or answer a question', and 'I am willing to approach the instructor of this class outside of class for help'. We analysed the responses to these two questions among students who mentioned the need to ask questions or seek help as characteristics of successful learners. A clear majority of these students agreed that they were willing to approach their teacher: over 85 per cent agreed or strongly agreed with the statement, while only 4 per cent disagreed and 10 per cent declined to give an opinion. In contrast, while over 35 per cent of students either agreed or strongly agreed with the statement 'I am willing to ask or answer a question in class', over 10 per cent disagreed and a surprisingly high 55 per cent declined to respond at all. We infer from this lack of response that a sizeable proportion of students do not find the learning environment comfortable enough to speak up in class, whether that is due to the classroom climate, the student's own degree of shyness or embarrassment, or any other factor.

What we can do

Ask your students to identify the most effective ways of engaging in class, such as contributing to discussions, note-taking and asking questions. Collate their suggestions on the board, and then **set students a goal** – perhaps negotiated with the group – to make a specific number of contributions in each class or to produce meaningful, comprehensible notes. For the latter, Phil Race (2007) suggests you ask students to switch notes partway through a class to check for understanding and seek clarification from you – a simple strategy that enables students to learn from one another, while you perform the role of sounding-board and clarifier.

Make it clear that you expect and welcome questions – especially those that test the boundaries of the students' understanding. As we suggested in Chapter 5, try to keep mundane administrative questions to a minimum by pointing students to relevant sources, like the VLE, course handbook or university regulations. To promote higher-order thinking in class, **engage students in an exercise based on Bloom's Taxonomy (Bloom et al. 1956) using Maynard's (n.d.) questions and problem statements**. First, pick a topic that all students know about (a recent event on campus, a major news story, a text or video that students have recently discussed in class). Give them a copy of Bloom's Taxonomy and explain that you're expecting them to demonstrate increasingly complex thinking on each topic, so that they're not stuck in the realms of regurgitating information. Show students John Maynard's question-openers and problem statements based on Bloom's

Taxonomy and give them up to 10 minutes in groups to devise a question or problem on your chosen topic for each level of the taxonomy. We use 'climate change' to illustrate this exercise in Table 7.5. Collate students' answers on the board so that they have examples on which to draw for future classes. In subsequent classes, you can **ask students to categorize their questions for you in relation to Bloom's Taxonomy**, so that you encourage them to correct misapprehensions early in discussions and then move on to more complex ideas that will stretch everyone's thinking.

Natural aptitude

While teachers in our study didn't emphasize natural aptitude as a characteristic of good students, 4 per cent of our students believed it to be important, citing qualities such as intelligence, analytical and logical skills, curiosity, patience and the ability to retain information.

Table 7.5 Example questions and problem statements on climate change based on Bloom's Taxonomy and Maynard's model questions (n.d.)

LEVEL OF BLOOM'S TAXONOMY	EXAMPLE QUESTIONS AND PROBLEM STATEMENTS
Knowledge	Define the 'greenhouse effect'.
	What physical evidence is there of climate change?
Comprehension	Give an example of how climate change has affected weather patterns.
	How do greenhouse gases relate to climate change?
Application	If the earth's temperature were to rise by a further 2°C, how would that affect people living on Pacific islands?
	From the list below, select the measures that will reduce greenhouse gas emissions.
Analysis	What motive is there to deny evidence of climate change?
	Distinguish evidence from conjecture in the following statement on sea temperatures.
Synthesis	How would you test for evidence of climate change in this city?
	Formulate a proposal for reducing carbon emissions in a household setting.
Evaluation	What inconsistencies do you see in each of the key arguments on climate change?
	Appraise the relative merits of nuclear energy and renewable energy for reducing carbon emissions.

One Constantia student wrote that 'you don't necessarily have to be intelligent', but most students who mentioned intelligence implied that you did. Another student felt that the most important aspect was an ability to follow instructions, while a third said 'Effectively demonstrating what the teacher wants to see, learning what the teacher wants.' We could interpret these comments as disappointing, in that they suggest a surface approach to learning, or as savvy, if we see them as a strategic approach responding to the circumstances of any given course.

What we can do

Only a small proportion of students mentioned natural aptitude. Even so, we believe it important to find ways to counter students' negative self-image or beliefs that they can't do something, be it a particular study skill, a habit of mind, or a facility with certain types of data or argumentation. These students are caught in a 'fixed mindset' and we know from Dweck's research that it can hinder students' ability to cope with adversity, overcome obstacles and reach their potential (Dweck 2008; see Chapter 6). To promote the 'growth mindset', wherever possible, point **out that many so-called 'intrinsic abilities' can be learned and developed**, including logical thinking, patience or the ability to retain information. For instance, what some students consider 'intelligence' might more accurately be described as skill at test-taking under pressure; 'quick thinking' might instead be a matter of well-honed techniques in memorization. If you're especially keen to build students' metacognitive skills and aid critical thinking, **use Reimers and Roberson's 'Perry Game'** (2001), as discussed in Chapter 6.

Over the last four chapters, we've explored teachers' preconceptions of 'good' students and students' beliefs about their successful peers. In each, we've suggested various activities and approaches we could use in response to these beliefs, regardless of whether they turned out to be upheld in our study. In Chapter 8, we address the thornier question of longer-term interventions to help colleagues acknowledge and overcome their preconceived ideas – and to help us police our own.

8
CHALLENGING OUR PRECONCEPTIONS

In this final chapter, we grapple with the underlying issues of this book: How do we challenge preconceptions, both our own and those of our colleagues? We start with a consideration of the reasons why we create preconceptions, or stereotypes, and why they might be unhelpful, before moving on to offer some practical advice to help overcome fixed mindsets.

Why do we have preconceptions?

Opinion varies on why we form preconceptions or stereotypes. But our brains are programmed to make and find patterns, to categorize and to make sense of the world; the human race has survived in part because of this ability (Shermer 2011). The 'economy model' of stereotype formation argues that if in every experience, we had to compute the myriad pieces of information that we sense from the environment, we would be swamped and unable to act (McGarty et al. 2002). Instead, we save time and mental effort by making classifications based on past experience and accrued cultural knowledge. Through repeated rehearsal, we internalize these classifications to the point of automaticity, where we act unconsciously. For example, if we classify all fire as hot, we don't need to touch it every time we come across it. Fire is always hot and potentially harmful, so this is a useful classification that leads us automatically to avoid touching fire. Other generalizations aid our survival as long as they are broadly correct. For instance, 'all snakes are venomous' might not be true, but knowing that most snakes are venomous is enough to deter us from seeking out the one or two that might be harmless.

What we might call the 'differentiation model' of stereotype formation counters that beliefs arise in order to explain differences between social groups. Spears (2002: 128) summarizes this model with four principles:

- the meaning principle, in which we make sense of a situation using available knowledge to categorize different groups
- the distinctiveness principle, whereby we create a distinct identity for our in-group
- the enhancement principle, where we seek to separate our group through positive attributes, rather than negatives
- the reality principle, in which we form beliefs by interpreting the real data around us.

So it can be argued that as humans evolved as social beings, we developed clans and a desire to belong, which we bolstered by generalizations about the in-group and out-groups; we created increasingly sophisticated rules and guidelines that served to increase our security and our chances of survival.

So stereotypes in this model are used to reinforce our world-view and to support our understanding in a complex environment. We tend to seek out people who are, in some way, like us – known in the literature as 'homophily' (see, for instance, Flynn et al. 2010) – and to be suspicious of those who are different. In contemporary society we see this mirrored in all aspects of life, from street gangs, to political allegiances, to interest groups. We form opinions that 'good' people (who are like us) behave, look, sound and dress in a particular way, while 'bad' people (who are not like us) behave, look, sound and dress another way.

Not only do we seek out people who we think will be like us but also we emphasize aspects that seem to support our view and ignore those that counter it, in a process called 'confirmation bias' (Dawson et al. 2002). We'll give you an example: Why do dog owners resemble their dogs? The answer is: they don't, in most instances. If you give people a selection of photos of individuals and asked them to pick out those that resemble dogs you will get a different response than if you give them photos of people *with* their dogs and ask if any of them resemble each other. In the latter case, confirmation bias kicks in and many people will look for characteristics that dog and owner seem to share (length of nose or snout, colour and texture of hair or fur, shape of face or head, and so forth), ignoring the many characteristics that are dissimilar. In a 2004 study, psychologists Roy and Christenfeld presented study participants with photographs of 45 dog owners and two pictures of dogs, one they owned and one they didn't. The participants were able to correctly link dogs to owners more than half the time, but only where the dog was a purebred, not where it was a mongrel. Even in this carefully controlled environment, most dog owners were not thought to resemble their pets, since most dogs in the study were not purebred. (Incidentally, the suggested reason why some owners might resemble their dogs is because of a tendency to *choose* an animal that resembles them [in other words, homophily]: we can predict the adult appearance of purebred puppies, but not of mongrels.)

We'll stay with dogs and owners for a moment, as we have another example that will help us think about how people form preconceptions. Hunter and Workman (2009) asked non-dog owners to identify the owners of three breeds of dog: Labrador, poodle and Staffordshire bull terrier. The participants correctly identified the dog owners more than half the time. However, the reasons they gave for allocating dogs to owner were based on assumed personality traits, such as levels of conscientiousness and emotional stability. When the researchers examined these qualities in the owners, they did not find a link. The participants relied on stereotypes to allocate dogs to their owners, but the stated links between owner and personality were incorrect. The three breeds used in the study carry connotations in UK society, and it is possible that some of the owners' choice of dog was influenced by these stereotypes. (For example, someone who wants to project a macho image is unlikely to choose a poodle). There are dangers in making links between disconnected characteristics, along the lines of fundamental attribution error (Ross and Nisbett 1991), where observers attribute an individual's actions to internal, personality-based issues and ignore the contextual factors in the situation. Here, for instance, we see unfounded beliefs that someone's personality can be determined from visual cues or that people who own a particular type of dog share common values, rather than considering the broader context: perhaps the poodle owner suffered from allergies and wanted a dog that would shed less fur; maybe the Labrador was an unexpected gift.

We give you this detailed example to illustrate a simple but uncomfortable point: the participants in these studies behave as most of us do. We take cues from appearance, behaviour, voice and accent. We automatically generalize from a few cues and classify people into expedient groups. We do this all the time to prevent the cognitive overload we would suffer if we had to process every piece of information consciously and to buttress the positive identity of our in-group. (This latter point helps explain why some preconceptions about student success seemed to relate more to the teachers' *own* behaviours as students, rather than to their students' behaviours.)

What's the problem with preconceptions?

If preconceptions and generalizations are useful for our survival, why do we need to challenge them? The obvious first answer is that **higher education isn't typically a matter of life and death**, so the stakes are low. Our survival does not depend on our ability to single out latecomers or nightshift workers, part-time students or athletes. Our cognitive abilities are better expended on strategies that promote learning and put all students at ease.

More salient is the fact that **generalizations ignore individual differences**. As a result, we miss the real person behind the preconception. From a selfish standpoint, if we believe that everyone in a particular group is hostile, then we won't take the time to seek out possible allies, potentially to our mutual disadvantage. From an altruistic standpoint, holding onto negative beliefs about a particular group excludes them, robbing them of opportunities and disadvantaging society as a whole.

One frequent concomitant of holding onto preconceived notions of specific groups is that **it helps maintain the status quo**. If we refuse to entertain the notion that individuals may benefit from higher education when they come from marginalized groups (ethnic minorities, first-generation students) or broader categories (Californians, people with dyslexia) or if they share specific circumstances (joined the degree programme late, attended a school that didn't encourage further study), then we continue to restrict higher education to those whose backgrounds, circumstances and attributes mirror our own, regardless of individuals' potential.

Generalizations result in poor decisions. Plenty of examples illustrate how erroneous negative beliefs can lead to unfair treatment. For instance, US citizens of Japanese heritage were imprisoned in the USA during World War II because of a belief they might sympathize with the Japanese forces. However, US citizens with German or Italian heritage were far less likely to be interned. It is thought that the reason for this discrimination was due to most Americans' European heritage: Japanese people were seen as 'other' and therefore not to be trusted (Ng 2002; Sundquist 1988).

So to recap in very simple terms: we all have preconceptions and make generalizations as a natural part of being human. At the same time, our preconceptions blind us from seeing each person in her or his own right. Since we rarely need to rely on generalizations for survival, we need to consider how we might learn to short-circuit our brains' standard operating procedures so that we come to value and more fairly evaluate individuals as they really are, based on their own individual behaviours and interactions.

Preconceptions in this study

We can loosely cluster the teachers' preconceptions from the study into five categories, where students are distinguished by their behaviours, circumstances and attitudes. In Table 8.1, we present all 37 preconceptions by these categories and remind you whether the preconception was upheld in the study.

We have debated some of our categorization here: by the time you meet your students, for instance, their previous academic achievements are now facts that cannot be altered; however, we see them as 'within the student's control' because we realize that a student's own actions did make a considerable difference to academic performance at school. Similarly, entering a programme prior to Clearing is generally dependent on prior academic success, so these two preconceptions belong together.

One preconception defies neat categorization: 'actively choose to take the course, rather than being required to do so' is within the student's control when the course is an elective and beyond the student's control when the course is a requirement; so for the sake of argument, we have put it in the twilight zone of an anomaly.

Table 8.1   All preconceptions from the study, categorized by type

DISTINCTIONS	UPHELD SUCCESSFUL STUDENTS:	NOT UPHELD TEACHERS BELIEVED THAT SUCCESSFUL STUDENTS:
In-class behaviours (3 out of 4 upheld)	1. are punctual for lectures and classes 2. prefer to sit towards the front in class 3. engage with orientation (induction) programme	4. talk with their teacher and ask questions
Out-of-class behaviours (3 out of 7 upheld)	1. keep up with assigned reading 2. access course information from the institution's VLE 3. spend a limited amount of time using social technologies	4. perform some paid, voluntary or service work, but not excessive hours 5. actively form their own study groups 6. use the learning centre or writing centre 7. regularly attend religious services
Circumstances typically beyond the student's control (0 out of 9 upheld)		1. belong to particular ethnic groups (white in most cases) 2. have a particular gender (differs depending on the subject studied) 3. do not have dyslexia 4. are independent thinkers whose parents encouraged debate 5. have at least one parent who completed university 6. were encouraged to attend university by their families 7. speak English at home 8. come from specific states (USA) 9. attended a high school where most of their peers expected to go to university
Circumstances typically within the student's control (1 out of 8 upheld)	1. are not in their first year of study (USA)	2. choose to come to university of their own volition, rather than to please others 3. attend full-time 4. have met previous academic targets 5. enter the programme prior to Clearing (UK) 6. are not married 7. are not student athletes 8. are not in their final year of study (USA)

Table 8.1   (Continued)

DISTINCTIONS	UPHELD SUCCESSFUL STUDENTS:	NOT UPHELD TEACHERS BELIEVED THAT SUCCESSFUL STUDENTS:
Attitudes (4 out of 8 upheld)	1. expect to develop different study habits from those that worked at high school 2. expect to perform well 3. enjoy reading in the discipline 4. show tenacity when faced with difficulty	5. have moderate anxiety 6. enjoy doing things in their leisure time that relate to the programme 7. feel that they belong at university 8. show an interest in current events and politics
Anomaly – either within or beyond the student's control (1 out of 1 upheld)	1. actively choose to take the course, rather than being required to do so	

What strikes us about this clustering of preconceptions is that only one cluster has *no* items that were upheld: *circumstances that are outside the student's control*. Since many of these immutable characteristics or situations form the basis of some of the more insidious stereotypes we see in our societies, we focus on them in our suggested strategies below. It's worth prefacing these suggestions with the observation that discrimination against people on grounds of sex, race, religion or belief, age, or disability is outlawed in many countries, including those in the European Union (Council Directive [EC] 2000/43 and 2000/78) and the USA (see, for instance, the US Equal Employment Opportunity Commission, n.d.). Despite this, groups or categories of people continue to experience inequitable treatment. So while laws may go some way to redressing social inequalities, they are clearly by no means sufficient. In addition, various minority groups continue to experience the injustice of unequal treatment: most notably in the USA, at the moment, the lesbian, gay, bisexual and transgender (LGBT) community. Although our study has touched on arguably five main aspects of diversity (gender, ethnicity, disability, belief system and language), the strategies we recommend here can relate more broadly to preconceptions in general.

What we can do

At the institutional level

Just as in teaching, where we need to find out a student's current level of knowledge so that we can build on it, it's essential to **establish the facts at your own institution**. Your Human Resources Department or Institutional Research Office should be able to provide you with general statistics about the proportion of employees at your institution in various categories of post by gender, ethnicity, and so forth. You and your colleagues may be surprised by the present diversity of employees or might detect clear absences or disparities that provide you opportunities to begin conversations with a wider circle of colleagues and university leaders.

- How does the profile of employees compare with that of students?
- Are there lessons to be learnt from these data?
- Is there a significant mismatch between groups of students on campus (women, people from minority ethnic groups) and their teachers?
- How will the university seek to redress imbalances that provide better role models of academic success for traditionally under-represented groups of students?

In part, that last question is answered by your institution's policies. Most universities in the UK, the USA, and in other countries operate equal opportunity policies designed to ensure fair treatment and in some instances to increase the proportion of certain under-represented groups in the workforce. How well is your university achieving this aim? Even the wording of your equal opportunities policy can make a difference. Steele (2010: 145–7) reports on a study examining how African-Americans responded to two types of policy: the first is described as 'colour-blind', where everyone is treated as individuals, while the second is a 'valuing-diversity' policy, where the organization welcomes the different backgrounds and perspectives that employees bring. Respondents did not trust the 'colour-blind' policy, but they felt they would be comfortable working for the 'valuing-diversity' company. So, **examine the wording of your university's equal opportunities policy** to see if it can be improved to encourage a more open and welcoming institutional culture. If some groups are *especially* under-represented (and this may be more apparent at a departmental rather than institutional level), can you identify any causes for this and potential remedies?

Steele (2010) also found that visibility made a difference to how individuals perceived an organization: if people from minority groups saw sufficient numbers of minorities represented in an organization's print materials, they felt they were more able to trust that it would be a good organization to work for. (In the study, the largest proportion of people from ethnic minorities in photos was one-third.) So you can challenge preconceptions if you **send signals in your online presence and your print materials that counter stereotypic expectations**. Many institutions have been doing this for a long time, but some still lag behind. Universities can highlight student successes or teachers who contradict stereotypes, ensuring diversity in materials. You can also check to see whether your wording is inclusive. When David was a head of department in the UK and worked on promotional materials for his degree programmes, he was asked to write a paragraph about the city: as well as talking about the general amenities for sports, culture and shopping, he added details on the churches, mosques and temples in the area, as well as the thriving gay scene. Students – and potential colleagues – who belong to these various groups will identify your institution as a safe place where they can be themselves; by presenting your university or programme in a way that welcomes diversity, you help gradually turn your institution into the place you'd like it to be.

As part of this visibility-raising exercise, **seek out potential allies who are keen to challenge preconceptions**. It may be the female engineer or the European mediaevalist who comes from Southeast Asia – their stories may well be more interesting and encouraging than reporting only on the majority: they have insights into the particular challenges you face when you put yourself in a position where you are in the minority. At the same time, as we have mentioned previously, it's key to avoid suggesting that these individuals can speak on behalf of all others like them: the experiences of one female engineer are just that, not those of an entire group.

For a more in-depth institutional view, **adapt our research to test out your own preconceptions**. Refer to our survey (see Appendix 1) for ideas and possible phrasing of questions. We are not suggesting you replicate our survey precisely. You will find it more useful if you identify the issues that seem to be important to you, your colleagues and your students in your specific context and devise your own survey. We have a few recommendations for this type of study:

- Pilot the survey with a few students to ensure that your questions elicit the information you intended to gather.
- Be sure that it includes the student's ID, so that later you can compare responses with the student's performance
- Consider whether to offer open text responses, and if so, how you will manage the data generated by these questions.
- Decide whether you want paper or electronic responses: paper surveys are easier to administer in a classroom than an online version, but the subsequent data entry can be daunting if you have large numbers of students. (We decided paper responses would lead to more responses.)
- The person administering the survey cannot be the teacher (who must leave the room altogether) and you have to reinforce to the students that the teacher will not see *any* individual responses – only aggregated data at a later stage, once all the grades have been confirmed.
- If you're using a paper-based system, administer the question-naire at the start or end of a scheduled class.
- Allow students 25–30 minutes to complete the survey; it's important to make arrangements early with the teachers to ensure they can find a session where they can spare the time.
- Consider whether you want to offer small incentives to students to complete the survey (such as providing food, snacks, or offering a small amount of credit).
- Most essentially, be sure to adhere to the ethical procedures in place at your university.

At the departmental or programme level

If, from institutional data or your own observations, you detect under-representation of certain groups of people in your department or on your programme, **focus on modifying the local culture**. Could a cause, for instance, be that the stereotypes of your subject area deter students or colleagues from minority groups? Can you counter those stereotypes to make the department or programme welcoming for all? Once you have identified the stereotypes you believe exist for your subject – whether internationally, nationally or simply within your institution, **brainstorm ways of countering those local stereotypes**. In the first phase of brainstorming (Race 2007), everyone offers their suggestions and you record all the ideas generated, regardless of practicality and without critique; this boosts creativity and can lead to some unexpected and smart proposals. Only once suggestions have dried up do you enter the second phase where you whittle down the list based on criteria of feasibility, appropriateness, manageability, and so on. From there, you are able to devise an action plan with your team. You may also find that during the conversation, and especially during the creative phase, further stereotypes occur to you or your colleagues, providing you a richer picture of how the department or programme appears to the outside world.

As well as gathering institutional data, we suggest you **review student data for your programmes**, and that you crunch the numbers in a variety of ways. Your student record system will probably allow you to separate out different groups of students (based on their demographic data) so you can identify groups who appear to be underachieving in comparison with their peers. **Check for in-built biases in your assessments**. We gave you the example in Chapter 4 of case studies involving the brewing industry when a sizable minority of students was teetotal and could not identify with the context well enough to perform well. In Chapter 2, we also mentioned Sax's (2008) summary of findings in which engineering is the *only* discipline where women are automatically predicted to score less well than men, so we'll use gender as our example here. If you suspect that there is a gender-based difference in performance in your programme, we suggest that you explore the assessment procedure: **Ask your programme team to engage in a norming session where they moderate a few student exam papers together** (where everyone grades the same four or five papers, then convenes to discuss grades given and agrees on norms) before taking further scripts away to grade alone. Ideally, ensure that two teachers grade each paper – one anonymized version, one named – to draw direct comparisons. What happens if half the scripts are anonymous and half show names? Do you find, for example, that women underperform when their names are on the scripts, but not when they are anonymous? Do your colleagues feel more comfortable grading papers without names (this is the norm in most UK universities already)? If you detect biases from these exercises, then can your programme agree that all assignments are anonymized and devise a procedure for it? A potential difficulty with this sort of norming procedure is that you could be accused of deception if your colleagues don't know what data you will be looking at later (such as gender differences). We suggest you take care with framing the exercise as being about developing a common standard for each level of your programme. If, however, it transpires from the norming that certain groups underperform by dint of their group membership, then you have every reason to show these data to your colleagues (removing the names of the individual teachers) to present the argument that grading practices may need to change department-wide. Once norming sessions are routinized in departments, most teachers find them beneficial and reassuring – they help you gauge whether your assignments and grading are out of kilter with the rest of the programme and allow you to make adjustments accordingly.

At the educational development level

In this section, we suggest a variety of workshops and events that educational (faculty) developers can run with teachers from across the university to help interrupt the process of forming preconceptions and stereotyping. We encourage you to take these ideas and adapt them for you own setting. Before getting into detail, we offer a few general pointers about this kind of professional development event.

As we noted in Chapter 1, the topic of this book is generally something that our colleagues do not want to talk about. If they've made it to a workshop that's clearly going to address the question of preconceptions, then it's paramount to acknowledge the difficulty of these discussions, to applaud them for participating and to endeavour not to leave them feeling guilty or humiliated. For this reason, several of the exercises encourage participants to work in groups on hypothetical situations, so that individuals do not feel unduly threatened. Some of them, however, take riskier strategies that require very careful handling and facilitation. The aim of these exercises is to encourage us all to be more sensitive to generalizations, to question their veracity and to be aware of the potential harm they can cause.

Opening up the dialogue: a demographics workshop

This short workshop activity is expanded from one that David used to run in the UK. Be warned that it can make participants very uncomfortable. The overarching topic is the student body on your campus, using your institution's latest data. At the start of the workshop, provide participants with a demographic form to fill out where they make estimates of the percentage breakdown of students in one of their classes or who study on their degree programme. Provide differentiation for each category (such as male/female for gender) with a space for their estimated percentages. While some categories are relatively straightforward for most teachers, others will make them uneasy or very awkward. We found that while UK teachers were happy to comment on gender or social class, they were less comfortable talking about ethnicity, admittedly clueless about religion, and squeamish about sexual orientation. Ask people how they felt while completing the survey. Past responses have included 'insulted to be asked', 'prurient', 'offended' and 'curious that I can't answer lots of these'. The overarching sense from participants was 'What does their religion/social class/sexual orientation have to do with me?' This response is the localized equivalent to the 'colour-blind' equal opportunities policy. It can then lead to a productive discussion of how we may or may not support our students if we are too uncomfortable or embarrassed to consider their identities and what those identities might mean in the classroom. Share your institution's demographic data towards the end of the session so that participants can compare their guessed percentages with the overarching university data (provide a breakdown by department if one is available); the conversation often moves on to the aspects of diversity for which the institution has no data and the complications, threats and anxieties involved when an organization asks for personal data in the first place.

Countering stereotypes: the lazy-brain workshop

This is probably the simplest-sounding workshop, but it is tricky to facilitate without becoming trite, so plan extremely carefully.

When we hear colleagues espouse shocking stereotypes or preconceptions, we are often so surprised that we are unable to respond. Many of these stereotypes can be attributed to intellectual laziness – the 'economy' model of stereotyping – so provide workshop participants an opportunity to practise their responses. Either prepare stereotypes yourself, or ask participants to write down (a) one stereotype or preconception they have heard more than once on campus and (b) one that especially upsets or offends them. Collect these responses, organize participants into triads and randomly distribute three participants' responses to each triad, so that no one knows where they came from. Triads examine their three preconceptions from part (a), and for each item, they generate two responses that courteously contradict the stereotype. The aim in each response should be to encourage the originator of the stereotype to step back and re-evaluate, so that the 'lazy-brain' model of stereotyping is short-circuited. Triads then share their best ideas with the entire group.

Now move to the trickier topics covered in part (b), where individuals' emotions are more tightly involved. Having heard everyone's suggestions from the previous exercise, they should be better placed to find thoughtful, productive (while still potentially pointed) responses to these new preconceptions. Again, share responses with the group and, once you've heard all suggestions, open the conversation up fully so that people can offer further ideas. Ideally, you'd compile these responses as they are raised so that you can distribute them to participants afterwards. They'll then be in a better position to counter colleagues' fixed ideas and preconceptions in a way that is calm and polite, while still refusing to accept unfounded, knee-jerk comments.

Stereotyping: the appearance–behaviour–circumstance workshop

This activity makes it personal. For the first minute, ask participants to write down a description of their appearance today – height, weight, clothing, and so on. They then have to put themselves into other people's shoes and list the stereotypes that they believe a complete stranger might have formed about them as they came onto campus, based purely on appearance. Next, everyone identifies any stereotypes that they conform to. In pairs or small groups, participants select from their stereotypes to discuss what negative effect these have, or could have, on them educationally, professionally and or socially.

In the second part, participants now add their observable behaviours from that morning: Did they talk with someone on the bus, wave to a colleague and smile, buy the newspaper without acknowledging the salesperson, order a grande skinny mocha latte with hazelnut as if it were the most normal thing in the world? How might this new information reinforce or mitigate against the preconceptions listed in part one? What new stereotypes might these behaviours have generate when combined with appearance? Which are accurate?

You know where this is going. Part three focuses on circumstances: What circumstantial information would allow people to form a more accurate judgement of the participants' appearance or behaviour this morning? ('People will think I'm disorganized because I'm dishevelled; I just flew back overnight from a conference, have no ironed clothes left and overslept. I was in such a hurry, I didn't even speak to the newspaper vendor who I usually joke with.') Again, how might this circumstantial evidence add to, or detract from, prior preconceptions and what are the implications for the individual?

The purpose of this gradual exercise is to encourage teachers to suspend their judgement as much as possible with their own students and with colleagues, to gather more information and evidence before they reach conclusions and to allow that their perceptions may still need to be modified as they learn more over time.

Stereotype short-circuiting: the 'Why?' and 'What if?' activity

For an alternative to the last exercise when working with a group that doesn't already know you, see David's Cultural Taboo and Transgression exercise in Chapter 1, where he asks participants to write down everything they *think* they know about him 10 minutes into a first encounter. The exercise relies on cues from both appearance and behaviour in the first 10 minutes. As a second element, rather than discussing the process of categorizing, as David does with his students, you could ask participants to provide a positive rationale for a few of their preconceptions. So for instance, if one observation is 'wears a suit', the corresponding preconception could be 'is formal and severe'. If you then ask 'Why does this person wear a suit for a workshop with teachers?' then participants may rationalize differently – he 'wants to demonstrate to participants that they are important enough for him to dress smartly', 'he's trying to set himself apart from the rest of us', 'he has a meeting with the vice-chancellor this afternoon'. You follow this rationalization with a 'What if?' question: What if the workshop facilitator were wearing a T-shirt and pair of jeans? How might you perceive him differently? What new preconceptions might it conjure? Debrief with a discussion of how to encourage participants to engage in this kind of self-questioning before acting on their preconceptions.

Debunking 'positive' stereotypes: a workshop with heightened anxiety

Some of our colleagues may wonder what the problem is with positive stereotypes. If, for instance, we hold the view that 'East Asian students work hard', then that's a good thing for their education and they will be pleased to hear that their teachers see them positively, right? Well, no. Positive stereotypes are still stereotypes, and they can cause anxieties. This exercise seeks to replicate those feelings and can be incorporated into a workshop on almost any topic. As with many of our suggestions here, it needs careful handling to succeed.

You begin as follows:

> To get a baseline of prior knowledge on the topic of this workshop, we're going to start with a quiz that's meant to be really hard, but I know you can all cope with it because teachers who come to these workshops are phenomenally smart. Then we'll switch papers and see how everyone scores and which department is the winner.

Then give participants a *genuinely* difficult quiz to do individually (one that requires detailed factual knowledge about the topic of a workshop that they has only just started) – and to take seriously because you're going to take in their answers and they'll be scored and returned later. Once they have run out of time (don't give them long!), you debrief:

- How did the quiz seem?
- How did participants feel while completing it?
- Did anything put them ill at ease?

Although a workshop for university teachers is a relatively low-stakes event, it should still have raised anxiety levels among participants. Conversation then moves onto problems with positive stereotypes.

Fundamental attribution error: a workshop on recruitment

Ruth Lawton at Birmingham City University runs a workshop on employability – an ongoing hot topic in UK universities – that we see as a neat way to raise fundamental attribution error with teachers. Her session ostensibly highlights the dangers of stereotypes in recruitment. Ruth provides groups or participants with three hand prints (taken from real people, including herself), and three samples of handwriting. Each of the three people who provided the hand prints have written out the same paragraph of text. Ruth asks the groups whether they can glean any information about a person from these items. She suggests things such as gender, age, educational attainment and social class, but participants are free to be as wide ranging in their assumptions as they wish. In many cases, participants are happy to share their presumptions based on this evidence. The groups report back their presumptions in plenary, which in most cases differ widely from group to group. This leads into a discussion about why each group thought as they did. Finally, Ruth reveals details about the real people behind the hand prints and handwriting (including the fact that one sample is her own). This light-hearted exercise can then lead into a discussion about the clues or cues that we use, and a debate around their validity. Airing the idea of fundamental attribution error in this final phase provides teachers a vocabulary with which to describe and check their own preconceptions:

- Am I making a fundamental attribution error in believing this about a person based on handwriting?
- In what circumstances do I make this kind of error?

- What questions can I ask myself to halt my preconceptions (for example, fact or supposition)?

Growth mindset: a learning styles workshop

Learning styles may seem out of place here, so we ask you to withhold judgement for a moment. Learning styles can be a helpful means of acknowledging the diverse ways in which students learn, and that, in certain circumstances, some students have preferences for the way they absorb information. In arguing the case for experiential learning, Kolb (1984) showed how students tend to have a preference for a particular type of learning – active learners, observers, and so on. Others (Fleming and Mills 1992) have explored how some people prefer to absorb information visually, some prefer auditory sources, others excel at reading and writing exercises, while a fourth group learns best kinaesthetically (collectively leading to the acronym VARK). Educational developers often include sessions on learning styles in their courses and workshops and many university teachers like to share these ideas with their students.

In the cases of both experiential learning and VARK, however, the theorists show that a preference is no more than that: it is not a direct order to learn in a particular way. Indeed, effective learners are able to learn in numerous ways; their approaches change according to experience and context, and the ability to learn to learn is possibly the most important skill of all. This requires a 'growth mindset' (Dweck 2008).

The danger with learning styles – one that we have seen and heard repeatedly among students *and* teachers – is that if mishandled, it can promote the 'fixed mindset': some students come to regard their learning abilities as immutable. They declare they are 'a visual learner', for example, and demand that the teacher respond to their specific needs accordingly or refuse to read a passage of text. This turns learning styles into a learning disability, an auto-stereotype that prevents students from developing as learners. So when running sessions on learning styles, we suggest you introduce Dweck's mindset research (2008), and that you strongly encourage teachers to focus on this bottom-line point: learning styles are best used to identify room for development. If students discover they are, say, visual learners, then it means they need to work harder to improve the other three styles so that they are more adaptable, flexible learners. Encourage your colleagues to avoid oversimplifying the learning process and to help students see that learning is complex, variable and often messy.

Confirmation bias: the scepticism workshop

Using the fiendishly complicated 'Wason selection task', Dawson et al. (2002) found that people with a more sceptical mindset were less likely to jump to conclusions or to stereotype. This scepticism was most likely to arise when individuals had a personal motivation to *disbelieve* a statement: they find themselves asking '*Must* I believe this?' Even with this motivation to disbelieve, though, people typically accepted the statement if they saw strong evidence that it was correct (Dawson et al. 2002: 1386). In contrast, if a statement worked in people's favour and early evidence supported the claim, individuals were less likely to seek out as much information to justify it, asking themselves only '*Can* I believe this?' (These findings provide examples of confirmation bias and the 'differentiation' model of stereotyping we discussed earlier in this chapter.)

Thus, people who would rather *disprove* a claim – and who ask 'Must I believe this?' – were more likely to reach an accurate conclusion because their evidentiary threshold was higher than those who ask 'Can I believe this?' and would like to uphold a claim. Uncertainty and doubt are tools that can help subvert the tendency to rely on generalizations. How do we turn this into an educational development event?

We suggest you first present a statement that university teachers are more likely to want to support: 'Research has found that university teachers are more thoughtful voters who are able to provide the clearest rationales for their voting habits.' Ask your workshop participants to call out the questions they would want to ask the researchers to check the veracity of that claim. Collate a list, as people volunteer their questions; when they dry up, solicit more. Once everyone has finished, conceal the list – people are not to see it for the next section.

Now you present a finding that you believe your audience will *not* want to support. For example: 'Research has found that university teachers are the least likely professionals to do volunteer work or to donate to charities.' Again, list the questions that participants would want to ask the researchers of this fictitious study. Hiding their previous list of questions means they have to start from scratch.

Once participants have exhausted their questions, compare the two lists. If Dawson et al.'s (2002) findings hold true, this second list will be longer because participants will be asking 'Must I believe this?' People trying to disprove a claim should seek a higher level of evidence. Share the research findings with the group and be sure to make it clear to everyone that you know of *no* research to support either assertion, but simply wanted to generate questions to test a theory.

At this point, participants can turn to one of their own courses and consider any specific findings or topics discussed in the course. For each of those topics, can the teachers think of an angle– whether true, false or still unclear – that their students typically want to disprove? (In criminal justice, 'Torture of terrorism suspects leads to reliable information that saves lives'; in engineering, 'The most common cause of building collapse in modern times is that engineers have misplaced a decimal point'.) Ask participants to share their ideas in small groups or in plenary so that everyone has a larger arsenal of possible constructions that should help galvanize students into sceptical thinking where they doubt, question and seek a higher level of evidence than they would normally. (For instance, the engineering example could be adjusted to say, 'Deaths in hospitals are mostly due to nurses misplacing a decimal point when dispensing medications'.)

To end the workshop, return to the stereotyping of students using preconceptions from this study that you believe are salient on your campus, or generate your own list based on conversations with colleagues: 'student athletes perform poorly'; 'successful students talk with their teachers'; 'students who join the university through Clearing underachieve'; and 'punctual students do well'. These can be preconceptions that were upheld or not; the key is to ask your participants to probe the statements and demonstrate greater scepticism in their thinking, using 'Must I believe this?' as their measuring stick. Having seen their varying levels of scepticism in the previous activities, this final stage should help them model suspension of judgement and higher-order thinking in their classes and in their communication with students.

The human face of preconceptions: workshops with student vignettes

We have intentionally saved vignettes to last: if we see our students as whole people, with all the complexity and messiness that entails, we will be better at suspending our judgement and treating them fairly. Based on real responses from students at the four universities, we have created four vignettes in Appendix 3 for you to use in workshops. Each vignette has four parts, though you may choose to break them up differently. We gradually reveal details about each student, with suggested questions at the end of each segment. Workshops with cases like this are most effective if participants have time to discuss each part of the vignette in small groups before contributing to a plenary discussion: it gives them time to test out their ideas and forms of expression. When running these events, be sure to hand out the stages separately, so that participants aren't tempted to read ahead. Depending on the needs and interests of the group, you may wish to alter the length of the session, but as a general guide we would suggest that one vignette would take around an hour in order to ensure time for good discussion.

Creating your own vignettes
You may prefer to tailor the vignettes to reflect the student groups that seem most relevant to your setting, or to write your own. They are somewhat tricky to write, so we'll share with you the method that has worked best for us. We suggest you start out by listing the preconceptions you'd like to touch upon in each vignette and then decide whether the student is going to reflect these preconceptions positively, negatively or ambiguously. Table 8.2 shows the first four preconceptions from our study and how we allocated those items across our four vignettes. Once you have decided the behaviours and attributes for your vignette, you can then choose which information will be revealed at which stage and begin writing.

Understanding undergraduates

At the very start of this book, we asked you to jot down your own thoughts on what makes a good student, a poor student and what you

Table 8.2 Format for planning vignettes

PRECONCEPTION	THEO	JULIA	KRISTEN	RYAN
Expect to develop different study habits from those that worked at high school	—	No	Yes	Yes
Are punctual for lectures and classes	No	—	Sometimes	—
Keep up with assigned reading	—	—	—	No
Prefer to sit towards the front in class	—	Yes	Yes	—

believe your *students* think makes a good student. If you managed to do that, we'd like you to return to your notes to remind yourself of what you wrote. It may be that some of your preconceptions coincided with those of the teachers in our study, and if so, you'll know whether we found them to be true of our students. Most likely, you'll also see other ideas that our teachers didn't raise.

So what might you do, or do differently, now that you have all this information about how and why we form preconceptions? As you walk into a classroom, as you prepare for office hours, as you encounter your students on campus, what will change? If you believe that particular behaviours, attitudes or changeable circumstances lead to underperformance, then the just response is proactively to build in strategies, activities and policies to help students circumnavigate these pitfalls. If you believe other behaviours, attitudes or changeable circumstances suggest success, then those warrant nurturing through your course or programme design so that all your students can benefit. If the focus of your beliefs is instead on certain *unchangeable* circumstances, then we challenge you to rethink: these factors are necessarily beyond your control and your students' control.

Clearly, we can't simply eradicate our judgement and cease to presume – as you've read in this chapter, detecting patterns and drawing inferences are a natural part of our humanity. Yet to hold onto those patterns as an irrefutable blueprint to which students will conform would be to deny the humanity of others. Even if our brains won't allow us to discard our preconceptions, we can still practise the skill of recognizing those intellectual shortcuts and take a moment to distinguish supposition from evidence. And even then, we can seek more evidence. Our classrooms are places where teachers and students gather to pool their array of backgrounds, traditions, experiences and attributes in search of learning. Ultimately, the more we get to know students as individuals in their own right, the better we are able to understand our undergraduates.

APPENDIX 1
STUDENT SURVEYS

Demographic data

Students' demographic data and final grade were supplied from central university records. Students signed consent forms attached to their surveys, where all demographic information to be collected was listed. Included in our surveys were the following:

> Age, sex, ethnicity, religious affiliation (if known, US), marital status, permanent address (US: city/state/zip code; UK: postcode), family income level (if known), year of study (US), major field of study (if decided, US), prior academic achievement (UK: GCSE and A levels/IB; US: SAT/ACT scores, AP scores), grade at the end of this course.

Example survey

The survey below is a composite of those used in the study, listing all the key questions we asked to elicit the information we have shared with you in this study. Here, we have used British English spellings.

A. About you

1 Student ID:

2 Which state were you living in prior to attending this university? (US)

3 Which year are you in? (UK: 1, 2, 3 or 4; US: freshman, sophomore, junior, senior)

4 'I am interested in current events and politics' (PLEASE CIRCLE)
Strongly agree | Agree | No opinion | Disagree | Strongly disagree

5 Did your parents complete university?
Yes, both | Yes, father | Yes, mother | No, neither

6 'I would gauge my use of social networking (such as text-messaging, Facebook, Twitter, etc.) as:'
Heavy use | Some use | Light use | Never use

7 While at high school, or equivalent, which language was most frequently spoken at home? (US)

_____

8 Do you regularly attend religious services? Yes | No (US)

9 Are you a student athlete? Yes | No (US)
If yes, which sport? _____

10 Have you been diagnosed as having dyslexia? Yes | No (UK)

B. Your experience of secondary school

1 Which of the following most closely describes your high school?
Public high school | Private high school | Home schooled | Other (specify) _____

2 What was the prevailing culture of your high school? (For example, valued academic achievement, sporting prowess, being street-wise, etc.)

_____

_____

_____

_____

3 What proportion of your peers at high school expected to go to university?
Most | Some | Few | None

4 'I was prepared appropriately for university work by my high-school experience.'
Strongly agree | Agree | No opinion | Disagree | Strongly disagree

5 'Before coming to university, I have been encouraged by my parents to question and to engage in debates.'
Strongly agree | Agree | No opinion | Disagree | Strongly disagree

C. Your experience of university

1 Why did you choose to come to this university? (For example: to please others, actively chose it myself, was attracted to the city, etc.)

_____

_____

_____

_____

2 How useful was any induction (UK)/ orientation (US) programme that you received?
Very useful | Quite useful | Not very useful | Not useful at all | I did not attend | It was not offered

3 What do you think are the characteristics of a successful learner?

_____

_____

_____

_____

4 'I have taken action to improve my learning skills.' (E.g. used the Learning Centre/Writing Centre)
Strongly agree | Agree | No opinion | Disagree | Strongly disagree

5 'I actively arrange to work with other students out of class.'
Strongly agree | Agree | No opinion | Disagree | Strongly disagree

6 Which of the following most closely describes your approach to your studies?
Often do less than I should/less than others do
Only do work that is going to be graded
Do just enough to get by
Usually do everything my instructor suggests I should do
Frequently do more than I am told to do, e.g. read around the subject, do additional exercises, etc.

7 When taking a course and you find the work difficult or challenging, what is the most important factor in keeping you going?
Family expectations | The prospect of future rewards (e.g. employment) | Your instructor's expectations | Your own desire to do well | Other (please specify): _____

8 Do you do paid work during the academic year? Yes | No
If Yes: How many hours per week? _____
          Where do you work? _____

9 Do you do voluntary or service work during the academic year? Yes | No
If Yes: How many hours per week? _____
          What do you do? _____

10 'In my leisure time I enjoy doing things that relate to my course.'
Strongly agree | Agree | No opinion | Disagree | Strongly disagree

11 'Outside class I enjoy reading that relates to my course.'
Strongly agree | Agree | No opinion | Disagree | Strongly disagree

12 'I feel I belong in this university.'
Strongly agree | Agree | No opinion | Disagree | Strongly disagree

13 'I actively chose to attend this university.'
Strongly agree | Agree | No opinion | Disagree | Strongly disagree

14 'My family encouraged me to attend university.'
Strongly agree | Agree | No opinion | Disagree | Strongly disagree

15 Did you join this university through Clearing? Yes | No (UK)

D. About this course

1 Which of the following describes your status on this course:
Full-Time | Part-Time | First attempt (UK) | Re-sit (UK)

2 When did you join this course? (UK)
Start of week 1 | Weeks 2 to 3 | Weeks 4 to 5 | After week 5

3   'Compared to my previous educational experience, I expected this course to require...'
    A lot more studying time | More studying time | About the same studying time | Less studying time | A lot less studying time

4   Compared to my high school experience this course requires a different approach
    Strongly agree | Agree | No opinion | Disagree | Strongly disagree

5   Was this course an elective? Yes | No (US)
    If no: if it had been elective, would you have chosen it? Yes | No
    If yes or if there was a choice of section: Why did you choose to take it?

    _____

    _____

    _____

    _____

6   How punctual are you for this class?
    Always on time | Occasionally a little late | Often late | Always late | Frequently do not attend (in other words, attend less than 50% of classes)

7   'I am willing to approach the instructor of this class outside of class for help.'
    Strongly agree | Agree | No opinion | Disagree | Strongly disagree

8   'I participate in the class.' (E.g. ask questions, join in debate.)
    Strongly agree | Agree | No opinion | Disagree | Strongly disagree

9   In this class, I prefer to sit:
    Near the front | In the middle | Near the back | Anywhere

10 What grade do you expect to get in this class? _____

11 I am anxious about failing (UK)
    Strongly agree | Agree | No opinion | Disagree | Strongly disagree

12 How frequently do you access course information on the VLE? (UK)
    Daily | Weekly | Occasionally | Infrequently | Never

Changing groups easily

Use the grids below to help you organize your students into different groups swiftly. Enter your students' names alphabetically in each grid so that they appear in the same cell each time. For any small-group discussion, you can reorganize the students randomly, knowing that they'll have chance to work with everyone in the class. You could also give your students their own copy of this grid (including names), so that they can organize themselves more readily.

A. Horizontal groups

1.	1.	1.	1.	1.
2.	2.	2.	2.	2.
3.	3.	3.	3.	3.
4.	4.	4.	4.	4.
5.	5.	5.	5.	5.

B. Vertical groups

1.	2.	3.	4.	5.
1.	2.	3.	4.	5.
1.	2.	3.	4.	5.
1.	2.	3.	4.	5.
1.	2.	3.	4.	5.

C. Diagonal groups

1.	2.	3.	4.	5.
5.	1.	2.	3.	4.
4.	5.	1.	2.	3.
3.	4.	5.	1.	2.
2.	3.	4.	5.	1.

D. Backslash groups (reverse diagonal)

1.	2.	3.	4.	5.
2.	3.	4.	5.	1.
3.	4.	5.	1.	2.
4.	5.	1.	2.	3.
5.	1.	2.	3.	4.

E. Knight groups (across two, down one, as a knight in chess)

1.	2.	3.	4.	5.
4.	5.	1.	2.	3.
2.	3.	4.	5.	1.
5.	1.	2.	3.	4.
3.	4.	5.	1.	2.

F. Extended knight groups (across *three*, down one)

1.	2.	3.	4.	5.
3.	4.	5.	1.	2.
5.	1.	2.	3.	4.
2.	3.	4.	5.	1.
4.	5.	1.	2.	3.

Appendix 3
Vignettes

Vignette 1: Theo, Arial University, UK

Theo, part one

You first notice Theo at the orientation for the degree programme, and for three distinct reasons: first, he is clearly older than the rest of the first-year students – perhaps in his late twenties; secondly, he arrives late with another male student halfway through the welcome address from the head of department; and thirdly, he looks as though he's spent the entire summer tanning himself on a Greek island, noticeably turning heads among his peers as he takes the one remaining seat toward the rear of the class.

From that first day, Theo is keen to join in the discussion, asks thoughtful questions and demonstrates that he's been reading around the subject for some time. You and your colleagues agree he is a great addition to the programme.

- Based on this limited information, what do you expect are Theo's strengths and weaknesses?
- What, if any, presumptions influenced your responses?

Theo, part two

Term starts well and Theo's contributions in your class demonstrate his commitment to the subject, though you sense that some of the other students think he dominates discussion. Through group consensus, you introduce some class guidelines that include providing space for more people to contribute and starting and ending class on time – Theo's tardiness from orientation has continued, and other students have been late, too.

Theo hands in his first written assignment in week 3; it's a borderline fail. Before meeting him to discuss it, you check his admissions file and see that he hadn't met the usual academic requirements, but was offered a place on the programme because of his enthusiasm, maturity and life experiences; even so, he scored B grades – higher than your programme requires – for GCSE English and mathematics when he was 16.

- Based on the information you have gleaned so far, what concerns do you have about Theo's chances of success on your course?
- Which information influences your thinking more heavily?
- What is your plan for this upcoming meeting?

Theo, part three

When you meet, Theo is unusually reticent and looks drained. You discover he has not joined a study group (which you had recommended) and that he doesn't feel part of the group: as he lives with his girlfriend off-campus, he has less time to mix socially with his year group and he finds the other students more immature than he'd expected.

Eventually, Theo tells you he is dyslexic, though he had been worried that the university wouldn't let him onto the course if he had declared this in his application. You explain that if his dyslexia is confirmed by Disability Services, he may be eligible for accommodations that will help level the playing field between him and his peers. Theo is visibly relieved. You walk him over to Disability Services and introduce him to the receptionist.

- How, if at all, does this new information affect your view of Theo and his prospects on the degree programme?
- What ideas might the course team be able to implement to support students like Theo?
- What presumptions have been confirmed or refuted in your encounters with him so far?

Theo, part four

Some weeks have passed and Disability Services have written to let you know what accommodations are needed for Theo. When he comes to thank you for taking the time to support him, you notice that he still looks worn out and stressed, so you ask how he is doing generally. While he is enjoying the course, the hour's commute to and from campus each day is tiring, as is the fact that he's working 15 hours a week in a bar to help pay the bills, on top of studying full-time. You remark that he must wish he were back on his summer holidays, at which point he looks at you quizzically: he spent the entire summer working long hours in a windowless office to help save up money for this first year of study. His girlfriend works full-time and has taken on more of their joint expenses, which makes him uncomfortable; he has taken out a personal loan and expects to graduate heavily in debt.

Even so, Theo is excited about his degree:

> I've withdrawn from a couple of programmes in the past, so you could say I've got a chequered history. So far in my life, I've disliked just about everything I've studied and everywhere I've worked. But here, I really think I've found something I'm passionate about.

- Based on all the information you have, what advice would you give Theo at this stage?
- What presumptions have you made about Theo's needs?
- If you had known all this information at the start of the year, how might you have acted differently?
- What actions can you take to mitigate against your own tendency to make presumptions?

Vignette 2: Julia, Baskerville University, UK

Julia, part one

Like most of her cohort, Julia has joined the medicine degree at Baskerville directly from secondary education, which in her case was a private school where virtually all pupils were expected to go to university. She must have done very well at school to make it onto the programme. In your large lecture course, you haven't really noticed her. She is one of a relatively competitive group of white, 18 to 19 year-old women who sit near the front.

- Based on this limited information, what do you expect are Julia's strengths and weaknesses?
- What, if any, presumptions influenced your responses?

Julia, part two

Early in the course, you encourage the students to discuss their previous experience and their reasons for studying medicine. As you wander around the room, you overhear that Julia comes from a privileged background (her father is a lawyer, her mother a dentist) and that she didn't really choose to study medicine at all: it was suggested to her by her parents and teachers, because she was slightly better at sciences than humanities. She had wondered about studying English, history or law, but in the end agreed to apply for medicine because she enjoys helping people.

Later in the session, when small groups are reporting back some of their thoughts, one student singles out Julia and says that unlike the rest of their group, she doesn't like to do anything related to medicine beyond studying – like watching hospital dramas or reading forensic mysteries. Julia is clearly anxious at being identified like this. At the end of class, you ask her to drop by during office hours for a chat to put her at ease.

- Based on the information you have gleaned so far, what concerns do you have about Julia's chances of success on your course?
- Which information influences your thinking more heavily?
- What is your plan for this upcoming meeting?

Julia, part three

When Julia eventually comes to see you – over a week later – it's apparent that she's uncomfortable talking with her teachers, or at least with you. To break the ice, you say,

> I really felt for you when your group member said you didn't like medical dramas, as if it were a crime against humanity! I'm with you: I never liked that stuff – and if I do happen to see it, I get irritated when they do something wrong. I don't want you to feel like a pariah for this!

Now seeing you as a potential ally, Julia begins to open up about her experience of the course so far.

> My school was all about independent learning, so I thought I knew what's in store when teachers talked about it during orientation. But this

is a *lot* more independent. I'm used to meeting with my teachers very regularly and getting feedback so that I can redo work if I've not done it well first time.

It becomes clear that Julia expects the strategies she used to get her through her A levels will suffice for university education.

- What advice would you give Julia at this point?
- What presumptions have you made about her needs in relation to the degree programme?
- Which presumptions have been confirmed or refuted in your encounters with her so far?

Julia, part four

After a long discussion on independent learning, you strongly encourage Julia to visit the learning centre and attend some workshops on study skills so that she can widen her repertoire for success.

In the week before mid-term assignments are due, you pull Julia aside during a break in the lecture. Although she still sits at the front of the class with her original group, you've noticed she doesn't appear as confident as at the start of term, so you ask how she is getting along with her study skills. It transpires that she has been trying to make do with her current strategies and has not attended any of the recommended workshops, because 'I'd feel a total failure if I had to attend one of *those*'. Her sister, a third-year dentistry student at another university, has assured her that the skills from secondary school are more than enough to do well, which has left Julia feeling even more of a failure for being unsure of her abilities. She is working very hard to keep up with all the required reading and checks everything on the VLE to make sure she has the right information, but is still worried that she is not going to pass the course.

- Based on all the information you have, what advice would you give Julia at this stage?
- How has your perception of her changed since the start of term?
- If you had known all this information at the start of the course, how might you have acted differently?

- What actions can you take to mitigate against your own tendency to make presumptions?

Vignette 3: Kristen, Constantia University, USA

Kristen, part one

Kristen comes up and introduces herself to you at the end of the first lecture of your introductory science course. She is evidently a self-confident drama and literature major who has transferred to Constantia from a prestigious, private university on the east coast and needs to fulfil her science requirements – which she has been dreading – before she can complete her studies in her majors. She is technically a junior (in other words, in year three of four) and just celebrated her twenty-first birthday last weekend. All of this she lets slip during a brief conversation in which she informs you she might occasionally arrive late because her baby's day-care opens only just before your 8:00 a.m. class and is a few blocks from campus. She asks you not to mention the baby to other students in the class.

- Based on this limited information, what do you expect are Kristen's strengths and weaknesses?
- What, if any, presumptions influenced your responses?

Kristen, part two

Ten days into the term, Kristen spots you in the library café and comes over to say hello. You discover that she has moved back to the area because she needed her family's support with the baby; her parents are both Constantia alumni and encouraged her to apply there.

When you ask how she is finding it coping with a new baby and full-time study, she says that she's in a much better position than her peers at high school.

> It was an alternative school. Most of the students were white, artistic 'rockers' and a majority of them smoked weed, many used other drugs. Class attendance was not required. The drop-out rate was fairly high, and many students had to attend for 5+ years to graduate.

Kristen tells you that, like many of her peers, she dropped out of school two years early, and completed a GED (General Educational

Development test) instead of gaining a high-school diploma. She says school didn't prepare her at all for the requirements of a university education, where she does a lot more work.

- Based on the information you have gleaned so far, what concerns do you have about Kristen's chances of success?
- Which information influences your thinking more heavily?

Kristen, part three

During a lab session, Kristen comes over to you looking pensive. Her lab partner and a few nearby students have been cracking jokes about Kristen being a slacker who's often late to class – they don't know about her baby. Their joking moved on to general comments about 'lazy Mexicans'.

Kristen feels she's in a bind. She wants to confront the others' prejudices, but feels she can only really do that if she lets them know she is Latina (which you didn't know either). If she tells them that, she worries that her arriving late to class will confirm their stereotypes. And if she tells them *why* she is late, that could make matters even worse.

- What advice do you give Kristen?
- How can *you* respond to the situation so that Kristen doesn't have to?
- What presumptions are you struggling with as you think this through?

Kristen, part four

While you were talking with Kristen, her lab partner comes and joins you to apologize for being offensive. A separate student, who has participated in intergroup dialogues on campus, had quietly discussed the negative impact of repeating stereotypes – even ones you don't believe – and the intellectual laziness of falling back on them. Kristen accepts and apology and you are relieved to see the class return to its usual level of energy.

Two weeks before final exams, Kristen comes to see you during office hours. She's finding it stressful juggling responsibilities as a young mother and a student, and she has no time for any paid work that might give her useful experiences for when she looks for a graduate-level job. She receives a scholarship from Constantia, for which she has to maintain her high grades. She has been trying to develop new study habits for your science course, since she suspects her successful tactics in humanities classes won't transfer. Competing demands of study, grades, childcare and a future job search are all taking their toll.

- Based on all the information you have, what advice would you give Kristen at this stage?
- How has your perception of her changed since the start of term?
- If you had known all this information at the start of the course, how might you have acted differently?
- What actions can you take to mitigate against your own tendency to make presumptions?

Vignette 4: Ryan, Delphin University, USA

Ryan, part one

Ryan is one of eight freshmen who attend an open workshop you run on students' expectations of university. Over the 90 minutes, he quietly contributes and you learn quite a bit about his background. Having participated in a mission abroad for the Church of Jesus Christ of Latter-day Saints, Ryan is a single, 20-year-old freshman who has moved to Delphin, partly to get away from his home town and most of his school friends, who are at other universities closer to home. He still attends religious services, but many other aspects of his life have changed. While he thought he was ready for university study, he has realized that he needs to develop new habits and is taking advantage of any event he can at the learning centre, which is why he has come to this workshop. Towards the end of the 90 minutes, Ryan volunteers to read his description of a successful learner:

> Not shy or afraid to make mistakes. Not a procrastinator. Being interested while in class and not texting or on Facebook. Willing to challenge their beliefs and preconceived notions: integrate whichever ideas are the best. Someone that can laugh. Not afraid of individual thought.

- Based on this limited information, what do you expect are Ryan's strengths and weaknesses?
- What, if any, presumptions influenced your responses?

Ryan, part two

In the following term, you discover Ryan has chosen your elective social studies course and see him in the first class, halfway back in the lecture theatre, close to the aisle. You are immediately surprised to see him not taking notes, but fumbling under the table while you are talking; when you walk towards the aisle, you can see he's texting and notice the white cable from an earphone sticking out above his collar. After the break, you reach an agreement with the class that technology will only be used for class-related activities.

You pull Ryan aside at the end of the session, though he's clearly not that willing to talk; he says he doesn't have much time because he works 30 hours a week in the computer labs on campus. When you mention his texting and the earphone, he laughs and apologizes. He calls himself a newly converted techno-addict, being a heavy user of social networks, constantly using his smart phone for Facebook and Twitter, plus commenting regularly on his favourite blogs. He promises to cut down his usage during class.

- Based on the information you have learned so far, what concerns do you have about Ryan's prospects in your class?
- Which information influences your thinking more heavily?

Ryan, part three

Your first large assignment is in the form of a public consultation on a polluted local river. Working in teams, students have to present the arguments of various stakeholders, drawing on the class content and relevant readings. At the end of a class where students have been preparing their presentations, two female students approach you about difficulties with Ryan. They say he hasn't done the reading, doesn't participate in their group preparations and has been listening to music during group discussion time. When they plead that they have already tried discussing his participation in the group, you decide to email Ryan to arrange a meeting.

- What is your plan for this upcoming meeting?
- Which information about Ryan influences your thinking more heavily?
- Which presumptions have been confirmed or refuted in your encounters with him so far?

Ryan, part four

Ryan is perplexed when you explain the purpose of the meeting. Yes, the other students have asked him to be more involved in the planning, but he has told them that he's not used to debating issues, so he'll wait until the end and then put together fantastic slides to back up whatever argument the team comes up with. He sees this as a fair distribution of labour.

When you raise the importance of groups working through an issue and developing their ideas together, he tells you he understands already (having been to a workshop on it), but hasn't actually put any of the ideas into practice:

> Those workshops were ok, you know, and the lunches were good, but a lot of it seems so obvious that I can't get excited about it. Don't get me wrong – I'm just saying. Now I'm getting used to it here, I don't think I need that stuff.

Ryan sees himself as a strong student who will do well in this course, regardless of how the group turns out.

- Based on all the information you have, what advice would you give Ryan at this stage?
- How has your perception of him changed since the start of the year?
- If you had known all this information at the outset, how might you have acted differently?
- What actions can you take to mitigate against your own tendency to make presumptions?

References

Ackerman, D.S. and Gross, B.L. (2010) Instructor feedback: How much do students really want? *Journal of Marketing Education*, 32(2), 172–81.

Ambrose, S.A., Bridges, M.W., DiPietro, M., Lovett, M.C. and Norman, M.K. (2010) *How learning works: Seven research-based principles for smart teaching*. San Francisco, CA: Jossey-Bass.

Aronson, J., Lustina, M.J., Good, C., Keough, K., Steele, C.M. and Brown, J. (1999) When white men can't do math: Necessary and sufficient factors in stereotype threat. *Journal of Experimental Social Psychology*, 35, 29–46.

Arum, R. and Roksa, J. (2011) *Academically adrift: Limited learning on college campuses*. Chicago, IL: University of Chicago Press.

Arvidson, P.S. (2008) *Teaching nonmajors: Advice for liberal arts professors*. Albany, NY: State University of New York Press.

Arvidson, P.S. (2011) Personal communication. E-mail (August 17, 2011).

Association for Learning Development in Higher Education (2011). Available at: http://www.aldinhe.ac.uk/ (accessed August 2011).

Aud, S., Hussar, W., Kena, G., Bianco, K., Frohlich, L., Kemp, J. and Tahan, K. (2011). *The condition of education 2011* (NCES 2011–033). US Department of Education, National Center for Education Statistics. Washington, DC: US Government Printing Office.

Aygün, Z.K., Arslan, M. and Güney, S. (2008) Work values of Turkish and American university students. *Journal of Business Ethics*, 80, 205–23.

Bach, S., Haynes, P. and Lewis Smith, J. (2007). *Online learning and teaching*. Maidenhead: Open University Press and McGraw-Hill.

Bandura, A. (1997) *Self-efficacy: The exercise of control*. New York: W.H. Freeman and Company.

Bandura, A. and Schunk, D.H. (1981) Cultivating competence, self-efficacy, and intrinsic interest through proximal self-motivation. *Journal of Personality and Social Psychology*, 41(3), 586–98.

Barfield, S., Hixenbaugh, P. and Thomas, L. (eds) (2006) *Critical reflections and positive interventions: An electronic casebook of good practice in personal tutoring*. York, UK: Higher Education Academy. Available online at: http://www.heacademy.ac.uk/resources/detail/resource_database/personal_tutoring_ecasebook_2006 (accessed August 2011).

Bean, J.C. (2011) *Engaging ideas: The professor's guide to integrating writing, critical thinking, and active learning in the classroom*, 2nd edn. San Francisco, CA: Jossey-Bass.

Beatty-Guenter, P. (1994) Sorting, supporting, connecting, and transforming: Retention strategies at community colleges. *Community College Journal of Research and Practice*, 18, 113–29.

Becher, T. and Trowler, P.R. (2001) *Academic tribes and territories: Intellectual enquiry and the cultures of disciplines*, 2nd edn. Buckingham, UK: Society for Research into Higher Education/Open University Press.

Beetham, H. and Sharpe, R. (2007) *Rethinking pedagogy for a digital age: Designing and delivering e-learning*. Abingdon, UK: Routledge.

Beven, R., Badge, J., Cann, A., Wilmott, C. and Scott, J. (2008) Seeing eye to eye? Staff and student views on feedback. *Bioscience Education E-Journal*, 12. Available online at: www.bioscience.heacademy.ac.uk/journal/vol12/beej-12-1.aspx (accessed May 2011).

Biggs, J. and Tang, C. (2007) *Teaching for quality learning at university: What the student does*, 3rd edn. Maidenhead, UK: Society for Research in Higher Education and Open University Press.

Biglan, A. (1973) Relationships between subject matter characteristics and the structure and output of university departments. *Journal of Applied Psychology*, 57(3), 204–13.

Black, P. and William, D. (1998) Assessment and classroom learning. *Assessment in Education*, 5(1), 7–74.

Bloom, B.S., Engelhart, M.D., Furst, E.J., Hill, W.H. and Krathwohl, D.R. (1956) *Taxonomy of educational objectives: The classification of educational goals; Handbook 1: Cognitive Domain*. New York: Longman.

Boice, R. (1996) Classroom incivilities. *Research in Higher Education*, 37(4), 453–86.

Boice, R. (2000) *Advice for new faculty members: Nihil nimus*. Needham Heights, MA: Allyn and Bacon.

Bourdieu, P. and Passeron, J.-C. (1965/1994). Introduction: Language and relationship to language in the teaching situation. In P. Bourdieu, J.-C. Passeron and M. de Saint Martin (eds), *Academic discourse: Linguistic misunderstanding and professorial power*, trans. Richard Teese (pp. 1–34). Cambridge: Polity Press.

Bradshaw, J., Ager, R., Burge, B. and Wheater, R. (2010) *PISA 2009: Achievement of 15 year olds in England*. Slough, UK: NFER. Available online at http://www.nfer.ac.uk/publications/NPDZ01 (accessed April 2011).

Bransford, J.D. and Schwartz, D.L. (1999) Rethinking transfer: A simple proposal with multiple implications. *Review of Research in Education*, 24, 61–100.

Brookfield, S.D. and Preskill, S. (2005) *Discussion as a way of teaching: Tools and techniques for democratic classrooms*, 2nd edn. San Francisco, CA: Jossey-Bass.

Brown-Glaude, W.R. (ed.) (2009) *Doing diversity in higher education: Faculty leaders share challenges and strategies*. New Brunswick, NJ: Rutgers University Press.

Bruff, D. (2009) *Teaching with classroom responses systems: Creating active learning environments*. San Francisco, CA: Jossey-Bass.

Bruner, J. (1966) *Towards a theory of instruction*. Cambridge: Cambridge University Press.

Campbell, F., Eland, J., Rumpus, A. and Shacklock, R. (2009) *Hearing the student voice: Involving students in curriculum design and delivery*. Edinburgh: Edinburgh Napier University.

Carnegie Foundation for the Advancement of Teaching (2010) Classification description. Available online at: http://classifications.carnegiefoundation. org/descriptions/basic.php (accessed April 2011).

Carroll, J. and Ryan, J. (eds) (2005) *Teaching international students: Improving learning for all*. SEDA Series. Abingdon, UK: Routledge.

Carver, R.P. (1992) Reading rate: Theory, research, and practical implications. *Journal of Reading*, 36(2), 84–95.

Casner-Lotto, J., Rosenblum, E. and Wright, M. (2009) *The ill-prepared U.S. workforce: Exploring the challenges of employer-provided workforce readiness training*. New York: The Conference Board.

Chan, A. and Lee, M.J.W. (2005) An MP3 a day keeps the worries away: Exploring the use of podcasting to address preconceptions and alleviate pre-class anxiety amongst undergraduate information technology students. In D.H.R. Spennemann and L. Burr (eds), *Good practice in practice: Proceedings of the Student Experience Conference* (pp. 59–71). Wagga Wagga, Australia: Charles Sturt University.

Chavous, T. (2002) Role of student background, perception of ethnic fit and racial identification in the academic adjustment of African American students at a predominantly white university. *Journal of Black Psychology*, 28(3), 234–60.

Chen, X. (2005) *First generation students in postsecondary education: A look at their college transcripts*. Washington, DC: National Center for Educational Statistics. Available online at: http://nces.ed.gov/pubsearch/pubsinfo. asp?pubid=2005171 (accessed August 2011).

Cheney, G., McMillan, J. and Schwartzman, R. (1997) *Should we buy the 'student-as-consumer' metaphor?* Available online at: http://mtprof.msun. edu/Fall1997/Cheney.html (accessed January 2011).

Cheng, D. and Reed, M. (2010) *Student debt and the class of 2009*. Oakland, CA: Project on student debt/Institute for College Access and Success. Available online at: http://projectonstudentdebt.org/files/pub/classof2009. pdf (accessed April 2011).

Clark, J.K., Eno, C.A. and Guadagno, R.E. (2011) Southern discomfort: The effects of stereotype threat on the intellectual performance of US southerners. *Self and Identity*, 10(2), 248–62.

Coker, A.D. (2003) African American female adult learners: Motivations, challenges, and coping strategies. *Journal of Black Studies*, 33(5), 654–74.

Cokley, K., Komarraju, M., Pickett, R., Shen, F., Patel, N., Belur, V. and Rosales, R. (2007) Ethnic differences in endorsement of the Protestant work ethic: The role of ethnic identity and perceptions of social class. *Journal of Social Psychology*, 147(1), 75–89.

Colliver, J.A., Feltovich, P.J. and Verhulst, S.J. (2003) Small group learning in medical education: A second look at the Springer, Stanne, and Donovan meta-analysis. *Teaching and Learning in Medicine*, 15(1), 2–5.

Conole, G. and Oliver, M. (2006) *Contemporary perspectives in e-learning research: Themes, methods and impact on practice.* Abingdon, UK: Routledge.

Cook, A. and Rushton, B. (2008) *Student transition: Practices and policies to promote retention.* SEDA Paper 121. London: SEDA.

Cooper, E. (2010) Tutoring center effectiveness: The effect of drop-in tutoring. *Journal of College Reading and Learning*, 40(2), 21–34.

Cotterell, S. (2008) *The study skills handbook*, 3rd edn. Basingstoke, UK: Palgrave Macmillan.

Council Directive (EC) 2000/43/EC 29 June 2000 implementing the principle of equal treatment between persons irrespective of racial or ethnic origin.

Council Directive (EC) 2000/78/EC 27 November 2000 establishing a general framework for equal treatment in employment and occupation.

Cousin, G. (2009) *Researching learning in higher education: An introduction to contemporary methods and approaches.* SEDA Series. Abingdon, UK: Routledge.

Covington, M.V., Spratt, M.F. and Omelich, C.L. (1980) Is effort enough, or does diligence count too? Student and teacher reactions to effort stability in failure. *Journal of Educational Psychology*, 72(6), 717–29.

Cramp, A. (2011) Developing first-year engagement with feedback. *Active Learning in Higher Education* 12(2), 113–24.

Crano, W.D. and Mellon, P.M. (1978) Causal influence of teachers' expectations on children's academic performance: A cross-lagged panel analysis. *Journal of Educational Psychology*, 70(1), 39–49.

Crowne, D.P. and Marlowe, D. (1960) A new scale of social desirability independent of psychopathology. *Journal of Consulting Psychology*, 24(4), 349–54.

Dawson, E., Gilovich, T. and Regan, D.T. (2002) Motivated reasoning and performance on the Wason selection task. *Personality and Social Psychology Bulletin*, 28(10), 1379–87.

Demmert, W.G. (2001) *Improving academic performance among Native Americans: A review of the literature.* Charleston, WV: ERIC Clearinghouse on Rural Education and Small Schools.

Department for Business, Innovation and Skills (2010) *Securing a sustainable future for higher education: An independent review of higher education and student finance.* Available online at: http://www.independent.gov.uk/browne-report (accessed January 2011).

Department for Education (2010) *The case for change.* Available online at: https://www.education.gov.uk/publications/eOrderingDownload/DFE-00564-2010.pdf (accessed May 2011).

Department for Education (2011a) *Participation in education, training and employment by 16–18 year olds in England.* Available at: http://www.education.gov.uk/rsgateway/DB/SFR/s001011/index.shtml (accessed August 2011).

Department for Education (2011b) *GCSE and equivalent results in England 2009/10 (Revised).* Available online at: http://www.education.gov.uk/rsgateway/DB/SFR/s000985/sfr01-2011.pdf (accessed April 2011).

Duncan, N. (2007) Feed-forward: Improving students' use of tutors' comments. *Assessment and Evaluation in Higher Education*, 32(2), 271–83.

Dweck, C.S. (2008) *Mindset: The new psychology of success.* New York: Ballantine.

Dyslexia Action (n.d.) What is dyslexia? Available online at: http://training.dyslexiaaction.org.uk/whatisdyslexia (accessed August 2011).

Education Scotland (n.d.) *What is curriculum for excellence?* Available online at: http://www.ltscotland.org.uk/understandingthecurriculum/whatis curriculumforexcellence/index.asp (accessed August 2011).

Eggens, L., van der Werf, M.P.C. and Bosker, R.J. (2008) The influence of personal networks and social support on study attainment of students in university education. *Higher Education*, 55(5), 553–73.

Elbow, P. (n.d.) *From grades to grids: Responding to writing with criteria.* Available online at: http://www.wsc.ma.edu/facultycenter/Elbows-grid.pdf (accessed August 2011).

Ellis, J.S., Hobson, R.S., Waterhouse, P.J., Meechan, J.G., Hoggs, S.D., Whitworth, J.M., and Thomason, J.M. (2006) Tutor perceptions of the use of a reflective portfolio within a pastoral tutor system to facilitate undergraduate personal development planning. *European Journal of Dental Education*, 10(4), 217–25.

Elton, L. (1996) Strategies to enhance student motivation. *Studies in Higher Education*, 21(1), 57–68.

Everatt, J., Steffert, B. and Smythe, I. (1999) An eye for the unusual: Creative thinking in dyslexics. *Dyslexia*, 5(1), 28–46.

Feagin, J.R. (2010) *The white racial frame: Centuries of racial framing and counter-framing.* New York: Routledge.

Ferguson, E., James, D. and Madeley, L. (2002) Factors associated with success in medical school: Systematic review of the literature. *British Medical Journal*, 324, 952–7.

Fleming, N.D. and Mills, C. (1992) Not another inventory, rather a catalyst for reflection. *To Improve the Academy*, 11, 137–49.

Flynn, F., Reagans, R. and Guillory, L. (2010) Do you two know each other? Transitivity, homophily, and the need for (network) closure. *Journal of Personality and Social Psychology*, 99(5), 855–69.

Forbes, C.E. and Schmader, T. (2010) Retraining attitudes and stereotypes to affect motivation and cognitive capacity under stereotype threat. *Journal of Personality and Social Psychology*, 99(5), 740–54.

Ford, M.E. and Smith, P.R. (2007) Thriving with social purpose: An integrative approach to the development of optimal human functioning. *Educational Psychologist*, 42(3), 153–71.

Francis, B. (2000) *Boys, girls and achievement: Addressing the classroom issues.* London: Routledge Falmer.

Francis, P. (2009) *Inspiring writing in art and design: Taking a line for a write.* Bristol, UK: Intellect.

Frederick, P. (1995) Walking on eggs: Mastering the dreaded diversity discussion. *College Teaching*, 43(3), 83–92.

Fry, H., Ketteridge, S. and Marshall, S. (2003) *A handbook for teaching and learning in higher education: Enhancing academic practice*, 2nd edn. London: Routledge Falmer.

Gardner, H. (1993) Educating for understanding. *American School Board Journal*, 180(7), 20–4.

Gardner, W. (n.d.) *Assessing individual contributions to group software projects.* Available online at: http://www.cs.ubc.ca/wccce/Program03/papers/Gardner-Group/Gardner-Group.htm (accessed January 2011).

Garrison, D.R. and Vaughan, N.D. (2008) *Blended learning in higher education: Framework, principles, and guidelines*. San Francisco, CA: Jossey-Bass.

Gibbs, G. (1992) *Improving the quality of student learning*. Bristol, UK: Technical and Educational Services.

Glaser, B.G. and Strauss, A.L. (1967) *The discovery of grounded theory: Strategies for qualitative research*. Chicago, IL: Aldine Publishing.

Goffman, E. (1959) *The presentation of self in everyday life*. Woodstock, NY: Overlook Press.

Golding, W. (1954) *Lord of the flies*. London: Faber and Faber.

Goldius, C. and Gotesman, E. (2010) The impact of assistive technologies on the reading outcomes of college students with dyslexia. *Educational Technology*, 50(3), 21–5.

Gonzales, P.M., Blanton, H. and Williams, K.J. (2002) The effects of stereotype threat and double-minority status on the test performance of Latino women. *Personality and Social Psychology Bulletin*, 28, 659–70.

Gorard, S., Smith, E., May, H., Thomas, E., Adnett, N. and Slack, K. (2006) *Review of widening participation research: Addressing the barriers to participation in higher education*. Bristol, UK: Higher Education Funding Council for England. Available online at http://www.hefce.ac.uk/pubs/rdreports/2006/rd13_06/barriers.pdf (accessed August 2011).

Gorham, J., Cohen, S.H. and Morris, T.L. (1999) Fashion in the classroom III: Effects of instructor attire and immediacy in natural classroom interactions. *Communication Quarterly*, 47(3), 281–99.

Graesser, A.C. and Person, N.K. (1994) Question asking during tutoring. *American Educational Research Journal*, 31(1), 104–37.

Grant, B. M., Lee, A., Clegg, S., Manathunga, C., Barrow, M., Kandlbinder, P., Brailsford, I., Gosling, D. and Hicks, M. (2009) Why history? Why now? Multiple accounts of the emergence of academic development. *International Journal for Academic Development*, 14(1), 83–6.

Gravestock, P. (2006) *Developing an inclusive curriculum: A guide for lecturers*. Cheltenham, UK: Geography Discipline Network, University of Gloucester. Available online at: http://www2.glos.ac.uk/gdn/icp/ilecturer.pdf (accessed August 2011).

Green, D.A. and Pilkington, R. (2006, June) 'Threshold concepts in educational development'. Workshop presented at the 2006 SEDA Spring Conference: Advancing evidence-informed practice in H.E. learning, teaching and educational development, Liverpool, UK.

Green, P. (2004) *Managing time: Loving every minute*, 2nd edn. Cookham, UK: Chartered Institute of Marketing.

Gupton, J.T., Castelo-Rodríguez, C., Martínez, D.A. and Quintanar, I. (2009) Creating a pipeline to engage low-income, first-generation college students. In S.R. Harper and S.J. Quaye (eds), *Student engagement in higher education: Theoretical perspectives and practical approaches for diverse populations* (pp. 243–60). New York: Routledge.

Halbesleben, J., Becker, J. and Buckley, M. (2003) Considering the labor contributions of students: An alternative to the student-as-customer metaphor. *Journal of Education for Business*, 78, 255–7.

Handal, G. (1999) Consultation using critical friends. *New Directions for Teaching and Learning*, 79, 59–70.

Harper, S.R. and Quaye, S.J. (2007) Student organizations as venues for black identity expression and development among African American male student leaders. *Journal of College Student Development*, 44(2), 127–44.

Harper, S.R. and Quaye, S.J. (eds) (2009) *Student engagement in higher education: Theoretical perspectives and practical approaches for diverse populations*. New York: Routledge.

Hassanien, A. and Barber, A. (2008) An evaluation of student induction in higher education. *International Journal of Management Education*, 6(3), 35–43.

Haswell, R.H. (1983) Minimal marking. *College English*, 45(6), 600–4.

Hawkins, P. (1999) *The art of building windmills: Career tactics for the 21st century*. Liverpool, UK: Graduate into Employment Unit, University of Liverpool.

HEFCE (2006) *Widening participation: A review*. Bristol, UK: Higher Education Funding Council for England. Available online at: http://www.hefce.ac.uk/widen/aimhigh/review.asp (accessed August 2011).

HEFCE (2009) *Supporting higher education in further education colleges: Policy, practice and prospects*. Bristol, UK: Higher Education Funding Council for England.

HEFCE (2010) *Student ethnicity: Profile and progression of entrants to full-time, first degree study May 2010/13*. Bristol, UK: Higher Education Funding Council for England. Available online at: http://www.hefce.ac.uk/pubs/hefce/2010/10_13/ (accessed July 2011).

HERI (2007) *First in my family: A profile of first-generation college students at four-year institutions since 1971*. Los Angeles, CA: Higher Education Research Institute. Available online at: http://www.heri.ucla.edu/PDFs/pubs/briefs/FirstGenResearchBrief.pdf (accessed August 2011).

Herzberg, F. (1968) One more time: How do you motivate employees? *Harvard Business Review*, 46, 53–62.

HESA (n.d.) Higher Education Statistics Agency: Headline Statistics. Available online at: www.hesa.ac.uk (accessed January 2012).

Hiedemann, B. and Jones, S.M. (2010) Learning statistics at the farmers market? A comparison of academic service learning and case studies in an introductory statistics course. *Journal of Statistics Education*, 18(3). Available online at: www.amstat.org/publications/jse/v18n3/hiedemann. pdf (accessed February 2011).

Higbee, K.L. (1979) Recent research on visual mnemonics: Historical roots and educational fruits. *Review of Educational Research*, 49(4), 611–29.

Hofstede, G. and Hofstede, G.J. (2005) *Cultures and organizations: Software of the mind*, 2nd edn. New York: McGraw-Hill.

Howe, N. and Strauss, W. (2000) *Millennials rising: The next great generation*. New York: Vintage.

Hunter, C. and Workman, L. (2009) Are pets like their owners? Dog ownership and personality traits in comparison with personality expectations. Paper presented at the Annual Conference of the British Psychological Society, April 2009, Brighton, UK.

Hurtado, S. and Carter, D.F. (1997) Effects of college transition and perceptions of the campus racial climate on Latino college students' sense of belonging. *Sociology of Education*, 70(4), 324–45.

Huston, T. (2009) *Teaching what you don't know*. Cambridge, MA: Harvard University Press.

Jackson, M. (2008) *Distracted: The erosion of attention and the coming dark age*. Amherst, NY: Prometheus Books.

Jacob, S.W., Wadlington, E. and Bailey, S. (1998) Accommodations and modifications for students with dyslexia in the college classroom. *College Student Journal*, 32(3), 364–9.

Janis, I.L. (1972) *Victims of groupthink: A psychological study of foreign-policy decisions and fiascoes*. Boston, MA: Houghton Mifflin.

Jansen, E.P.W.A. (2004) The influence of the curriculum organization on study progress in higher education. *Higher Education*, 47(4), 411–35.

Jenkins, A. (1996) Discipline-based educational development. *International Journal for Academic Development*, 1(1), 50–62.

Jones-London, M.D. (2006) DCDC2: Demystifying and decoding dyslexia. Press release. Bethesda, MD: National Institute of Neurological Disorders and Stroke. Available online at: http://www.ninds.nih.gov/news_and_events/news_articles/news_article_dyslexia_DCDC2.htm (accessed August 2011).

Kaye, T., Bickel, R. and Birtwistle, T. (2006) Criticizing the image of the student as consumer: Explaining legal trends and administrative responses in the US and the UK. *Education and the Law*, 18(2–3), 85–129.

King, A. (1992) Facilitating elaborative learning through guided student-generated questioning. *Educational Psychologist*, 27(1), 111–26.

Knowles, M. (1980) *The modern practice of adult education*. Cambridge, UK: Prentice-Hall.

Knowles, M. (1990) *The adult learner: A neglected species*. Houston, TX: Gulf Publishing.

Kolb, D.A. (1984) *Experiential learning experience as the source of learning and development*. Englewood Cliffs, NJ: Prentice-Hall.

Laurillard, D. (2002). *Rethinking university teaching*, 2nd edn. London: Routledge Falmer.

Lave, J. and Wenger, E. (1991) *Situated learning: Legitimate peripheral participation*. New York: Cambridge University Press.

Laycock, M. (2009) *Personal tutoring in higher education: Where now and what next?* SEDA Special 25. London: Staff and Educational Development Association.

Learning and Skills Improvement Service (LSIS) (2004) *A framework for understanding dyslexia*. Nottingham: QIA Publications. Available online at: http://www.excellencegateway.org.uk/page.aspx?o=124856 (accessed June 2011).

Lewis, K. (2001) Using midsemester student feedback and responding to it. *New Directions for Teaching and Learning*, 87(3), 33–44.

McCulloch, A. (2009) The student as co-producer: Learning from public administration about the student–university relationship. *Studies in Higher Education*, 34(2), 171–83.

McGarty, C., Spears, R. and Yzerbyt, V.Y. (2002) Conclusion: Stereotypes are selective, variable and contested explanations. In C. McGarty, V.Y. Yzerbyt and R. Spears (eds), *Stereotypes as explanations: The formation of meaningful beliefs about social groups* (pp. 186–99). Cambridge, UK: Cambridge University Press.

McManus, I.C., Richards, P., Winder, B.C., Sprotson, K. and Styles, V. (1995) Medical school applicants from ethnic minority groups: Identifying if and when they are disadvantaged. *British Medical Journal*, 310, 496–500.

Marton, F. and Säljö, R. (1976a) On qualitative differences in learning I: Outcome and process. *British Journal of Educational Psychology*, 46, 4–11.

Marton, F. and Säljö, R. (1976b) On qualitative differences in learning II: Outcome as a function of the learner's conception of the task. *British Journal of Educational Psychology*, 46, 115–27.

Marton, F., Hounsell, D.J. and Entwistle, N.J. (1997) *The experience of learning: Implications for teaching and studying in higher education*, 2nd edn. Edinburgh: Scottish Academic Press.

Maslow, A.H. (1954) *Motivation and personality*. New York: Harper and Row.

Mason, R. and Rennie, F. (2006) *E-learning: The key concepts*. Abingdon, UK: Routledge.

Massey, D.S., Charles, C.Z., Lundy, G.F. and Fischer, M.J. (2003) *The source of the river: The social origins of freshmen at America's selective colleges and universities*. Princeton, NJ: Princeton University Press.

Maynard, J. (n.d.) Bloom's taxonomy model questions and key words. Available online at: http://www.lifelearning.utexas.edu/SI/TestQuestion Keywords. pdf (accessed August 2011).

Meyer, J.H.F. and Land, R. (eds) (2006a) *Overcoming barriers to student understanding: Threshold concepts and troublesome knowledge*. London: Routledge.

Meyer, J.H.F. and Land, R. (2006b) Threshold concepts and troublesome knowledge: An introduction. In J.H.F. Meyer and R. Land (eds),

Overcoming barriers to student understanding: Threshold concepts and trouble-some knowledge. London: Routledge.

Middlemas, B. (n.d.) *What's it worth? Developing equivalency guidelines for the assessment of multi-format coursework.* Available online at: http://jisctech-dis.ac.uk/techdis/pages/detail/floating_pages/Developing_Equivalency_ Guidelines_Assessment_Multi-Format_Coursework (accessed August 2011).

Moon, J.A. (2004) *A handbook of reflective and experiential learning: Theory and practice.* London: RoutledgeFalmer.

Moxley, D., Najor-Durack, A. and Dumbrigue, C. (2001) *Keeping students in higher education: Successful practices and strategies for retention.* London: Kogan Page.

Mulcahy-Ernt, P.I. and Caverly, D.C. (2009) Strategic study-reading. In R.F. Flippo and D.C. Caverly (eds), *Handbook of college reading and study strategy research*, 2nd edn. (pp. 177–198). New York: Routledge.

Myers, J. (2008) Is personal tutoring sustainable? Comparing the trajectory of the personal tutor with that of the residential warden. *Teaching in Higher Education*, 13(5), 607–11.

Myers, S.A. (2010) Using the Perry Scheme to explore college student classroom participation. *Communication Research Reports*, 27(2), 123–30.

National Center for Education Statistics (2011) Enrollment trends by age. Available online at: http://nces.ed.gov/programs/coe/indicator_ope.asp (accessed August 2011).

National Center on Universal Design for Learning (2011) *UDL guidelines: Version 2.0.* Available online at: http://www.udlcenter.org/aboutudl/ udlguidelines (accessed May 31, 2011).

Nederhof, A.J. (1985) Methods of coping with social desirability bias: A review. *European Journal of Social Psychology*, 15(3), 249–61.

Neville L. (2007) *The personal tutor's handbook.* Basingstoke, UK: Palgrave Macmillan.

Ng, W.L. (2002) *Japanese American internment during World War II: A history and reference guide.* Westport, CT: Greenwood Press.

Nilson, L.B. (2010) *Teaching at its best*, 3rd edn. San Francisco, CA: Jossey-Bass.

Northedge, A. (2005) *The good study guide.* Milton Keynes, UK: Open University.

Norton, M.I., Sommers, S.R., Apfelbaum, E.P., Pura, N. and Ariely, D. (2006) Color blindness and interracial interaction: Playing the political correct-ness game. *Psychological Science*, 17(11), 949–53.

NSSE (National Survey of Student Engagement) (2010) *Major differences: Examining student engagement by field of study – annual results 2010.* Bloomington, IN: Indiana University Center for Postsecondary Research. Available online at http://nsse.iub.edu/html/annual_results.cfm (accessed February 2011).

NUS (National Union of Students) (n.d.) Available online at: www.nus.org.uk (accessed April 2011).

OECD (Organisation for Economic Co-operation and Development) (2009) *Education at a glance 2009: OECD indicators.* Paris: OECD Publishing. Available online at http://www.oecd.org/dataoecd/41/25/43636332.pdf (accessed April 2011).

Orwell, G. (1949) *Nineteen Eighty-Four.* London: Secker and Warburg.

Ouellett, M.L. (ed.) (2005) *Teaching inclusively: Resources for course, department and institutional change in higher education.* Stillwater, OK: New Forums Press.

Owens, L.D. and Walden, D.J. (2001) Peer instruction in the learning laboratory: A strategy to decrease student anxiety. *Journal of Nursing Education,* 40(8), 375–7.

Parkinson, M. (2009) The effect of peer assisted learning support (PALS) on performance in mathematics and chemistry. *Innovations in Education and Teaching International,* 46(4), 381–92.

Parliamentary Office of Science and Technology (2004) *Dyslexia and dyscalculia.* Postnote 226. London: POST. Available online at: http://www.parliament.uk/documents/post/postpn226.pdf (accessed April 2011).

Pascarella, E.T. and Terenzini, P.T. (2005) *How college affects students: A third decade of research,* 2nd edn. San Francisco, CA: Jossey-Bass.

Pennington, B.F. (1991) *Diagnosing learning disorders: A neuropsychological framework.* New York: Guilford Press.

Perry, W.G. (1970) *Forms of intellectual and ethical development in the college years: A scheme.* New York: Holt, Rinehart and Winston.

Pitt, R.N. (2006). Downlow Mountain? De/stigmatizing bisexuality through pitying and pejorative discourses in media. *Journal of Men's Studies,* 14(2), 254–8.

Plank, K. and Zakrajsek, T. (2011, June) Intro to generational theory (millennial students). Workshop presented at the 2011 International Institute for New Faculty Developers, Atlanta, GA.

Poole, L. and Lefever, R. (2009) *The Leeds Met book of resilience.* Leeds, UK: Leeds Metropolitan University. Available online at: http://www.leedsmet.ac.uk/091124-36595_Book_of_Resilience_LoRes.pdf (accessed August 2011).

Popovic, C. (2007) 'Why do medical students fail? A study of first year medical students and the educational context', unpublished thesis, University of Birmingham. Available online at http://etheses.bham.ac.uk/223/ (accessed January 2012).

Popovic, C. (2010) Myth busting: An examination of teachers' beliefs about first-year medical students. How well do teachers know their students? *Innovations in Education and Teaching International,* 27(2), 141–54.

Provitera McGlynn, A. (2007) *Teaching today's college students: Widening the circle of success.* Madison, WI: Atwood.

Purcell, K. and Elias, P. (2010) Evidence for UK longitudinal studies on the impact of higher education on equality of opportunity. In S. Pavlin and A. N. Judge (eds), *Development of competencies in the world of work and education: Conference proceedings* (pp. 11–22). Ljubljana, Slovenia: University of Ljubljana.

Purcell, K., Elias, P. and Atfield, G. (2009) *Analysing the relationship between higher education participation and educational and career development patterns and outcomes: A new classification of higher education institutions.* Coventry, UK: IER University of Warwick.

QAA (2009) *Academic credit in higher education in England: An introduction.* Gloucester, UK: Quality Assurance Agency for Higher Education.

Race, P. (2001) *A briefing on self, peer and group assessment.* Assessment Series 9. York, UK: Learning and Teaching Support Network Generic Centre.

Race, P. (2007) *The lecturer's toolkit: A practical guide to learning, teaching and assessment,* 3rd edn. Abingdon, UK: Routledge.

Race, P. (2010) *Making personal tutoring work.* Leeds, UK: Leeds Metropolitan University.

Ramsden, P. (2003) *Learning to teach in higher education,* 2nd edn. Abingdon, UK: Routledge Falmer.

Redmond, P. (2008) Here comes the chopper. *The Guardian,* education supplement, 2 January. Available online at: http://www.guardian.co.uk/education/2008/jan/02/students.uk (accessed July 2011).

Reimers, C. and Roberson, W. (2004) The Perry Game. *The National Teaching and Learning Forum,* 14(1). Available online at: http://www.ntlf.com/html/lib/suppmat/1401.htm (accessed August 2011).

Reynolds, G. (2008) *Presentation Zen: Simple ideas on presentation design and delivery.* Berkeley, CA: New Riders.

Rheinheimer, D.C., Grace-Odeleye, B., Francois, G.E. and Kusorgbor, C. (2010) Tutoring: A support strategy for at-risk students. *Learning Assistance Review (TLAR),* 15(1), 23–33.

Robertson, M., Line, M., Jones, S. and Thomas, S. (2000) International students, learning environments and perceptions: A case study using the Delphi technique. *Higher Education Research and Development,* 19(1), 89–102.

Rockquemore, K.A. and Laszloffy, T. (2008) *The black academic's guide to winning tenure – without losing your soul.* Boulder, CO: Lynne Rienner.

Rosenthal, R. and Jacobson, L. (1968) *Pygmalion in the classroom: Teacher expectations and pupils' intellectual development.* New York: Holt, Rinehart and Winston.

Ross, L. and Nisbett, R.E. (1991) *The person and the situation: Perspectives of social psychology.* New York: McGraw-Hill.

Rothenberg, P.S. (2008) *White privilege: Essential readings on the other side of racism,* 3rd edn. New York: Worth.

Roxå, T. and Mårtensson, K. (2009) Significant conversations and significant networks: Exploring the backstage of the teaching arena. *Studies in Higher Education,* 34(5), 547–59.

Roy, M. and Christenfeld, N.J.S. (2004) Do dogs resemble their owners? *Psychological Science,* 15(5), 361–3.

Ruppert, B. and Green, D.A. (2012) Practicing what we teach: Credibility and alignment in the business communication classroom. *Business Communication Quarterly,* 75. Advance online publication. doi:10.1177/1080569911426475.

Rybczynski, S.M. and Schussler, E.E. (2011) Student use of out-of-class study groups in an introductory undergraduate biology course. *CBE - Life Sciences Education*, 10(1), 74–82.

Salmon, G. (2011) *E-moderating: The key to online teaching and learning*, 3rd edn. New York: Routledge.

Salmon, G. and Edirisingha, P. (eds) (2008) *Podcasting for learning in universities*. Maidenhead, UK: Society for Research in Higher Education and McGraw Hill.

Savin-Baden, M. (2007) *A practical guide to problem-based learning online*. London: Routledge.

Savin-Baden, M., and Major, C. (2004) *Foundations of problem-based learning*. Maidenhead, UK: Open University Press and Society for Research in Higher Education.

Sax, L.J. (2008) *The gender gap in college: Maximizing the developmental potential of women and men*. San Francisco, CA: Jossey-Bass.

Schmader, T., Johns, M. and Forbes, C. (2008) An integrated process model of stereotype threat effects on performance. *Psychological Review*, 115(2), 336–56.

Schmitt, D. (2005) Writing in the international classroom. In J. Carroll and J. Ryan (eds), *Teaching international students: Improving learning for all* (pp. 63–74). Abingdon, UK: Routledge.

Schroeder, C.C. (1993) New students - new learning styles. *Change*, 25(5), 21–7.

Schwartz, P., Mennin, S. and Webb, G. (eds) (2001) *Problem-based learning: Case studies, experience and practice*. Abingdon, UK: Routledge.

Scouller, K. (1998) The influence of assessment method on students' learning approaches: Multiple choice question examination versus assignment essay. *Higher Education*, 35, 453–72.

Sebastian, R.J. and Bristow, D. (2008) Formal or informal? The impact of style of dress and forms of address on business students' perceptions of professors. *Journal of Education for Business*, 83(4), 196–201.

SEDA (n.d.) Staff and Educational Development Association. Available online at: http://www.seda.ac.uk (accessed July 2011).

Shapiro, J.R. (2011) Different groups, different threats: A multi-threat approach to the experience of stereotype threats. *Personality and Social Psychology Bulletin*, 37(4), 464–80.

Sharpe, R., Beetham, H. and Freitas, S.D. (2010) *Rethinking learning for a digital age: How learners are shaping their own experiences*. Abingdon, UK: Routledge.

Shermer, M. (2011) *The believing brain*. New York: Times Books.

Simkins, S. and Maier, M.H. (2010) *Just-in-time teaching: Across the disciplines, across the academy*. Sterling, VA: Stylus.

Smith, L.J. (2008) Grading written projects: What approaches do students find most helpful? *Journal of Education for Business*, 83(6), 325–30.

Spears, R. (2002) Four degrees of stereotype formation: Differentiation by any means necessary. In C. McGarty, V.Y. Yzerbyt and R. Spears (eds),

Stereotypes as explanations: The formation of meaningful beliefs about social groups (pp. 127–56). Cambridge, UK: Cambridge University Press.

Springer, L., Stanne, M.E. and Donovan, S.S. (1999) Effects of small-group learning on undergraduates in science, mathematics, engineering, and technology: A meta-analysis. *Review of Educational Research,* 69(1), 21–51.

Steele, C. (1997) A threat in the air: How stereotypes shape intellectual identity and performance. *American Psychologist,* 52(6), 613–29.

Steele, C.M. (2010) *Whistling Vivaldi: How stereotypes affect us and what we can do.* New York: Norton.

Steele, C. and Aronson, J. (1995) Stereotype threat and intellectual test performance of African Americans. *Journal of Personality and Social Psychology,* 69(5), 797–811.

Stone, J. (2002) Battling doubt by avoiding practice: The effects of stereotype threat on self-handicapping in white athletes. *Personality and Social Psychology Bulletin,* 28, 1667–78.

Stuart, M. (2003) Widening participation: The changing agenda. *Directions in Legal Education,* 6. Available online at http://www.ukcle.ac.uk/resources/directions/previous/issue6/access/ (accessed July 2011).

Sue, D.W. (2010a) *Microaggressions in everyday life: Race, gender, and sexual orientation.* Hoboken, NJ: Wiley.

Sue, D.W. (ed.) (2010b) *Microaggressions and marginality: Manifestation, dynamics, and impact.* Hoboken, NJ: Wiley.

Sundquist, J. (1988) The Japanese-American internment: A reappraisal. *American Scholar,* 57(4), 529–47.

Sweller, J. (2006) The worked example effect and human cognition. *Learning and Instruction,* 16(2), 165–9.

Tang, T.L.-P. (1990) Factors affecting intrinsic motivation among university students in Taiwan. *Journal of Social Psychology,* 130(2), 219–30.

Terry, J. (2007) *Moving on.* Coventry and Worcester, UK: Collaborative Widening Participation Project. Available online at www2.warwick.ac.uk/fac/sci/dcs/teaching/movingon/ (accessed August 2012).

Thomas, C.A., Davies, I.K., Openshaw, D. and Bird, J.B. (1963/2007) *Programmed learning in perspective: A guide to program writing.* New Brunswick, NJ: Aldine Transaction.

Thomas, L. and Hixenbaugh, P. (eds) (2006) *Personal tutoring in higher education.* London: Trentham Books.

Tinto, V. (1993) *Leaving college: Rethinking the causes and cures of student attrition,* 2nd edn. Chicago, IL: University of Chicago Press.

Trompenaars, F. and Hampden-Turner, C. (1998) *Riding the waves of culture: Understanding diversity in global business,* 2nd edn. Boston, MA: Nicholas Brealey.

Twenge, J.M. (2006) *Generation me: Why today's young Americans are more confident, assertive, entitled – and more miserable than ever before.* New York: Free Press.

UCAS (2010) Decade ends with record student numbers. Available online at: http://www.ucas.ac.uk/about_us/media_enquiries/media_releases/2010/210110 (accessed July 2011).

University of Nottingham (2011) *Schools and colleges liaison.* Available online at: http://www.nottingham.ac.uk/ugstudy/introduction/visiting-us/schools-liaison (accessed February 2011).

University of Southampton School of Social Sciences (2008) *Teaching citizenship in higher education.* Southampton, UK: University of Southampton. Available at: http://www.soton.ac.uk/citizened/ (accessed August 2011).

Upcraft, M.L., Gardner, J.N. and Barefoot, B.O. (2005) Introduction: The first year of college revisited. In M.L. Upcraft, J.N. Gardner and B.O. Barefoot (eds), *Challenging and supporting the first-year student: A handbook for improving the first year of college* (pp.1–14). San Francisco, CA: Jossey-Bass.

US Census Bureau (2009) *2005–2009 American Community Survey.* Available online at: http://factfinder.census.gov/servlet/STTable?_bm=y&-geo_id=01000US&-qr_name=ACS_2009_5YR_G00_S1201&-ds_name=ACS_2009_5YR_G00_ (accessed August 2011).

US Census Bureau (2011) Educational attainment in the United States: 2010 – detailed tables. Available online at: http://www.census.gov/hhes/socdemo/education/data/cps/2010/tables.html (accessed August 2011).

US Department of Education (2008) Structure of the US Education System: Credit systems. Available at www2.ed.gov/about/offices/list/ours/international/usnei/us/credits.doc (accessed January 2012).

US Equal Employment Opportunity Commission (n.d.) Laws enforced by EEOC. Available online at: http://www.eeoc.gov/laws/statutes/index.cfm (accessed August 2011).

van Schalkwyk, S., Menkveld, H. and Ruiters, J. (2010) What's the story with class attendance? First-year students: Statistics and perspectives. *South African Journal of Higher Education,* 24(4), 630–45.

Veerman, A., Andriessen, J. and Kanselaar, G. (2002) Collaborative argumentation in academic education. *Instructional Science,* 30(3), 155–86.

Vygotsky, L. (1987) *Collected works, vol. 1.* New York: Plenum.

Wareing, S. (2009) Disciplines, discourse, and Orientalism: The implications for postgraduate certificates in learning and teaching in higher education. *Studies in Higher Education,* 34(8), 917–28.

Warner, S.L. (1999) The Protestant work ethic and academic achievement, ERIC ED447166. Available online at: http://www.eric.ed.gov/ERICWebPortal/detail?accno=ED447166 (accessed August 2011).

Waterfield, J., West, B. and Chalkley, B. (2006) *Developing an inclusive curriculum for students with dyslexia and hidden disabilities.* Cheltenham, UK: Geography Discipline Network, University of Gloucester. Available online at: http://www2.glos.ac.uk/gdn/icp/idyslexia.pdf (accessed May 2011).

Watts, M. and de Jesus, H.P. (2005) The cause and affect of asking questions: Reflective case studies from undergraduate sciences. *Canadian Journal of Science, Mathematics and Technology Education,* 5(4), 437–52.

Weaver, M.R. (2006) Do students value feedback? Student perceptions of tutors' written responses. *Assessment and Evaluation in Higher Education,* 31(3), 379–94.

Weber, M. (1904–05) *The Protestant work ethic and the spirit of capitalism with other writings on the rise of the West*, 4th edn, trans. and intr. Stephen Kalberg (2009). New York: Oxford University Press.

Weimer, M. (2002). *Learner-centered teaching: Five key changes to practice.* San Francisco, CA: Jossey-Bass.

Weller, M. (2007) *Virtual learning environments: Using, choosing and developing your VLE.* Abingdon, UK: Routledge.

Wentworth, D.K. and Chell, R.M. (1997) American college students and the Protestant work ethic. *Journal of Social Psychology*, 137(3), 284–96.

Wenz, M. and Yu, W.C. (2010) Term-time employment and academic performance of undergraduates. *Journal of Education Finance*, 35(4), 353–73.

West, T.G. (1997) *In the mind's eye: Visual thinkers, gifted people with dyslexia and other learning difficulties, computer images and the ironies of creativity*, 2nd edn. Amherst, NY: Prometheus.

White, S.A. and Carr, L.A. (2005) Brave new world: Can we engineer a better start for Freshers? In *Proceedings of 35th annual ASEE/IEEE Frontiers in Education Conference: Pedagogies and technologies for the emerging global economy* (pp. 26–31). Piscataway, NJ: IEEE. Available online at: http://eprints.ecs.soton.ac.uk/11631/ (accessed August 2011).

Wiggins, G. and McTighe, J. (1998) *Understanding by design.* Alexandria, VA: Association for Supervision and Curriculum Development.

Wilcox, P., Winn, S. and Fyvie Gauld, M. (2005) 'It was nothing to do with the university, it was just the people': The role of social support in the first-year experience of higher education. *Studies in Higher Education*, 30(6), 707–22.

Wilson, J. and Sweet, J. (2003) Supporting students. In J. Sweet, S. Huttley and I. Taylor (eds), *Effective learning and teaching in medical, dental and veterinary education.* London: Kogan Page.

Wisker, G., Exley, K., Antoniou, M. and Ridley, P. (2007) *Working one to one with students: Supervising, coaching, mentoring and personal tutoring.* London: Routledge.

Witte, J. (1990) *Entry into marriage and the transition to adulthood among recent birth cohorts of young adults in the United States and the Federal Republic of Germany.* SIPP working papers. Washington, DC: US Bureau of the Census. Available online at: http://www.census.gov/sipp/workpapr/wp128_9023.pdf (accessed August 2011).

Wlodkowski, R.J. (2008) *Enhancing adult motivation to learn: A comprehensive guide for teaching all adults*, 3rd edn. San Francisco, CA: Jossey-Bass.

Wolff, U. and Lundberg, I. (2002) The prevalence of dyslexia among art students. *Dyslexia*, 8(1), 34–42.

Yourglich, A. (1955) Study on correlation between college teachers' and students' concepts of 'ideal-student' and 'ideal-teacher'. *Journal of Educational Research*, 49(1), 59–64.

Zepke, N., Leach, L. and Prebble, T. (2006) Being learner-centred: One way to improve student retention? *Studies in Higher Education*, 31(5), 587–600.

Index